WITHDRAWN BY THE
UNIVERSITY OF MICHIGAN

The Politics of Executive Privilege

BY THE SAME AUTHOR

Nazi Saboteurs on Trial:
A Military Tribunal & American Law (2003)

American Constitutional Law (5th ed., 2003)

Religious Liberty in America: Political Safeguards (2002)

Political Dynamics of Constitutional Law
(With Neal Devins, 3d ed., 2001)

Congressional Abdication on War and Spending (2000)

The Politics of Shared Power:
Congress and the Executive (4th ed., 1998)

Constitutional Conflicts
Between Congress and the President (4th ed., 1997)

Presidential War Power (1995)

Encyclopedia of the American Presidency
(with Leonard W. Levy, 1994)

Constitutional Dialogues:
Interpretation as Political Process (1988)

The Constitutional Between Friends:
Congress, the President, and the Law (1978)

Presidential Spending Power (1975)

President and Congress:
Power and Policy (1972)

THE POLITICS OF
EXECUTIVE PRIVILEGE

Louis Fisher

CAROLINA ACADEMIC PRESS
Durham, North Carolina

Copyright © 2004
Louis Fisher
All Rights Reserved

Library of Congress Cataloging-in-Publication Data

Fisher, Louis
  The politics of executive privilege / by Louis Fisher
    p. cm.
  Includes bibliographical references and index.
  ISBN 0-89089-416-7 (paperback)
  ISBN 0-89089-541-4 (hardcover)
    1. Executive privilege (Government information—United States. 2. Executive power—United States. 3. Legislative power—United States. 4. Separation of powers—United States. I. Title.

JK468.S4F57 2003
352.23'5'0973—dc22

2003060238

CAROLINA ACADEMIC PRESS
700 Kent Street
Durham, NC 27701
Telephone (919) 489-7486
Fax (919) 493-5668
www.cap-press.com

Cover art by Scot C. McBroom for the Historic American Buildings Survey, National Parks Service. Library of Congress call number HABS, DC, WASH, 134-1.

Printed in the United States of America

*To Morton Rosenberg,
public servant*

Contents

Foreword	xi
Introduction	xv
1. Constitutional Principles	3
Early Skirmishes	6
Robert Morris Inquiry	6
Steuben's Annuity	7
St. Clair Investigation	10
Investigating Hamilton	11
Diplomatic Correspondence with France	13
The Contempt Power	14
Judicial Guidelines	17
Presidential Challenges	19
2. The Appropriations Power	27
Power of the Purse	27
Warm-Up Debates in 1789	28
Treaty Disputes, 1791–96	30
Algerine Treaty	30
Jay Treaty	33
Louisiana Purchase	39
House Participation in Treaty Power	40
Funding the Contras	45
Legislative Vetoes	46
3. The Impeachment Power	49
Presidential Policies	49
Andrew Jackson Fights Back	51
The Senate Resolution	51
The House Investigation	52
Impeaching Andrew Johnson	57

Watergate	58
Iran-Contra	62
Clinton's Impeachment	64
Is Censure an Option?	67

4. The Appointment Power — 71
Kleindienst Nomination	71
L. Patrick Gray III	74
Judicial Nominations	76
Rehnquist for Chief Justice	76
Robert Bork	77
Stephen Trott	79
Miguel Estrada	79
Ambassador to Guyana	81
Environmental Crimes Section (DOJ)	82
Senate "Holds"	84
Must the Senate Always Act?	88

5. Congressional Subpoenas — 91
Issuing a Subpoena	91
Immunity	94
The *Ashland* Case	95
DOJ Opinion: Seizing Suspects Abroad	97
DOJ Documents: The Inslaw Affair	100
Whitewater Notes	103
FBI Corruption in Boston	106

6. The Contempt Power — 111
Actions from 1975 to 1981	112
Rogers C. B. Morton	112
David Mathews	114
Henry Kissinger	116
Joseph A. Califano, Jr.	118
Charles W. Duncan, Jr.	121
James B. Edwards	123
James Watt	124
Gorsuch Contempt	126
Travelgate and Jack Quinn	130
Contempt Action against Reno	132

7. HOUSE RESOLUTIONS OF INQUIRY	135
Origins of the Procedure	136
Committee and Floor Procedures	138
Administrative Discretion	140
Committee Review	142
Committee Amendments	143
Adverse Reports	144
Competing Investigations	147
Discharging a Committee	149
Military Operations in Vietnam	150
Forcing Other Legislative Actions	154
Supplemental Hearings	154
Triggering Legislation	156
Mexico Rescue Package	157
Iraq's Declaration on WMD	158
8. THE "SEVEN MEMBER RULE"	161
Origin of the Statute	161
Applying the Statute	165
The Waxman Request	167
District Court Decision	168
Request for Reconsideration	172
Briefs for the Ninth Circuit	173
9. GAO INVESTIGATIONS	179
Statutory Authorities	179
Problems of Access	180
The GAO-Cheney Face-Off	183
The Legislative Request	184
Challenging GAO's Legal Authority	187
The Demand Letter	189
Going to Court	192
The Court Decides	195
Lieberman's Subpoenas	196
10. TESTIMONY BY WHITE HOUSE OFFICIALS	199
Watergate and Its Aftermath	199
Cutting One's Losses	202
The Clinton Years	203
White House-Treasury Contacts	204
Travel Office Firings	205

Security of FBI Files	206
Presidential Pardons	208
Scope of the Power	208
Basic Procedures	210
FALN Clemency	211
Marc Rich et al.	216
Clinton's Defense	219
Grand Jury Probe	222
Tom Ridge	224

11. National Security Claims — 229

Controlling National Security Information	230
Commander in Chief	231
Head of the Executive Branch	233
"Sole Organ" in Foreign Affairs	236
Role of the Courts	237
The Pentagon Papers	238
Recent Statutory Changes	240
Department of the Navy v. Egan (1988)	241
The Garfinkel Case	243
Settling Executive-Legislative Collisions	245
The AT&T Cases	246
Proceedings against Henry Kissinger	247
The James Watt Episode	248
Charges about Congressional "Leaks"	248
Congressional Access to Executive Branch Employees	251
The Lloyd-LaFollette Act	251
Whistleblower Protection Act of 1989	254
Congressional Action in 1998	254

Conclusions   257

Subject Index   261

Index of Cases   270

Foreword

For over two hundred years, Congress and the President have locked horns on an issue that will not, and cannot, go away: legislative access to executive branch information. Presidents and their advisers often claim that the sought-for information is covered by the doctrine of executive privilege and other principles that protect confidentiality among presidential advisers. In terms of constitutional principles, I see these battles as largely a standoff, with each side presenting fairly reasonable arguments either to get information (Congress) or to deny it (executive officials). Court decisions in this area are interesting but hardly dispositive. What usually breaks the deadlock is a political decision: the determination of lawmakers to use the coercive tools available to them, and political calculations by the executive branch whether a continued standoff risks heavy and intolerable losses for the President.

I take a few liberties with the title of this book, but not much. On many of the conflicts that I describe, the President or agency officials did not formally invoke or suggest executive privilege. Statutory grounds and other reasons were offered. However, whether executive privilege is exercised or not, the argument from the executive branch is couched in essentially the same terms: citing the constitutional need of the President and his advisers for confidentiality and candor when discussing and formulating national policy.

The emphasis on "politics," both in the title and the general theme, is not meant to belittle or neglect legal and constitutional arguments. Congress is not entitled to everything it asks for, and the executive branch cannot expect to win every time it says "deliberative process" or "active litigation files." Those are opening, not closing, arguments. In a system of separated powers, some autonomy is needed for each branch, but so is there a need for compromise and closure. Many useful and thoughtful standards have been developed to provide guidance for executive-legislative disputes over access to information. Those standards, constructive as they are, are set aside at times to achieve what both branches may decide has higher importance: settling differences and moving on.

I developed the theme of this book in several earlier articles: "Invoking Executive Privilege: Navigating Ticklish Political Waters," William & Mary Bill of Rights Journal, Vol. 8, No. 3 (April 2000), and "Congressional Access to Information: Using Legislative Will and Leverage," Duke Law Journal, Vol. 52, No. 2 (November 2002). I appreciate the courtesy of both journals for allowing me to reprint material from those articles. Over the years, I published many of these ideas in my books and in such articles as "Grover Cleveland Against the Senate," Capitol Studies, Vol. 7, No. 1 (Spring 1979); "Congressional Access to Executive Branch Information: Lessons from Iran-Contra," Government Information Quarterly, Vol. 6, No. 4 (1989); "Congressional Participation in the Treaty Process," University of Pennsylvania Law Review, Vol. 137, No. 5 (May 1989); "Congressional-Executive Struggles Over Information: Secrecy Pledges," Administrative Law Review, Vol. 42 (Winter 1990); "White House Aides Testifying Before Congress," Presidential Studies Quarterly, Vol. 27, No. 1 (Winter 1997); "When Presidential Power Backfires: Clinton's Use of Clemency," Presidential Studies Quarterly, Vol. 32, No. 3 (September 2002); and "Congressional Access to Presidential Documents: The House Resolution of Inquiry," Presidential Studies Quarterly, Vol. 33, No. 4 (December 2003).

Other sources for this book come from my work as Research Director of the House Iran-Contra Committee, where I analyzed the national security arguments of the Reagan administration to withhold information from Congress or even mislead it. Also, over the years I have testified on various aspects of executive privilege, particularly before the House Committee on Government Operations, the Senate Select Committee on Intelligence, and the House Permanent Select Committee on Intelligence.

For many decades it has been my good fortune to have close friends who study with great care congressional investigations, legislative oversight, and executive privilege. In particular, I want to single out Neal Devins, Fred Kaiser, Walter Oleszek, Harold Relyea, Morton Rosenberg, Mark Rozell, Stephen Stathis, and Charles Tiefer. All have made significant contributions to understanding these executive-legislative struggles. Mort and Charles read the manuscript and offered valuable comments. H. Jefferson Powell provided insights on the executive perspective. I appreciate the continued support of Keith Sipe of Carolina Academic Press, which recently published the fifth edition of my book, *American Constitutional Law*. I greatly respect the professionalism and integrity of the press. In both books I had the pleasure of working with Tim Colton, who handles production and has a talented eye for selecting and designing attractive covers.

I dedicate this book to Mort Rosenberg, a friend and colleague for three decades. To his training as a lawyer he adds a love of history and a keen sense of politics. In studying past disputes over documents or testimony, I frequently came upon his detailed memos preserved in committee reports, hearings, or the *Congressional Record*, setting forth with great clarity the issues that need consideration. Year in, year out, Mort shows how one person can make a difference in keeping our political institutions healthy and giving life to checks and balances.

Introduction

Presidents and their advisers cite various legal principles when they withhold documents from Congress and refuse to allow executive officials to testify before congressional committees. Congress can marshal its own impressive list of legal citations to defend legislative access to information, even when Presidents assert executive privilege. These legal and constitutional principles, finely-honed as they might be, are often overridden by the politics of the moment and practical considerations. Efforts to discover enduring and enforceable norms in this area invariably fall short.

This book explains the political settlements that decide most information disputes. Courts play a role, but it is a misconception to believe that handy cites from judicial opinions will win the day. Efforts to resolve interbranch disputes on purely legal grounds may have to give ground in the face of superior political muscle by a Congress determined to exercise the many coercive tools available to it. By the same token, a Congress that is internally divided or uncertain about its institutional powers, or unwilling to grind it out until the documents are delivered, will lose out in the quest for information. Moreover, both branches are at the mercy of political developments that can come around the corner without warning and tilt the advantage decisively to one side.

I begin by reviewing the constitutional principles at stake when presidential decisions to withhold documents from Congress collide with the needs of lawmakers for information about the executive branch. Which implied power should yield to the other? The next chapter analyzes the use of a fundamental legislative tool—the appropriations power—to extract information from the President. Subsequent chapters focus on other forms of congressional leverage: impeachment, the appointment power, congressional subpoenas, holding executive officials in contempt, House resolutions of inquiry, the "Seven Member Rule," investigations conducted by the General Accounting Office, and requests to White House aides to testify, all of which may force executive officials to release documents and discuss matters they would otherwise prefer to keep private and confidential.

The final chapter is devoted to executive claims of national security, which has special importance after the terrorist attacks of 9/11 and the U.S. military operations in Afghanistan and Iraq. Many scholars, judges, lawmakers, and executive officials believe that a President has great leverage when he withholds information in the areas of foreign policy and national defense. They think that a presidential assertion of executive privilege over this domain enjoys especially powerful, if not unreviewable, authority. I strongly disagree. Courts may decide to back off when Presidents assert that claim, but lawmakers have no reason to acquiesce. The Constitution grants them specific powers and duties in foreign and military affairs.

It is tempting to see executive-legislative clashes only as a confrontation between two branches, yielding a winner and a loser. It is more than that. Congressional access represents part of the framers' belief in representative government. When lawmakers are unable (or unwilling) to obtain executive branch information needed for congressional deliberations, the loss extends to the public, democracy, and constitutional government. Ever since World War II, there has been a steady flow of political power to the President. Some are comfortable with that trend because they believe that power is exercised more efficiently and effectively by the executive branch. The cost is great, however, to the checks and balances and separation of powers that the framers knew were essential to protect individual rights and liberties.

The Politics of Executive Privilege

1

Constitutional Principles

No constitutional language authorizes the President to withhold documents from Congress, nor does any provision empower Congress to demand and receive information from the executive branch. The Supreme Court has recognized the constitutional power of Congress to investigate,[1] and the President's power to withhold information,[2] but those powers would exist with or without judicial rulings. Over the past two centuries, both branches have insisted that their powers are necessarily implied in the effective functioning of government. No doubt they are. The difficult and unpredictable issue is how to resolve two implied powers when they collide.[3] Court cases occasionally provide guidance, but most of the disputes are resolved through political accommodations.

A lengthy study by Herman Wolkinson in 1949, expressing the executive branch position, asserted that federal courts "have uniformly held that the President and the heads of departments have an uncontrolled discretion to withhold the information and papers in the public interest, and they will not interfere with the exercise of that discretion."[4] That statement, incorrect when written, is even less true today as a result of litigation and political precedents established over the past half century. Similarly inaccurate is the claim that "in every instance where a President has backed the refusal of a head of a depart-

---

1. McGrain v. Daugherty, 273 U.S. 135, 175 (1927) ("A legislative body cannot legislate wisely or effectively in the absence of information respecting the conditions which the legislation is intended to affect or change.")

2. United States v. Nixon, 418 U.S. 683, 711 (1974 ("To the extent this interest relates to the effective discharge of a President's powers, it is constitutionally based.").

3. For a careful analysis of the constitutional arguments for and against executive privilege, see Mark J. Rozell, Executive Privilege (2d ed. 2002).

4. Herman Wolkinson, "Demands of Congressional Committees for Executive Papers" (Part I), 10 Fed'l Bar J. 103, 103 (1949). At the time he wrote his article, Mr. Wolkinson served as an attorney with the U.S. Department of Justice.

ment to divulge confidential information to either of the Houses of Congress, or their committees, the papers and the information requested were not furnished."[5] Congress and its committees have enjoyed more success than that. Wolkinson asserted that Congress could not, "under the Constitution, compel heads of departments by law to give up papers and information, regardless of the public interest involved; and the President is the judge of that interest."[6] He seriously understated the coercive powers of Congress by claiming that the heads of departments "are entirely unaffected by existing laws which prescribe penalties for failure to testify and produce papers before the House of Representatives or the Senate, or their committees."[7] Congress may hold both executive officials and private citizens in contempt.

What informs the process of congressional access to executive branch information is the constitutional structure of separation of powers and the system of checks and balances. Neither political branch has incontestable authority to withhold information or force its disgorgement. When these executive-legislative clashes occur, they are seldom resolved judicially. Accommodations are usually entered into without the need for litigation. In 1982, President Ronald Reagan set forth the governing procedure for responding to congressional requests for information: "Historically, good faith negotiations between Congress and the Executive Branch have minimized the need for invoking executive privilege, and this tradition of accommodation should continue as the primary means of resolving conflicts between the Branches."[8]

On those rare occasions where these executive-legislative disputes enter the courts, judges typically reject sweeping claims of privilege by elected officials while encouraging the two branches to find a satisfactory compromise.[9] Courts rely on legal precedent, "and legal precedent is much too inflexible to apply in individual cases of executive-legislative disputes."[10] The outcome is more likely decided by the persistence of Congress and its determination to punish executive noncompliance. Congress can win most of the time—if it has the will—because its political tools are formidable.

---

5. Id. at 104.
6. Id. at 107.
7. Id.
8. Memorandum from President Reagan to the Heads of the Executive Departments and Agencies, "Procedures Governing Responses to Congressional Requests for Information, November 4, 1982, paragraph 1.
9. E.g., United States v. AT&T, 567 F.2d 121 (D.C. Cir. 1977); United States v. American Tel. & Tel. Co., 551 F.2d 384 (D.C. Cir. 1976).
10. Joel D. Bush, "Congressional-Executive Access Disputes: Legal Standards and Political Settlements," 9 J. Law & Pol. 719, 745 (1993).

Political confrontations between Congress and the executive branch attract the media, which loves a good fight. Knock-down battles dominate the press and remain within our collective memory, but little attention is devoted to the week-to-week cooperative efforts that characterize much of executive-legislative operations. Government cannot function in a constant state of strife, agitation, and enmity. Lawmakers and agency officials necessarily devise compromises to break deadlocks and move public policy forward.[11]

Although the congressional power to investigate is not expressly stated in the Constitution, the framers understood that legislatures must oversee the executive branch. Under British precedents, lawmakers developed procedures to hold administrators accountable. James Wilson, one of the framers and later a Justice on the Supreme Court, expected the House of Representatives to "form the grand inquest of the state. They will diligently inquire into grievances, arising both from men and things."[12] In an essay in 1774, he described members of the British House of Commons as "grand inquisitors of the realm. The proudest ministers of the proudest monarchs have trembled at their censures; and have appeared at the bar of the house, to give an account of their conduct, and ask pardon for their faults."[13]

At the Philadelphia Convention, George Mason emphasized that members of Congress "are not only Legislators but they possess inquisitorial powers. They must meet frequently to inspect the Conduct of the public offices."[14] Charles Pinckney submitted a list of congressional prerogatives, including: "Each House shall be the Judge of its own privileges, and shall have authority to punish by imprisonment every person violating the same."[15] The Constitution, however, provided no express powers for Congress to investigate or to punish for contempt. What was left silent would be filled within a few years by implied powers and legislative precedents.

---

11. Stephen W. Stathis, "Executive Cooperation: Presidential Recognition of the Investigative Authority of Congress and the Courts," 3 J. Law & Pol. 183 (1986).
12. 1 The Works of James Wilson 415 (1967 ed.).
13. 2 Id. 731 (essay "Considerations on the Nature and Extent of the Legislative Authority of the British Parliament").
14. 2 The Records of the Federal Convention of 1787, at 206 (Farrand ed. 1937 (hereafter "Farrand"). See also Mason's comments as reported by Madison, id. at 199.
15. Id. at 341.

Early Skirmishes

The Constitution makes no specific reference to a presidential power to withhold documents from Congress, nor does it expressly recognize a congressional need for information to legislate. Yet it is routine to consider both powers implied in the operation of the executive and legislative branches. Long before the Supreme Court acknowledged that fact, the political branches had already reached a rough understanding and worked out accommodations. When these two implied powers collide, which should give way? No magic formula yields a ready and reliable answer, for too much depends on individual circumstances and political requirements.

Robert Morris Inquiry

During the First Congress, the House debated a request from Robert Morris to investigate his conduct as Superintendent of Finance during the period of the Continental Congress.[16] The matter was referred to a select committee consisting of James Madison, Theodore Sedgwick, and Roger Sherman.[17] The House learned a day later that the Senate had passed a resolution authorizing President George Washington to appoint three commissioners to inquire into the receipts and expenditures of public moneys during Morris's administration and to report the results to Congress.[18] Thus, while the House was determined to conduct its own inquiry, the Senate initially entrusted the matter to the President.

The select committee of Madison, Sedgwick, and Sherman issued a report, recommending that a committee of five be appointed to examine Morris's performance in office. John Laurance and William Smith were added to the three already in place.[19] Elbridge Gerry objected that the House was pretending it still had the power of the Continental Congress, when it possessed both legislative and executive powers. He insisted that the President was "the only competent authority to take cognizance of the conduct of officers in the Executive Department; if we pursue the proposed plan of appointing committees, we destroy the responsibility of Executive officers, and divest the House

---

16. 1 Annals of Cong. 1168 (February 8, 1790).
17. Id. at 1204 (February 10, 1790).
18. Id. at 1233 (February 11, 1790).
19. 2 Annals of Cong. 1514 (March 19, 1790) (spelled "Lawrence" in the Annals).

of a great and essential privilege, that of impeaching our Executive offices for maladministration."[20] Gerry favored the Senate's approach of appointing three commissioners to do the job.[21] Theodorick Bland regarded the appointment of commissioners as "an unnecessary expense."[22] Madison supported the five-man committee, arguing that the House "should possess itself of the fullest information in order to doing [sic] justice to the country and to public officers."[23] Gerry persisted in his belief that "the several branches of Government should be kept separate."[24] The committee was appointed and issued a report on February 16, 1791.[25]

The committee investigation did not represent a full-fledged collision between Congress and the Washington administration. The controversy centered on a holdover dispute from the previous Continental Congress. Still, Congress ended up debating an important issue: Which branch of government—legislative or executive—was the proper party for investigating executive matters? The House decided, as Madison noted, that Congress needed information to "do justice" to the country and to public officers.

Steuben's Annuity

A 1790 request from Treasury Secretary Alexander Hamilton to Congress, seeking financial compensation for Baron von Steuben, triggered an early executive-legislative clash over access to documents. Initially, the administration withheld some materials from Congress. In the end, after a confrontation, lawmakers received sufficient documents to pass the bill for Steuben. The controversy involved both principle and personalities, a mix that continues to this day.

On January 27, 1790, Steuben detailed for Hamilton his military assistance to America during the Revolutionary War. Trained in the Prussian army, Steuben accepted a commission in the American Continental army in 1777. Among his duties: training, disciplining, and reorganizing the troops under General George Washington, preparing regulations for military discipline, and commanding one of the three divisions at Yorktown.[26] Steuben told Hamilton

---

20. Id. at 1515.
21. Id.
22. Id.
23. Id.
24. Id. at 1515–16.
25. Id. at 2017 (February 16, 1791).
26. For some of the history on Steuben's effort to seek financial compensation from Congress, see 7 Documentary History of the First Federal Congress of the United States of

that to "decline all compensation for the Sacrifices I had made" would appear to be the conduct of "a Lunatic or a Traitor." Either he fit the first category, for coming "from another part of the globe to serve a Nation unknown to him," or the second, "as it might appear that his making such generous proposals to introduce himself into your army was with the most dangerous views, for which he probably received compensation from the enemy."[27]

On April 6, 1790, the House received from Hamilton a memorial requesting financial assistance for Steuben.[28] The memorial consisted mainly of statements by those who knew Steuben and could vouch for his contributions to the country. Hamilton believed that legislation offering compensation would be "most consistent with the dignity and equity of the United States."[29] He recommended three types of compensation: a lump sum of $7,396.74, an annuity for life, and "a moderate grant of land."[30]

Upon receipt of Hamilton's memorial, the House appointed a committee to report a bill.[31] The House bill proposed an annuity for life of $2,706, plus "____ thousand acres of land in the Western Territory of the United States."[32] After omitting the grant of land, the House settled on a fixed sum of $7,000 and an annuity of $2,000 for life.[33] The Senate, notified that the House had passed the bill for Steuben, assigned the matter to a committee consisting of William Maclay, Caleb Strong, Ralph Izard, Oliver Ellsworth, and Samuel Johnston.[34]

Maclay called on the Commissioner of Army Accounts, who "furnished me with all [the information] in his power."[35] Discovering that the Continental Congress had previously given Steuben $7,000, Maclay met with Joseph Nourse, Register of the Treasury Department, and asked for the receipts. Nourse assured Maclay that his request would be complied with. Told by Maclay that he needed the documents that day, Nourse gave assurances that the deadline would be honored.[36] A little over an hour later Nourse gave

---

America 201–06 (1997). For documents related to his petition to Congress, see id. at 206–46.
27. 6 The Papers of Alexander Hamilton 221 (Syrett ed. 1962).
28. 2 Annals of Cong. 1572 (April 6, 1790).
29. 6 The Papers of Alexander Hamilton 326.
30. Id. at 326–27.
31. 2 Annals of Cong. 1584 (April 19, 1790).
32. Id. at 1606.
33. Id. at 1609–10.
34. 1 Annals of Cong. 972.
35. Kenneth R. Bowling and Helen Veit, eds., The Diary of William Maclay 265 (1988).
36. Id. at 266.

Maclay some information, indicating that the warrants were deposited at the U.S. Bank. Maclay subsequently learned that "some books papers or property of that kind was lodged at the Bank by Mr. Hamilton, Who had the Keys and Care of them."[37]

Maclay told Hamilton what he wanted and was refused "in pretty stiff terms." Hamilton saw no grounds for opening "any Gentlemen's Papers." Maclay insisted that the papers "belonged to the public & to no private Gentleman," and that Hamilton was in no position "to refuse information to a Committee of Congress." When Hamilton offered to deliver the papers if the committee voted for them, Maclay replied that "any Member of Congress, had a right to any Papers in any Office Whatever. That as Chairman of the Committee I had promised to procure What Papers were necessary."[38] The leverage here lay with Congress. If Hamilton chose to stonewall, Maclay and his committee members could withdraw support for the Steuben bill.

Following this exchange, Maclay said he expected to hear from Hamilton in half an hour. After that time had come and gone, Maclay went to the Treasury. The warrant "was delivered to me with all the pomp of official ceremony."[39] Maclay was still waiting for a document that Hamilton had promised to provide. After Maclay was "admitted into the Sanctum Sanctorum," he told "his Holiness that he had been good enough to promise me a note which was not come to my hands."[40] Hamilton admitted that the papers were on the premises, but in a desk that was locked and "bound round with tape."[41] Maclay wrote in his diary: "A School Boy should be Whipped for such pitiful Evasions."[42]

Maclay continued collecting "documents & papers" to support the bill for Steuben. Whether he obtained the papers in the bound desk is not known from available records. Maclay was incensed at Hamilton's request, saying he had never seen "so Villainous an Attempt to rob the public, as the System which has been brought forward by the Secretary of the Treasury."[43] Maclay and the other committee members examined the papers regarding the bill for Steuben.[44] They deleted the lump sum of $7,000 and reduced the annuity to

---

37. Id.
38. Id.
39. Id. at 267.
40. Id.
41. Id.
42. Id.
43. Id. at 270.
44. Id.

$1,000.[45] After the Senate accepted and rejected some amendments, Congress settled on a private bill that granted Steuben an annuity of $2,500 for life.[46]

St. Clair Investigation

Two years later, on March 27, 1792, the House appointed a committee to inquire into the heavy military losses suffered by the troops of Maj. Gen. Arthur St. Clair to Indian tribes. Out of 1,400 U.S. troops, 657 were killed and another 271 wounded.[47] The House empowered the committee "to call for such persons, papers, and records, as may be necessary to assist their inquiries."[48] William Giles, who regarded the inquiry as "indispensable" and "strictly proper," called the House "the proper source, as the immediate guardians of the public interest."[49] Similar to the Morris inquiry, some members of the House thought the investigation should be conducted by President Washington. A motion to that effect was rejected 21 to 35, after which the House supported the inquiry 44 to 10.[50]

According to the account of Thomas Jefferson, President Washington convened his Cabinet to consider the extent to which the House could call for papers and persons. The Cabinet agreed

> first, that the House was an inquest, and therefore might institute inquiries. Second, that it might call for papers generally. Third, that the Executive ought to communicate such papers as the public good would permit, and ought to refuse those, the disclosure of which would injure the public: consequently were to exercise a discretion. Fourth, that neither the committee nor House had a right to call on the Head of a Department, who and whose papers were under the President alone; but that the committee should instruct their chairman to move the House to address the President.[51]

The Cabinet concluded that "there was not a paper which might not be properly produced."[52] President Washington instructed Secretary of War

---

45. Id. at 274; 1 Annals of Cong. 978 (May 25, 1790).
46. 6 Stat. 2 (1790); 1 Annals of Cong. 978–80; The Diary of William Maclay, at 276–78.
47. George C. Chalou, "St. Clair's Defeat, 1792," in Congress Investigates, 1792–1974, at 7 (Arthur M. Schlesinger, Jr. & Roger Bruns, eds. 1975).
48. 3 Annals of Cong. 493 (March 27, 1792).
49. Id. at 490.
50. Id. at 493.
51. 1 The Writings of Thomas Jefferson 304 (Bergh ed. 1903).
52. Id. at 305.

Henry Knox to "lay before the House of Representatives such papers from your Department, as are requested by the enclosed Resolution."[53] Washington also thought it appropriate for St. Clair, who had expressed an interest in retiring, to make himself fully available to the House: "I should hope an opportunity would thereby be afforded you, of explaining your conduct, in a manner satisfactory to the public and yourself."[54] The House committee examined papers furnished by the executive branch, listened to explanations from department heads and other witnesses, and received a written statement from General St. Clair.[55] The general principle of executive privilege had been established because the President could refuse papers "the disclosure of which would injure the public." The language here is significant. The injury had to be to the *public*, not to the President or his associates. Presidents were not entitled to withhold information simply because it might embarrass the administration or reveal improper or illegal activities.

Investigating Hamilton

Early in 1793, Rep. William Giles introduced a series of resolutions charging that Secretary Hamilton had violated an appropriations law, deviated from the instructions given to him by President Washington, failed to give Congress official information "in due time," failed to give official information to commissioners regarding the purchase of the public debt, and had been guilty of "an indecorum to this House, in undertaking to judge of its motives in calling for information which was demandable of him, from the constitution of his office; and in failing to give all the necessary information within his knowledge."[56] The House agreed to delete the charge regarding a violation of an appropriations law, but took votes on the other resolutions.

In debating these resolutions, part of the discussion concerned the degree of discretionary authority that must be available to top executive officials.[57] Also of concern was the procedure available to Hamilton, who was forced to submit lengthy reports without the opportunity to come before the House to explain his conduct. Rep. William Smith explained:

---

53. 32 The Writings of George Washington 15 (John C. Fitzpatrick ed. 1939).
54. Id. at 16.
55. 3 Annals of Cong. 1106–13 and Appendix (1052–59, 1310–17).
56. Id. at 900 (February 28, 1793).
57. Id. at 901–02.

> The Secretary of the Treasury was…not even permitted to come to the bar to vindicate himself. Through the imperfect medium of written reports he was compelled, when called upon for information, to answer, as it were by anticipation, charges which were not specific, without knowing precisely against what part of his administration subsequent specific charges would be brought to bear.
>
> If in his reports he was concise, he was censured for suppressing information; if he entered into a vindication of the motives which influenced his conduct, he was then criminated for stuffing his reports with metaphysical reasonings. A gentleman from Pennsylvania [Mr. FINDLEY] had said that the Secretary's reports were so voluminous that he was quite bewildered by them, and that instead of their throwing any light on the subject, he was more in the dark than ever....[58]

Whatever dispute there might have been over Hamilton's record in office, there was little question about the right of the House to whatever documents it needed to complete the investigation. For example, on the issue of Hamilton deviating from presidential instructions, Smith said those instructions "have been laid before the House."[59] Exactly what the House received is uncertain. Smith claimed that the instructions were not from Washington to Hamilton but from Hamilton to his agents.[60] Rep. William Findley disagreed:

> The PRESIDENT did give commission and instructions, and those are fully communicated to us. If he conceived we had no right to demand them, he would have told us so; if he had kept any part of them back, he would have informed us, and assigned his reasons for doing so. I presume that the PRESIDENT has acted the part of a candid, honest man; the gentleman [Smith] presumes the reverse. The suggestion that this House, which has the exclusive right of originating the appropriation of money, has no right to be informed of the application of it, is so novel and extraordinary, so inconsistent with every idea of propriety and good Government, that it requires no reply.[61]

James Madison discussed an instruction that Washington had given Hamilton.[62] In an investigation of this nature, involving the application of public

---

58. Id. at 912.
59. Id. at 913.
60. Id. at 916.
61. Id. at 919.
62. Id. at 940.

funds, it would have been of great risk for the administration to do anything other than comply fully with the legislative request. Any resistance could be interpreted as a cover-up, fueling suspicions, heightening passions, and hardening positions. In such situations, non-cooperation may escalate a dispute to a motion for contempt of Congress and even impeachment.

The resolutions were rejected by large margins, the votes ranging from 40–12 to 33–8. Having watched the resolutions defeated one by one, Smith said it "had been already clearly shown, by documents in the possession of the House, that the necessary information had been communicated."[63] The final resolution, charging that Hamilton had been guilty of an indecorum to the House "in undertaking to judge of its motives in calling for information, which was demandable of him, from the constitution of his office, and in failing to give all the necessary information within his knowledge," lost on a vote of 34 to 7.[64]

Diplomatic Correspondence with France

In 1794, the Senate adopted a resolution requesting President Washington to submit certain diplomatic correspondence concerning U.S. policy with France.[65] At a Cabinet meeting he received advice from Secretary of War Knox that "no part of the correspondence should be sent to the Senate." Secretary Hamilton agreed with Knox, adding that "the principle is safe, by excepting such parts as the President may choose to withhold." Attorney General Edmund Randolph, about to become Secretary of State, said that "all the correspondence proper, from its nature, to be communicated to the Senate, should be sent; but that what the President thinks improper, should not be sent."[66] William Bradford, replacing Randolph as Attorney General, was of the opinion that "it is the duty of the Executive to withhold such parts of the said correspondence as in the judgment of the Executive shall be deemed unsafe and improper to be disclosed."[67]

Washington, carving out some room, notified the Senate that he had directed copies and translations to be made "except in those particulars which, in my judgment, for public considerations, ought not to be communicated."[68]

---

63. Id. at 960.
64. Id. at 960–63. For background on the House investigation of Hamilton, see 2 Broadus Mitchell, Alexander Hamilton 245–86 (1962).
65. 4 Annals of Cong. 38 (January 24, 1794).
66. 4 The Works of Alexander Hamilton 505–06 (John C. Hamilton ed.).
67. Id. at 494–95.
68. 4 Annals of Cong. 56 (February 26, 1794).

Apparently the Senate accepted this arrangement, but had Senators wanted to press the matter they might have forced the release of more material. As noted by Abraham Sofaer, "nothing would have prevented a majority from demanding the material, especially in confidence, or from using their power over foreign policy, funds and offices to pressure the President to divulge."[69]

The Contempt Power

The first use of the investigative power to protect the dignity of the House occurred in 1795. William Smith, a Representative from South Carolina, announced that a Robert Randall had confided in him a plan to seek a grant of some 20 million acres from Congress, to be divided into 40 shares. More than half that amount would be reserved to lawmakers who assisted him. Rep. William Murphy had also been sounded out by Randall. One of Randall's associates, Charles Whitney, got in touch with Rep. Daniel Buck to see if he was interested. The House passed a resolution directing the Sergeant at Arms, upon the order of the Speaker, to arrest Randall and Whitney.[70]

On January 6, 1796, the House concluded that Randall had been guilty of contempt and a breach of House privileges by attempting to corrupt the integrity of its members. Randall was brought to the bar of the House, reprimanded by the Speaker, and recommitted to custody. At that time, the House had a jail within its building. Because Whitney had attempted to bribe Buck when he was a member-elect, the House discharged Whitney from custody without charging him with contempt. A week later it voted to release Randall.[71]

Four years later, the Senate opened an investigation into material published by William Duane, editor of the *Aurora* newspaper.[72] On March 18, 1800, the Federalist Senate voted 20 to 8 along party lines for this language: "the said publication contains assertions, and pretended information, respecting the Senate, and the Committee of the Senate, and their proceedings, which are false, defamatory, scandalous, and malicious; tending to defame the Senate of the United States, and to bring them into contempt and disrepute, and to excite against them the hatred of the good people of the United States."[73] By a

---

69. Abraham D. Sofaer, "Executive Privilege: An Historical Note," 75 Colum. L. Rev. 1318, 1321 (1975).
70. Annals of Cong., 4th Cong., 1st Sess. 155–70 (1795).
71. Id. at 171–245, passim. For further details on Congress's power to punish for contempt, see 2 Hinds' Precedents §§ 1597–1640.
72. Annals of Cong., 6th Cong., 1st-2d Sess. 63 (February 26, 1800).
73. Id. at 111–12.

vote of 17 to 11 it regarded the content of the newspaper "a high breach of the privileges of this House."[74] Duane was ordered to appear at the bar of the Senate on March 24 to defend his conduct.[75] After hearing the charges and appearing before the Senate, he asked for the assistance of counsel, which the Senate granted.[76] He then refused to return, explaining that he was "bound by the most sacred duties to decline any further voluntary attendance upon that body, and leave them to pursue such measures in this case as, in their *wisdom*, they may deem meet."[77]

It was for that action, and not the published material, that the Senate voted 16–12 to hold him in contempt.[78] A warrant was issued for his arrest, but Duane managed to stay a step ahead of the Sergeant at Arms.[79] On May 14, the Senate adopted a resolution (13 to 4) requesting the President to prosecute Duane in the courts. The Senate asked that a proper law officer prosecute Duane "for certain false, defamatory, scandalous, and malicious publications...tending to defame the Senate of the United States, and to bring them into contempt and disrepute, and to excite against them the hatred of the good people of the United States."[80] Duane was indicted by a federal grand jury, but after several postponements was never convicted. The grand jury's failure to find "any legal basis for the Senate's complaint clearly branded the original action by the Federalist majority as a usurpation of authority."[81]

During the debate, Senator Charles Pinckney questioned the authority of Congress to punish members of the press simply because "they thought they had a right to attack, by argument, proceedings which appeared to them unconstitutional."[82] It seemed plain to Pinckney that "for all libels or attacks on either branch of the Legislature, in writing or in print, the mode must be prosecution...."[83] In these indictments for libel "the *Jury* shall have a right to determine the law, and the fact, under the direction of the court, as in other

---

74. Id. at 112.
75. Id. at 113.
76. Id. at 117–18.
77. Id. at 122 (emphasis in original).
78. Id. at 123.
79. James Morton Smith, Freedom's Fetters: The Alien and Sedition Law and American Civil Liberties 297–98 (1956).
80. Annals of Cong., 6th Cong., 1st–2d Sess. at 184.
81. Smith, Freedom's Fetters, at 306; see also Ernest J. Eberling, Congressional Investigations 42–53 (1928).
82. Annals of Cong. 6th Cong., 1st–2d Sess. at 73.
83. Id. at 75.
84. Id. at 76 (emphasis in original).

cases."[84] Other Senators recognized the option of transferring this type of dispute "to the judicial courts, and that the Attorney General should be directed to prosecute."[85]

Thomas Jefferson, Presiding Officer of the Senate in 1800, summarized the legislative action on Duane. He noted that Congress had a right to protect itself so that it did not "sit at the mercy of every intruder who may enter our doors or gallery, and, by noise and tumult, render proceeding in business impracticable."[86] He suggested in his parliamentary manual that it might be wise for Congress, given the uncertain state of the law of contempt of Congress, to "declare by law what is necessary and proper to enable them to carry into execution the powers vested in them, and thereby hang up a rule for the inspection of all, which may direct the conduct of the citizen, and at the same time test the judgments they shall themselves pronounce in their own case."[87]

The first committee witness punished for contempt of the House was Nathaniel Rounsavell, a newspaper editor, charged in 1812 with releasing sensitive information to the press. He admitted to a select committee that he had leaked secret House debates on a proposed embargo, and that part of the source was overhearing a conversation between members of the House. Nevertheless, he refused to identify the lawmakers or say where the conversation took place. The House put him in the custody of the Sergeant at Arms and brought him before the bar to be questioned. Once against he declined to name the lawmakers.

On the following day, still in custody, Rounsavell drafted a letter in which he disclaimed any intention of showing disrespect to the House. He said that overhearing the conversation was inadvertent and explained that he had declined to give the select committee the information it requested because he thought it might incriminate lawmakers who had committed, in his view, no crime. Only because of previous knowledge, which he obtained from other sources, was he aware that the conversation involved an embargo. At this point in the proceedings, John Smilie of Pennsylvania identified himself as the member who Rounsavell had overheard. Smilie regarded the information that appeared in the newspaper "of no importance." If the House wanted a victim, he offered himself as a substitute for Rounsavell.

The House now wanted to discharge Rounsavell without compromising its rights and dignity. The Speaker put to him the question: "Are you willing to answer such questions as shall be propounded by you by order of the House?"

---

85. Id. at 91 (Senator Joseph Anderson).
86. Jefferson's Manual, §297; H. Doc. No. 106-320, at 134.
87. Id. at §299, at 136–37.

Rounsavell said he was prepared to do that. The House then moved that Rounsavell, having purged himself of contempt, be released. The motion carried without opposition.[88]

Judicial Guidelines

The British Parliament treated the contempt power and legislative privileges as wholly within the power of the legislative branch, without any interference from the judiciary. A different practice developed in the United States. The Supreme Court has held that the congressional authority to punish citizens for contempt because of a breach of legislative privileges "can derive no support from the precedents and practices of the two Houses of the English Parliament, nor from the adjudged cases in which the English courts have upheld these practices."[89]

The Court first placed limits on congressional investigations in *Anderson* v. *Dunn* (1821). Rep. Lewis Williams informed the House that a Col. John Anderson had offered him $500 if he would reciprocate with certain favors. The House ordered the Sergeant at Arms to take Anderson into custody. After interrogation by the Speaker, the House voted Anderson in contempt and in violation of the privileges of the House. The Speaker reprimanded him and released him from custody.[90] The Supreme Court upheld the House action as a valid exercise in self-preservation. Without the power to punish for contempt, the House would be left "exposed to every indignity and interruption that rudeness, caprice, or even conspiracy may meditate against it."[91] However, the Court ruled that the power to punish for contempt was not unlimited. The House had to exercise the least possible power adequate to fulfill legislative needs (in this case, the power of imprisonment), and the duration of punishment could not exceed the life of the legislative body. Thus, imprisonment had to cease when the House adjourned at the end of a Congress.[92]

---

88. Annals of Cong., 12th Cong., 1st Sess. 1255–74. Additional cases where the House punished witnesses for contempt are discussed in 3 Hinds' Precedents §§ 1666–1701.
89. Kilbourn v. Thompson, 103 U.S. 168, 189 (1881). See also Marshall v. Gordon, 243 U.S. 521, 533–41 (1917) and Watkins v. United States, 354 U.S. 178, 192 (1957).
90. Annals of Cong., 15th Cong., 1st Sess. 580–83, 592–609, 777–90 (1818).
91. Anderson v. Dunn, 6 Wheat. 204, 228 (1821).
92. The Senate, a continuing body, is not limited by the expiration of a Congress; McGrain v. Daugherty, 273 U.S. 135, 181–82 (1927).

As a result of this decision, it would be possible for someone to violate the dignity of the House in the closing days of a Congress and be punished only for the remaining period. To handle such situations, Congress passed legislation in 1857 to enforce the attendance of witnesses on the summons of either House. If an individual fails to appear or refuses to answer pertinent questions, that person can be indicted for misdemeanor in the courts.[93]

Initially, the Court defined the legislative power to investigate somewhat narrowly. In 1881, it spoke of Congress investigating only with "valid legislation" in mind.[94] That particular case concerned the power of Congress to investigate the affairs of private citizens engaged in a real-estate pool. If the individuals committed a crime or offence, the Court said the judiciary would be the proper branch to act. The Court worried about "a fruitless investigation into the personal affairs of individuals."[95]

Later judicial rulings came to recognize a much greater sweep to congressional authority. In 1927, the Court faced a situation where Congress looked not into the activities of people in the private sector but rather the conduct of the executive branch, particularly the administration of the Justice Department. The Court first stated that "the power of inquiry—with process to enforce it—is an essential and appropriate auxiliary of the legislative function."[96] Congress could not legislate "wisely or effectively in the absence of information."[97] Unlike the decision in 1881, the Court in 1927 did not confine congressional investigations to "valid legislation." Congress had a right to seek information "for legislative purposes."[98] The Court recognized that the Senate resolution that launched the investigation of the Justice Department

> does not in terms avow that it is intended to be in aid of legislation; but it does show that the subject to be investigated was the administration of the Department of Justice—whether its functions were being properly discharged or were being neglected or mistreated, and particularly whether the Attorney General and his assistants were per-

---

93. 11 Stat. 155 (1857), amended by 12 Stat. 333 (1862). The 1857 law, as amended, was upheld by the Supreme Court; In re Chapman, 166 U.S. 661 (1897). As amended in 1936 (49 Stat. 2041) and 1938 (52 Stat. 942), this law is codified at 2 U.S.C. §§ 192–94 (2000).
94. Kilbourn v. Thompson, 103 U.S. 168, 195 (1881).
95. Id.
96. McGrain v. Daugherty, 273 U.S. at 174.
97. Id. at 175.
98. Id. at 177.

forming or neglecting their duties in respect of the institution and prosecution of proceedings to punish crimes and enforce appropriate remedies against the wrongdoers—specific instances of alleged neglect being recited.[99]

It was enough, said the Court, that the subject of investigation "was one on which legislation could be had and would be materially aided by the information which the investigation was calculated to elicit."[100] That is, a *potential* for legislation was sufficient. A congressional investigation could have legislation as a possible, but not a necessary, outcome. Investigation as pure oversight into the operations of the executive branch was adequate justification.

To accomplish the purpose of legislation or oversight, each House is entitled to compel witnesses to provide testimony pertinent to the legislative inquiry.[101] Even the "potential" theory too narrowly circumscribes legislative investigations. Courts recognize that committee investigations may take researchers up "blind alleys" and into nonproductive enterprises: "To be a valid legislative inquiry there need be no predictable end result."[102]

Presidential Challenges

As implied in President Washington's response to the St. Clair investigation, administrations were prepared to withhold information from Congress if disclosure "would injure the public: consequently were to exercise a discretion." In the nineteenth century, one of the most effective presidential challenges to a legislative demand for documents came from Grover Cleveland. Under great pressure, he refused to buckle to principles he considered fundamental to the effective discharge of executive duties. His steadfastness led to repeal of the Tenure of Office Act, which had given the Senate a major role in the suspension and removal of executive branch employees.

In 1886, the Senate voted to condemn Attorney General Augustus Garland for refusing, "under whatever influence" (meaning Cleveland), to send copies of papers called for in a Senate resolution. For 24 years, from Abraham Lincoln through Chester Arthur, Republicans held control of the White House. Cleveland's election in 1884 interrupted this period of Republican dominance,

---

99. Id.
100. Id.
101. Id. at 180.
102. Eastland v. United States Servicemen's Fund, 421 U.S. 491, 509 (1975).

and he took office in the shadow of the Pendleton Act of 1883, which promised the nation a new breed of nonpartisan civil servant. Cleveland discussed civil service reform in his inaugural address of March 4, 1885, stating that the people had a right to be protected from the "incompetency of public employees who hold their places solely as the reward of partisan service." He decried this "corrupting influence" and insisted that an able citizen who sought public service had the right to expect that "merit and competency shall be recognized instead of party subserviency or the surrender of honest political belief."[103] In his first annual message to Congress, on December 8, 1885, he ventured the hope that "we shall never again be remitted to the system which distributes public positions purely as rewards for partisan service."[104]

Cleveland took care to sprinkle in a few qualifiers, such as "solely" and "purely." It was never his intention to exclude partisan considerations, particularly after inheriting a federal bureaucracy estimated to be "at least" 95 percent Republican.[105] Any official who attended county, district, state, or national conventions of the Republican party, or who had been an active partisan in elections, became a candidate for suspension, no matter how "capable, faithful, and efficient in the discharge of his official duties."[106]

Cleveland's plans for replacing Republicans with Democrats depended upon the advice and consent of the Senate, which remained under Republican control. The Tenure of Office Act of 1867 had given the Senate a role in the suspension and removal of executive officials. The statute required the President to report to the Senate the "evidence and reasons" for suspending an official. If the Senate refused to concur in the suspension, the officer should "forthright resume the functions of the office."[107] After Ulysses S. Grant replaced Andrew Johnson in the White House, Congress revised the statute to give the President greater discretion over suspensions while retaining the Senate's role in the removal process.[108]

The revised legislation provided that during any recess of the Senate the President could, "in his discretion," suspend any civil officer appointed by and with the advice and consent of the Senate, except judges of the federal courts, until the end of the next session of the Senate. The President was further au-

---

103. 10 A Compilation of the Messages and Papers of the Presidents 4887 (James D. Richardson ed.) (hereafter "Richardson").
104. Id. at 4948.
105. S. Rept. No. 135 (Part 2), 49th Cong., 1st Sess. 1 (1886).
106. Id. at 22.
107. 14 Stat. 430 (1867).
108. 16 Stat. 6, §2 (1869).

thorized to designate a suitable person, "subject to be removed in his discretion by the designation of another," to perform the duties of the suspended officer. Within 30 days after the commencement of each session of the Senate, the President would nominate persons to fill all vacancies that existed at the last meeting of the Senate as well as those for places occupied by the suspended officers. If the Senate refused to consent to the appointment of a replacement for a suspended officer, the President was required to nominate another person as soon as practicable.

In his first ten months in office, Cleveland sent to the Senate a list of 643 suspensions,[109] but the Senate refused to act on his nominations to replace the suspended officers. On July 17, 1885, after Cleveland had suspended George M. Duskin from the office of U.S. Attorney for the southern district of Alabama, he designated John D. Burnett to perform the duties of that office, and on December 14, when the Senate returned, he submitted Burnett's nomination.

On December 16, George F. Edmunds of the Senate Judiciary Committee asked Attorney General Garland for all papers and information concerning the conduct and administration of Duskin, as well as the character and conduct of Burnett. On January 25, 1886, after numerous delays convinced the committee that it could not rely on this informal process for obtaining the information, the committee persuaded the Senate to adopt a resolution directing Garland to transmit to the Senate copies of all documents and papers filed in the Justice Department since January 1, 1885, relating to the management and conduct of the office of U.S. Attorney for the southern district of Alabama.[110]

Garland responded that the papers regarding Burnett's fitness for office had already been delivered to the committee, but that it "is not considered that the public interest will be promoted" by transmitting the documents on Duskin to the committee.[111] The committee insisted that under the Constitution either House of Congress must have "at all times the right to know all that officially exists or takes place in any of the Departments of Government."[112] The committee recognized some limits to the investigative power. The House of Representatives could not demand papers relating to treaties still under con-

---

109. S. Rept. No. 135 (Part 1), 49th Cong., 1st Sess. 12–13 (1886). See also Grover Cleveland, The Independence of the Executive 43–45 (1913).
110. 25 Journal of the Executive Proceedings of the Senate 294 (1901).
111. S. Rept. No. 135 (Part 1), 49th Cong., 1st Sess. 3 (1886).
112. Id. at 4.
113. Id. at 4–5.

sideration by the President and the Senate, and papers might be refused in cases where Congress had granted the President a discretionary authority.[113] But just as Congress could claim an implied power to investigate, so could Cleveland claim the implied power to remove executive officials or to withhold documents concerning their removal.

The report from the Senate Judiciary Committee, indirectly criticizing the President, provoked Cleveland to make his views known, and he did so in a communication to the Senate on March 1, 1886. He justified his refusal to give the Senate the papers it wanted on two grounds: statutory interpretation and constitutional authority. Under the revised Tenure of Office Act, the Senate did not appear to have any role in suspensions. It could not explore the reasons for a suspension or put the suspended person back in office. Under the 1869 statute the President did not have to disclose his reasons for suspending an officer, for he acted "in his discretion."

The Senate Judiciary Committee claimed that the Senate was not interested in the "reasons or motives" behind the suspensions, and yet those were precisely what the committee sought. Regarding Duskin's suspension, the committee said "it is plain that the conduct and management of the incumbent is a matter absolutely essential to be known to the Senate in order that it may determine whether it can rightly advise his removal...."[114] Cleveland said that the Senate's request for papers and documents assumed the right "to sit in judgment upon the exercise of my exclusive discretion and Executive function, for which I am solely responsible to the people from whom I have so lately received the sacred trust of office."[115]

Turning to constitutional grounds, Cleveland denied that he had withheld any official or public papers. He regarded the papers and documents addressed to him, or intended for his use, "purely unofficial and private, not infrequently confidential, and having reference to the performance of a duty exclusively mine." Although the papers were kept in the files of the Justice Department, they were deposited there "for my convenience, remaining still completely under my control." Cleveland believed that it would be entirely proper to take them into his own custody, "and if I saw fit to destroy them no one could complain."[116]

He claimed that the President was at liberty to suspend public officers in the absence of any papers or documents. He noted that many suspensions

---

114. S. Rept. No. 135 (Part 1), 49th Cong., 1st Sess. 9 (1886).
115. 10 Richardson 4966.
116. Id. at 4963.

from office were more the result of oral representations made to him by citizens of known good repute, including members of Congress, than of letters and documents presented for his examination.[117] In the event the Senate refused to confirm one of his nominees, he would not assume the right to ask the reasons for the Senate's action, and he did not want the Senate inquiring into his reasons for suspensions or removals.[118] It was Cleveland's position that the power to remove or suspend public officials was vested in the President alone. The Constitution expressly provided that the executive power be vested in the President, and that he shall take care that the laws be faithfully executed.[119] His message suggested that the Tenure of Office Act, however interpreted, intruded upon the constitutional powers of the President.[120]

Because of Democratic control of the House of Representatives, the Senate was unable to act legislatively against Cleveland. Instead, the Judiciary Committee reported four Senate resolutions to the floor for consideration. The first resolution was a motion to adopt and agree to the committee report. The second expressed the Senate's "condemnation of the refusal of the Attorney-General, under whatever influence," to send copies of papers called for by the Senate resolution of January 25. The third resolution, which represented the ultimate sanction, stated that it was the duty of the Senate, under the circumstances then prevailing, to refuse to give advice and consent to proposed removals of officers. The fourth resolution suggested that Cleveland had violated a public law that gave preference to persons seeking civil office who had been honorably discharged from the military service by reason of disability incurred in the line of duty.[121] According to information available to Democrats on the committee, Duskin had never been a Union soldier. He was either a member of the Confederate army or a Confederate sympathizer in his native state of North Carolina.[122]

During floor debate, Senator Edmunds denied that Presidents had exclusive control over "unofficial and private" papers. Any papers located within a department, he said, must of necessity be public papers available to Congress.[123] A Democrat on the committee, James Lawrence Pugh, charged that the whole proceeding was in vain because Duskin's term of office had expired

---

117. Id. at 4964.
118. Id. at 4967.
119. Id. at 4964.
120. Id. at 4965–66.
121. S. Doc. No. 135 (Part 1), 49th Cong., 1st Sess. 12 (1886).
122. S. Doc. No. 135 (Part 2), 49th Cong., 1st Sess. 22 (1886).
123. 17 Cong. Rec. 2214 (1886).

on December 20, 1885. What possible purpose could the Senate have in asking for papers? If Senators decided that the suspension was improper or unwise, they could not restore Duskin to an office that had expired. Pugh said that "the Senate is thrown into a moot-court in discussing a purely abstract question."[124]

By considering a resolution to condemn the Attorney General, the Senate marched into territory reserved by the Constitution to the House of Representatives. Did the Senate intend to usurp the power of impeachment by pronouncing a judgment of conviction before the official had been tried?[125]

After a debate occupying almost 200 pages of the *Congressional Record* (printed with much smaller type than at present), the Senate voted on the four resolutions. Had they been adopted, they would have had no legal effect. Senate resolutions merely express the sentiment of a majority of that body. The first resolution, adopting the committee report, passed by a strictly partisan vote of 32 to 26. The second, expressing condemnation of the Attorney General, passed along partisan lines, 32 to 25. The third, concerning the duty of the Senate to refuse its advice and consent to Cleveland's proposed removal of officers, passed 30 to 29. Two Republicans (John H. Mitchell of Oregon and Charles H. Van Wyck of Nebraska) and a Readjuster (Harrison H. Riddleberger of Virginia) voted with the Democrats.[126] The final resolution, about giving preference to disabled veterans, could have been for mother or apple pie. It passed 56 to one.[127]

Even after its amendment in 1869, there had been strong doubts about the constitutionality and propriety of the Tenure of Office Act. The suspicion was strongly held that Congress, intoxicated by its assertions of authority during the Andrew Johnson administration, had arrogated unto itself a power that belonged to the President. The House of Representatives had voted almost unanimously in 1869 to repeal the act, but the Senate succeeded in preserving some role for itself in removals.

On December 14, 1885, before the Senate had made headlines with its resolutions against the Attorney General and the President, Senator George Hoar (R-Mass.) introduced a bill for the total and complete repeal of the Tenure of Office Act. The bill passed the Senate on December 17, 1886, by a vote of 30 to 22. Four Republicans—Jonathan Chase of Rhode Island, George Hoar,

---

124. Id. at 2247.
125. Id. at 2617.
126. Id. at 2810–14.
127. Id. at 2814.
128. 13 Cong. Rec. 248 (1886).

John J. Ingalls of Kansas, and John H. Mitchell of Oregon—joined with the Democrats to form the majority.[128] The bill found easy acceptance in the House of Representatives and was enacted into law on March 3, 1887. Cleveland had not only prevailed in his confrontation with the Senate over documents, but had helped lay the foundation for the repeal of a troubled, and troubling, statute.[129]

Subsequent chapters explore the use of particular congressional powers to force the release of documents or testimony by executive officials: the appropriations power, impeachment, Senate advice and consent on appointments, congressional subpoenas, the contempt power, and House resolutions of inquiry. Other chapters deal with a particular statute (the "Seven Member Rule"), access by the General Accounting Office, testimony by White House officials, and claims by administrations that documents related to national security may be kept from Congress.

---

129. 24 Stat. 500 (1887). For more details on the conflict between Cleveland the Senate over documents, see Louis Fisher, "Grover Cleveland Against the Senate," 7 Capitol Studies 11 (1979).

2

The Appropriations Power

Presidents may decide to surrender documents—even sensitive or confidential—as the price for obtaining funds for programs considered important to the executive branch. This congressional leverage appears in a number of early executive-legislative confrontations, when lawmakers flexed their muscles in exercising the traditional power of the purse. Acting out of an abundance of caution, Presidents may decide to share treaty documents with the House in order to obtain funds to implement a treaty. Administrations can also act recklessly by ignoring prohibitions in appropriations bills, as with funding the Contras during the Reagan years. To conceal such activities, executive officials may decide to testify falsely and either withhold documents or doctor them. Finally, although the administration may treat the carrying out of statutory programs as purely an executive power, congressional committees are often included in administrative decisions because they are key to authorizing and appropriating funds. In sharing those decisions, committee members will have access to the documents they need.

Power of the Purse

The framers were familiar with efforts by English kings to rely on extraparliamentary sources of revenue for their military expeditions and other activities. Some of the payments came from foreign governments. Because of those transgressions, England lurched into a civil war and Charles I lost both his office and his head.[1] The rise of democratic government is directly traceable to legislative control over all expenditures.

The U.S. Constitution attempted to avoid the British history of civil war and bloodshed by vesting the power of the purse squarely in Congress. Under

---

1. Paul Einzig, The Control of the Purse 57–62, 100–06 (1959).

Article I, Section 9, "No Money shall be drawn from the Treasury, but in Consequence of Appropriations made by Law." In Federalist No. 48, James Madison explained that "the legislative department alone has access to the pockets of the people." The power of the purse, he said in Federalist No. 58, represents the "most complete and effectual weapon with which any constitution can arm the immediate representatives of the people, for obtaining a redress of every grievance, and for carrying into effect every just and salutary measure."

Warm-Up Debates in 1789

One of the first responsibilities awaiting Congress in 1789 was the creation of the executive departments. The Departments of Foreign Affairs and War were recognized as executive in nature and assigned directly to the President. Those departmental heads were under no obligation to come before Congress and present reports. No such deference was extended to the Secretary of the Treasury. It was proposed on June 25, 1789, that the Secretary not only digest plans for the improvement and management of the revenue but also *report* them. Some lawmakers objected to this opportunity for executive influence over Congress, but Benjamin Goodhue saw no grounds for concern:

> We certainly carry our dignity to the extreme, when we refuse to receive information from any but ourselves. It must be admitted, that the Secretary of the Treasury will, from the nature of his office, be better acquainted with the subject of improving the revenue or curtailing expense, than any other person; if he is thus capable of affording useful information, shall we reckon it hazardous to receive it?[2]

Thomas Fitzsimons of Pennsylvania suggested that the bill be amended by striking out the word "report" and inserting prepare in its place. The bill enacted into law reflected that change: "...it shall be the duty of the Secretary of the Treasury to digest and prepare plans for the improvement and management of the revenue, and for the support of public credit; to prepare and report estimates of the public revenue, and the public expenditures...." However, he was also required to "make report, and give information to either branch of the legislature, in person or in writing (as he may be required), re-

---

2. 1 Annals of Cong. 594 (June 25, 1789).

specting all matters referred to him by the Senate or House of Representatives, or which shall appertain to his office."[3]

Although the Senate is the only legislative chamber with an express role in treaty-making, most treaties require appropriations and it is through that process that the House is able to insist on documents from the executive branch. The first such debate occurred on August 11, 1789, when the House took up a bill to provide expenses for Indian treaties. Rep. Theodore Sedgwick, a Federalist from Massachusetts, "thought it a dangerous doctrine to be established, that the House had any authority to intervene in the management of treaties."[4] To Sedgwick, the Constitution gave the treaty power solely to the President and the Senate.

Rep. John Page of Virginia, who would join forces with the Jeffersonian Democrats, disagreed. Members of the House "had a right to say what money should be expended in this way. They had a right to say whether they would grant any or not; otherwise the President and Senate might do as they pleased with respect to negotiations, and call upon the House in all cases to defray their expense."[5] With regard to the Indian treaty, how much should the House appropriate? As was the custom at that time, the funding bill contained a blank. The first motion was to fill the blank with $41,000. Rep. Thomas Sumter, a South Carolinian Democrat, objected that the House had "no data to govern them in making the provisions; consequently, gentlemen were to judge from their own opinions what would be a proper sum." He suggested $16,000.[6]

If data was lacking, the House could have requested additional documentation from President Washington, or the administration—aware of concern in the House—could have volunteered the information. Rep. Abraham Baldwin, a Federalist from Georgia, said he had seen an estimate that mentioned two sums that justified the full $41,000: $25,000 for the Creeks, and $16,000 for the Wabash Indians.[7] The House vote on the $41,000 failed, 23 to 24. James Madison then moved to fill the blank with $40,000, "which was a round sum." His motion was agreed to, 28 to 23.[8] The reduction was fairly insignificant, but the House had sent an important signal: On treaty matters it would not roll over and passively endorse whatever the President and the Senate agreed to.

---

3. 1 Stat. 65, §2 (1789).
4. 1 Annals of Cong. 690 (August 11, 1789).
5. Id. at 691.
6. Id. at 698.
7. Id. at 701.
8. Id. at 703.

Treaty Disputes, 1791–96

President George Washington inherited the noxious American practice of paying annual bribes ("tributes") to four countries in North Africa: Morocco, Algiers, Tunis, and Tripoli. The United States made regular payments to allow American merchant vessels to operate in those waters without interference.[9] Those countries also held a number of American seamen in prison. Washington knew that whatever he wanted to do in this area required support from the House of Representatives.

Algerine Treaty

President Washington told the Senate on February 22, 1791, that he would "take measures for the ransom of our citizens in captivity in Algiers, in conformity with your resolution of advice in the first instance, *so soon as the moneys necessary shall be appropriated by the Legislature*, and shall be in readiness."[10] The Senate was not happy about including the House as a participant in the treaty process.[11]

On March 11, 1792, Secretary of State Thomas Jefferson offered advice to Washington on whether he should make a treaty with the Algerines "on the single vote of the Senate, without taking that of the Representatives."[12] Jefferson, who generally defended executive prerogatives, did not seek refuge behind narrow legal reasoning and argue that the House had no constitutional role in the treaty-making process. He analyzed the issue pragmatically: "We must go to Algiers with cash in our hands. Where shall we get it? By loan? By converting money now in the treasury?"[13] He reasoned that a loan might be obtained on presidential authority, "but as this could not be repaid without a subsequent act of legislature, the Representatives might refuse it. So if money in the treasury be converted, they may refuse to sanction it."[14]

Next, Jefferson said that just as Senators "expect to be consulted beforehand" about a pending treaty, if Representatives need to fund a treaty "why

---

9. Gerhard Casper, Separating Power: Essays on the Founding Period 45–50 (1997); Louis Fisher, Presidential War Power 24 (1995).
10. 1 American State Papers: Foreign Relations 128 (1833) (emphasis added).
11. Roy Swanstrom, "The United States Senate, 1789–1801," S. Doc. No. 64, 87th Cong., 1st Sess. 120 (1961).
12. "The Anas," 1 Writings of Thomas Jefferson 294 (Bergh ed. 1903).
13. Id.
14. Id.

should not they expect to be consulted in like manner, when the case admits?"[15] Here Jefferson distinguished between the President's latitude in entering into treaties that can be implemented without appropriations (self-executing treaties) and those that are dead in the water unless Congress decides to provide funds:

> A treaty is a law of the land. But prudence will point out this difference to be attended to in making them; viz. where a treaty contains such articles only as will go into execution of themselves, or be carried into execution by the judges, they may be safely made; but where there are articles which require a law to be passed afterwards by the legislature, great caution is requisite.[16]

After advising "against hazarding this transaction without the sanction of both Houses," Jefferson said that the President concurred.[17] Having resolved a potential collision between the President and the House, Jefferson now learned about a dispute between the Senate and the House. He found out that the Senate was willing to pay an annual tribute to Algiers "to redeem our captives," but was "unwilling to have the lower House applied to previously to furnish the money; they wished the President to take the money from the treasury, or open a loan for it."[18] Jefferson said that Senators feared that if the President consulted the House on one occasion, this "would give them a handle always to claim it, and would let them into a participation of the power of making treaties, which the Constitution had given exclusively to the President and Senate."[19]

Senators tried to bolster their prerogative with another argument, but this one backfired. If the House voted for a particular sum, Senators warned, "it would not be a secret."[20] Washington decided against trying to circumvent the House by making a loan. Moreover, he "had no confidence in the secrecy of the Senate, and did not choose to take money from the Treasury or to borrow."[21] Washington did not like having to persuade the House to fund a treaty that he thought it should support as a constitutional duty,[22] but Jefferson ad-

---

15. Id.
16. Id.
17. Id. at 295.
18. Id. at 305.
19. Id. at 305–06.
20. Id. at 306.
21. Id.
22. Id.

vised that "wherever the agency of either, or both Houses would be requisite subsequent to a treaty, to carry it into effect, it would be prudent to consult them previously, if the occasion admitted."[23] Advance consultation with the House was necessary, "especially in the case of money, as they held the purse strings, and would be jealous of them."[24]

Washington followed Jefferson's advice. In a message to Congress on December 16, 1793, regarding a treaty with Morocco for the payment of ransom and establishing peace with Algiers, Washington forwarded to both the Senate and the House communications and confidential letters that he asked the lawmakers to keep secret.[25] Throughout the process of treaty-making with Algiers, whatever information Washington "sent to the Senate he submitted also to the Representatives."[26] Later that month, the House went into secret session to debate the treaty, clearing the chamber "of all persons but the members and clerk."[27] Some members objected that "secrecy in a Republican Government wounds the majesty of the sovereign people," but in reply to such arguments it was said that

> because this Government is Republican, it will not be pretended that it can have no secrets. The PRESIDENT OF THE UNITED STATES is the depository of secret transactions; his duty may lead him to delegate those secrets to the members of the House, and the success, safety, and energy of the Government may depend on keeping those secrets inviolably.[28]

Lawmakers argued that the public had "interests as well as rights," and it was the duty of Congress "to take every possible measure to promote those interests."[29] Discussing secret matters publicly "was the ready way to sacrifice the public interest, and to deprive the Government of all foreign information."[30] The galleries were cleared. For several days the House debated, in secret, the confidential documents that Washington had entrusted to them.[31] With this close cooperation between Washington and the House, Congress authorized

---

23. Id. at 307.
24. Id.
25. 4 Annals of Cong. 20–21 (1793).
26. Ralston Hayden, The Senate and Treaties, 1789–1817, at 52 (1920).
27. 4 Annals of Cong. 150.
28. Id.
29. Id.
30. Id.
31. Id. at 151–55.

and funded the treaty with Algiers.[32] The treaty included an annual amount to be paid to the Dey of Algiers.[33]

Jay Treaty

Having worked closely with both Houses on the Algerine Treaty, President Washington pursued an entirely different strategy with the Jay Treaty. In his long and honorable career, his conduct on the Jay treaty marked a rare occasion where a public statement by Washington could be called trite and disingenuous. He now argued that (1) the House could not be trusted with secret communications and (2) treaty-making—within the legislative branch—lay solely with the Senate. On March 1, 1796, he advised Congress that the Jay Treaty had been ratified.[34] The House had to decide whether to pass the necessary legislation to put the treaty into effect.

The treaty was controversial in many respects. First, a number of lawmakers had objected to the nomination of Chief Justice John Jay to negotiate the treaty. They said it would have been better for someone within the administration to handle the matter, instead of delegating the task to a special envoy outside the executive branch. Also, the treaty might come to Jay later for judicial consideration.[35] Second, Jay decided to depart from his instructions and agree to various restrictions on American commerce.[36] With its express constitutional responsibilities over foreign commerce, the House had a right to take a close look. A rejected Senate resolution stated that the treaty "asserts a power in the President and Senate, to control, and even annihilate the constitutional right of the Congress of the United States over their commercial intercourse with foreign nations."[37] Third, the Senate ratified the treaty by a bare minimum, voting along party lines to produce the required two-thirds majority, 20 to 10.

Alexander Hamilton advised Washington not to release the treaty instructions to the House, describing the instructions as "in general a crude mass" that would do "no credit to the administration."[38] Washington knew his po-

---

32. 8 Stat. 133 (1795); see Casper, Separating Power, at 51–65.
33. 8 Stat. 136 (Art. XXII).
34. Annals of Cong., 4th Cong., 1st Sess. 394 (Mar. 1, 1796).
35. Hayden, The Senate and Treaties, at 69–70.
36. Abraham D. Sofaer, War, Foreign Affairs and Constitutional Power: The Origins 85 (1976).
37. Hayden, The Senate and Treaties, at 82n.
38. Id. at 90.

litical footing was precarious. In a letter to Hamilton, he said that "at present the cry against the Treaty is like that against a mad-dog; and every one, in a manner, seems engaged in running it down."[39] Washington acted not on constitutional principles but on a political calculation. Withholding the documents from the House, he knew, would enrage some members. Releasing the documents, he feared, might make matters worse. He decided to take a chance: Keep the documents from the House and see what happened. If the votes went against him, he could always take the next step and negotiate a settlement with members of the House.

Rep. Edward Livingston took the lead in requesting documents from the administration, stating that "it was very desirable, therefore, that every document which might tend to throw light on the subject should be before the House."[40] He offered a resolution that President Washington "be requested to lay before this House a copy of the instructions given to the Minister of the United States who negotiated the Treaty with Great Britain,... together with the correspondence and other documents relative to the said Treaty."[41] Recognizing that some of the negotiations might be unfinished, he modified his resolution by adding this language: "Excepting such of said papers as any existing negotiation may render improper to be disclosed."[42] Addressing the role of the House in the treaty process, Livingston cautioned that the House possessed "a discretionary power of carrying the Treaty into effect, or refusing it their sanction."[43] Without the papers, the House might decide to retaliate by refusing the funds needed to implement the treaty. Rep. Albert Gallatin agreed that the House did not have to acquiesce in decisions reached by the President and the Senate if a treaty encroached upon powers expressly reserved to the House, such as the regulation of trade.[44]

After weeks of debate, the House supported the Livingston resolution by a margin of 62 to 37.[45] Some of the documents had already been shared with the House. Livingston, as chairman of the House Committee on American Seamen, "together with the whole committee, had been allowed access to these papers, and had inspected them. The same privilege, he doubted not, would be given to any member of the House who would request it."[46] During this

---

39. 34 The Writings of George Washington 262.
40. Annals of Cong., 4th Cong., 1st Sess., at 400.
41. Id. at 400–41.
42. Id. at 426.
43. Id. at 427–28.
44. Id. at 437, 466–74.
45. Id. at 759.
46. Id. at 461 (remarks of Rep. Harper).

same period Congress had passed legislation to provide for the relief and protection of American seamen, many of whom had been impressed by Great Britain.[47] One member of the House said that with respect to the papers on the Jay Treaty, "he did not think there were any secrets in them. He believed he had seen them all."[48] He remarked that "[f]or the space of ten weeks any member of that House might have seen them."[49] Another member of the House noted that his colleagues could have walked over to the office of the Secretary of the Senate to see the papers, but why, he said, "depend upon the courtesy of the Clerk for information which might as well be obtained in a more direct channel?"[50]

Madison, who voted for Livingston's resolution, elaborated on his own views regarding executive-legislative struggles over information. He began by avowing his intent to proceed "with the utmost respect to the decorum and dignity of the House, with a proper delicacy to the other departments of Government, and, at the same time, with fidelity and responsibility, for our constituents."[51] However, he wanted the resolution drafted in such a form "as not to bear even the appearance of encroaching on the Constitutional rights of the Executive."[52] Livingston's amendment to the resolution, Madison felt, went a long way toward removing constitutional objections.[53] Madison proposed the following language to further ease the tensions between the branches: "Except so much of said papers as, in his judgment, it may not be consistent with the interest of the United States, at this time, to disclose."[54] Madison's amendment failed, 37 to 47.[55]

In denying the House access to documents, Washington cited a number of reasons, including the need for caution and secrecy in foreign negotiations, as well as the exclusive role of the Senate to participate as a member of the legislative branch in treaty matters.[56] He reasoned that the only ground on which the House might request documents regarding treaty instructions and negotiations would be impeachment, "which the resolution has not expressed."[57]

---

47. Id. at 802–20.
48. Id. at 642 (remarks of Rep. Williams).
49. Id.
50. Id. at 588 (remarks of Rep. Freeman).
51. Id. at 437.
52. Id. at 438.
53. Id.
54. Id.
55. Id.
56. Id. at 759.
57. Id. at 760.

His decision to withhold documents from the House was not an exercise of executive privilege, because he acknowledged that "all the papers affecting the negotiation with Great Britain were laid before the Senate, when the Treaty itself was communicated for their consideration and advice."[58]

Washington's message to the House is unpersuasive on several grounds. First, members of the House were not requesting documents as part of the treaty process. They did not need the President to tell them the Constitution excludes the House from treaty-making. They knew that. But the treaty process was complete; the Jay Treaty had been negotiated, approved by the Senate, and ratified. The House was now requesting documents as part of the *post*-treaty process: the appropriation of funds needed to implement the treaty. The House had a right to whatever papers it needed to make an informed legislative judgment. Washington seemed to understand that right. A letter from Hamilton to Washington implies that Washington had initially considered giving the House access to the papers it requested:

> The course you suggest has some obvious advantages & merits careful consideration. I am not however without fears that there are things in the *instructions* to Mr. Jay which good policy, considering the matter *externally* as well as *internally*, would render it inexpedient to communicate. This I shall ascertain to day. A middle course is under consideration — that of not communicating the papers to the house but of declaring that the Secretary of State is directed to permit them to be *read* by the *members individually*.[59]

In other words, because Washington seemed prepared to submit the papers to the House, Hamilton was offering an intermediate position of retaining the papers in the custody of the Secretary of State while allowing members of the House to come and read them in his presence. The editor of Hamilton's papers reported that, in an unfound letter to Hamilton, Washington "apparently suggested that he planned to comply with the request in Livingston's resolution."[60]

Hamilton, no longer in the administration, later advised President Washington to deny the House the documents it requested on the Jay Treaty. He thought that production of the papers "cannot fail to start [a] new and unpleasant Game — it will be fatal to the Negotiating Power of the Government

---

58. Id. at 761.
59. Letter from Hamilton to Washington (March 24, 1796), in 20 The Papers of Alexander Hamilton 81–82 (Syrett ed. 1974) (emphasis in original).
60. Editor's Introductory note to letter from Hamilton to Washington (March 7, 1796), id. at 66.

if it is to be a matter of course for a call of either House of Congress to bring forth all the communication however confidential."[61] Having taken a hard line, Hamilton cautioned Washington not to appear too abrupt or imperious when communicating to the House: "[A] too peremptory and unqualified refusal might be liable to just criticism."[62]

Shortly after Washington's message to the House on the papers, Rep. Thomas Blount introduced two resolutions (both adopted 57 to 35), stating that although the House of Representatives had no role in making treaties,

> ...when a Treaty stipulates regulations on any of the subjects submitted by the Constitution to the power of Congress, it must depend, for its execution, as to such stipulations, on a law or laws to be passed by Congress. And it is the Constitutional right and duty of the House of Representatives, in all such cases, to deliberate on the expediency or inexpediency of carrying such Treaty into effect, and to determine and act thereon, as, in their judgment, may be most conducive to the public good.[63]

Madison, supporting the Blount resolutions, said that the House "must have a right, in all cases, to ask for information which might assist their deliberations on the subjects submitted to them by the Constitution; being responsible, nevertheless, for the propriety of their measures."[64] Madison was "as ready to admit that the Executive had a right, under a due responsibility, also, to withhold information, when of a nature that did not permit a disclosure of it at the time."[65] Yet he expressed some misgivings about Washington's premise that the papers were not related to any objective of the House:

> [The rationale] implied that the Executive was not only to judge of the proper objects and functions of the Executive department, but, also, of the objects and functions of the House. He was not only to decide how far the Executive trust would permit a disclosure of information, but how far the Legislative trust could derive advantage from it. It belonged, he said, to each department to judge for itself. If the Executive conceived that, in relation to his own department,

---

61. Letter from Hamilton to Washington (March 7, 1796), id. at 68.
62. Id. at 69.
63. Annals of Cong., 4th Cong., 1st Sess. 771 (1796). For the votes, see id. at 782–83.
64. Id. at 773.
65. Id.

papers could not be safely communicated, he might, on that ground, refuse them, because he was the competent though a responsible judge within his own department. If the papers could be communicated without injury to the objects of his department, he ought not to refuse them as irrelative to the objects of the House of Representatives; because the House was, in such cases, the only proper judge of its own objects.[66]

The House had driven home its point: If a treaty entered into by the President and the Senate required legislation and appropriations to be carried out, the House would be strongly positioned to insist on whatever papers and documentation it needed to judge the merits of the treaty. Denied such information, it could threaten to block implementation. It might easily tell the President: "Sorry, but without additional documents supplied by you, we have inadequate grounds to pass the necessary legislation."

Precisely those conditions prevailed in 1796 because President Washington needed the support of both Houses to pass an appropriation of $90,000 to implement the Jay Treaty.[67] Rep. Samuel Maclay lamented the situation, noting that members of the House, having been denied the papers they requested, "were left to take their measures in the dark; or, in other words, they were called upon to act without information."[68] He proposed the following preamble and resolution:

> The House…are of opinion that [the treaty] is in many respects highly injurious to the interests of the United States; yet, were they possessed of any information which could justify the great sacrifices contained in the Treaty, their sincere desire to cherish harmony and amicable intercourse with all nations, and their earnest wish to cooperate in hastening a final adjustment of the differences subsisting between the United States and Great Britain, might have induced them to waive their objection to the Treaty;…Therefore,
>
> *Resolved*, That, under the circumstances aforesaid, and with such information as the House possess, it is not expedient at this time to concur in passing the laws necessary for carrying the said Treaty into effect.[69]

The House never voted on Maclay's language. After a lengthy debate, the bill to appropriate funds to implement the treaty passed by the narrow mar-

---

66. Id.
67. Id. at 991.
68. Id. at 970.
69. Id. at 970–71.

gin of 51 to 48.[70] James Madison voted against the bill. An earlier test vote showed the House divided 49 to 49, with the Speaker willing to break the tie to support the treaty.[71] The appropriation was enacted into law.[72] Given the closeness of the vote, had the opposition maintained a narrow margin, it seems reasonable that President Washington would have shared with the House—or with a few selected opponents—the documents needed to swing some votes.

Louisiana Purchase

In 1803, the Jefferson administration entered into discussions with France to purchase territory in the south. Starting with a provisional appropriation of $2 million from Congress to be applied toward the purchase of New Orleans and the Floridas, his negotiators reached agreement to buy the whole of the Louisiana Territory. The purchase would extend the country west of the Mississippi River to the Rocky Mountains, doubling its size. The vast size of the territory convinced Jefferson that he needed the support of both Houses to implement the treaty: "This treaty must of course be laid before both Houses, because both have important functions to exercise respecting it."[73] The executive officials who negotiated the terms, Jefferson said, "have done an act beyond the Constitution."[74] Because Congress would have to "ratify and pay for it,"[75] support would be needed from the House of Representatives.

Legal issues were further complicated by the fact that the Constitution does not explain how the government may annex new territory.[76] In his past public statements, Jefferson had argued strongly in favor of a strict interpretation of the Constitution. Was it necessary to amend the Constitutional to allow for what was not expressly authorized? Jefferson decided against an amendment.

---

70. Id. at 1291.
71. Id. at 1280.
72. 1 Stat. 459 (1796).
73. Letter from Jefferson to Thomas Breckenridge, August 12, 1803; 10 The Writings of Thomas Jefferson 410 (Bergh ed. 1907).
74. Id. at 411.
75. Id.
76. Art. IV, §3, seems to give that authority to both Houses by empowering Congress "to dispose of and make all needful Rules and Regulations respecting the Territory or other Property belonging to the United States."

As he ventured to Levi Lincoln, his Attorney General, the "less that is said about any constitutional difficulties, the better."[77]

Jefferson sent copies of the ratified treaty to both Houses, explaining: "You will observe that some important conditions can not be carried into execution but with the aid of the Legislature, and that time presses a decision on them without delay."[78] The House debated at length a resolution asking Jefferson to submit certain papers and documents relating to the treaty.[79] Some portions of the resolution were adopted, others rejected. The resolution as a whole went down to defeat, 57 to 59.[80] With or without the resolution, there is little doubt that the administration was willing to provide the House with whatever documents it needed to support the treaty. The House subsequently joined the Senate in passing legislation to enable Jefferson to take possession of the Louisiana Territory.[81]

House Participation in Treaty Power

Having established its constitutional position with the Jay Treaty and the Louisiana Purchase, the House continued to insist on its right to deny funding for treaties it opposed. Debate on a commercial treaty with Great Britain in 1816 featured lengthy discussion of the types of treaties that invaded House prerogatives. Rep. John Forsyth (D-Ga.) issued this warning: "take from Congress the regulation of commerce and give it to the treaty-making power, and you entirely exclude from that important power all that branch of the Government which represents the people directly."[82] Each time members of the House made this argument credibly, they increased their chances of gaining access to treaty documents that the administration had shared with the Senate.

Two of the treaties fought out on this battleground were the Gadsden purchase treaty with Mexico in 1853 and the Alaskan purchase treaty with Russia in 1867. The first agreed to pay Mexico $10,000,000 for territory that now

---

77. 10 The Writings of Thomas Jefferson 417 (letter from Jefferson to Attorney General Levi Lincoln, August 30, 1803).
78. 1 Richardson 362–63; see also Annals of Cong., 8th Cong., 1st Sess. 18, 382 (1803).
79. Annals of Cong., 8th Cong., 1st Sess. 385 (1803).
80. Id. at 385–419.
81. 2 Stat. 245, 247 (1803).
82. Annals of Cong. 14th Cong., 1st Sess. 480 (1816).

forms the southern parts of New Mexico and Arizona.[83] A year later, Congress appropriated the funds to implement the treaty.[84] The second offered Russia $7,200,000 for the land that is now Alaska.[85] Some lawmakers denied that Congress, after a treaty has been ratified by the Senate, was obliged "to make an appropriation to execute it as it is to provide for the payment of the salaries of the judges and President, or to vote money to pay an acknowledged debt."[86] During floor debate, some members insisted that the House could refuse funds for treaties it objected to.[87] The following provision failed by the narrow margin of 78 to 80:

> *Provided*, That no purchase in behalf of the United States of any foreign territory shall be hereafter made until after provision by law for its payment; and it is hereby declared that the powers vested by the Constitution in the President and Senate to enter into treaties with foreign Governments do not include the power to complete the purchase of foreign territory before the necessary appropriation shall be made therefor by act of Congress.[88]

The House supported the appropriation of $7,200,000, voting 113 to 43.[89] The appropriations statute, however, carried this warning: "whereas said stipulations [regarding rights and immunities of the inhabitants of the territory] cannot be carried into full force and effect except by legislation to which the consent of both houses of Congress is necessary."[90] Had members of the House concluded that the funds needed for the Gadsden or Alaskan territories were excessive, they could have voted down the appropriation and forced the treaty negotiators to begin again.

House leverage is particularly strong when treaties attempt to change tariffs and duties, because that power is vested expressly in both Houses of Congress. For example, a commercial reciprocity treaty with the Hawaiian Islands in 1875 established new schedules for duties on various goods and articles. To respect the constitutional prerogatives of the House, the treaty specified that it would take effect only after a law "to carry it into operation shall have been

---

83. 10 Stat. 1031 (1853).
84. 10 Stat. 301, ch. 71 (1854).
85. 15 Stat. 539, 543 (Art. VI) (1867).
86. H. Rept. No. 37, 40th Cong., 2d Sess. 45 (1868).
87. Cong. Globe, 40th Cong., 2d Sess. 4053 (1868).
88. Id. at 4055.
89. Id.
90. 15 Stat. 198, ch. 247 (1868).

passed by the Congress of the United States."[91] In 1880, the House declared that the negotiation of a commercial treaty that fixes the rates of duty to be imposed on foreign imports would be "an infraction of the Constitution and an invasion of one of the highest prerogatives of the House of Representatives."[92] Three years later a commercial treaty with Mexico contained language making its validity dependent on action by both Houses of Congress.[93] Although subsequent treaties extended the time available for congressional approval, the House did not support the treaty and it was not implemented.[94]

During this period, the House also challenged the Senate's monopoly over Indian treaties. Article I, Section 8, of the Constitution empowers Congress to "regulate Commerce with foreign Nations, and among the several States, and with the Indian Tribes." For nearly a century Congress treated the tribes as independent nations, subject to the treaty-making power of the President and the Senate. The House began to voice strong opposition to this practice. In 1869, when the Senate inserted funds in a bill to fulfill treaties it had ratified with the Indians, the House withheld its support. The session expired without an appropriation for the Indian Office. Finally, a bill enacted in 1871 contained this language: "*Provided*, That hereafter no Indian nation or tribe within the territory of the United States shall be acknowledged or recognized as an independent nation, tribe, or power with whom the United States may contract by treaty."[95]

In 1880, the House declared that the negotiation of a commercial treaty, fixing the rates of duty to be imposed on foreign imports, would be "an infraction of the Constitution and an invasion of one of the highest prerogatives of the House of Representatives."[96] A commercial treaty with Mexico in 1883 contained a clause making its validity dependent on action by both Houses. The House did not support the treaty and it did not take effect.[97]

---

91. 19 Stat. 627 (Art. V) (1875).
92. 2 Hinds' Precedents § 1524.
93. 24 Stat. 975, 983 (Art. VIII) (1883).
94. 25 Stat. 1370, 1371 (1885); 2 Hinds' Precedents §§ 1526–28. For studies that explore the role of the House in implementing treaties, see Chalfant Robinson, "The Treaty-Making Power of the House of Representatives," 12 Yale Rev. 191 (1903), and Ivan M. Stone, "The House of Representatives and the Treaty-Making Power," 17 Ky. L. J. 216 (1929).
95. 16 Stat. 566 (1871). See also U.S. Department of the Interior, Federal Indian Law 138–214 (1958).
96. 2 Hinds' Precedents § 1524.
97. 24 Stat. 975 (1883); 25 Stat. 1370 (1885); 24 Stat. 1018 (1886); and 2 Hinds' Precedents §§ 1526–28.

The House continues to make its will felt in treaty matters. Although the Ford administration believed it could enter into an executive agreement with regard to military bases in Spain, the Senate insisted it be done by treaty.[98] The administration conceded that point, but then ran into trouble when members of both the House and the Senate objected to language in the treaty that appeared to make appropriations mandatory over a five-year period. The administration also maintained that the treaty constituted an *authorization* to have funds appropriated, thus threatening to bypass the jurisdiction of the Senate Committee on Foreign Relations and the House Committee on Foreign Affairs. The Senate Resolution of Advice and Consent contained a declaration that the sums referred to in the Spanish treaty "shall be made available for obligation through the normal procedures of the Congress, including the process of prior authorization and annual appropriations."[99] This guaranteed congressional involvement for the authorizing and appropriating committees of *both* Houses. Congress enacted legislation in 1976 to authorize the appropriation of funds needed to implement the treaty.[100] If in considering this legislation the authorizing and appropriating committees in the House wanted additional documents, the executive branch was in no position to withhold the information by claiming that the treaty power is reserved to the President and the Senate.

The Spanish Bases Treaty was replaced by an executive agreement in 1982. The agreement stipulates that the supply of defense articles and services are subject to "the annual authorizations and appropriations contained in the United States security assistance legislation." Although the agreement promised support "in the highest amounts, the most favorable terms, and the widest variety of forces," it also conditioned such support on what "may be lawful and feasible."[101] In short, U.S. officials could negotiate whatever they liked; what Spain actually received depended on action by both Houses.

There are no clear guidelines on the types of national policy that must be included only in a treaty and not in a statute. After the Senate failed to support a treaty for the annexation of Texas, President John Tyler advised the House that the power of Congress is "fully competent in some other form of

---

98. Louis Fisher, Constitutional Conflicts between Congress and the President 239 (1997).

99. S. Rept. No. 94-941, 94th Cong., 2d Sess. 2 (1976).

100. 90 Stat. 765, §507 (1976); 90 Stat. 2498 (1976).

101. "Agreement on Friendship, Defense, and Cooperation Between the United States of America and the Kingdom of Spain," Complementary Agreement Three, Article 2 (signed July 2, 1982).

proceeding to accomplish everything that a formal ratification of the treaty could have accomplished."[102] He gave the House the rejected treaty "together with all the correspondence and documents which have heretofore been submitted to the Senate in its executive sessions."[103] The papers embraced not only the series made public by order of the Senate, "but others from which the veil of secrecy has not been removed by that body, but which I deem to be essential to a just appreciation of the entire question."[104] The joint resolution for annexing Texas to the United States passed Congress and became law.[105]

The coequal role of the House in international agreements was evident in 1994 when President Bill Clinton submitted the Uruguay Round Agreements to Congress as a bill rather than as a treaty. The purpose of the bill was to implement the worldwide General Agreements on Tariffs and Trade (GATT). Although Laurence H. Tribe testified that the proposal had such impact on federalism that it required presentation as a treaty rather than a bill,[106] the subject matter of NAFTA and GATT—international trade—was certainly within the jurisdiction of Congress as a whole to "regulate Commerce with foreign Nations,"[107] and therefore merited action by both Houses through the regular statutory process. The bill was enacted into law on December 8, 1993.[108]

In 2001, the Eleventh Circuit ruled that the issue of whether NAFTA was a "treaty" requiring Senate ratification pursuant to the Treaty Clause, or could instead be enacted as a statute, represented a nonjusticiable political question.[109] It found that the Treaty Clause failed to "outline the circumstances, if any, under which its procedures must be adhered to when approving international commercial treaties."[110]

---

102. 5 Richardson 2176.
103. Id.
104. Id.
105. 5 Stat. 797 (1845). For other joint resolutions used to accomplish a public policy that had failed through the treaty process, see Louis Fisher, Constitutional Conflicts between Congress and the President 238 (4th ed. 1997).
106. "S. 2467, GATT Implementing Legislation," hearings before the Senate Committee on Commerce, Science, and Transportation, 103d Cong., 2d Sess. 302–12 (1994).
107. Bruce Ackerman and David Golove, "Is NAFTA Constitutional?," 108 Harv. L. Rev. 799 (1995); Laurence H. Tribe, "Taking Text and Structure Seriously: Reflections on Free-Form Method in Constitutional Interpretation," 108 Harv. L. Rev. 1223 (1995).
108. 107 Stat. 2057 (1993).
109. Made in the USA Foundation v. United States, 242 F.3d 1300 (11th Cir. 2001), cert. denied, sub nom. United Steelworkers of America, AFL-CIO, et al., 534 U.S. 1039 (2001).
110. 242 F.3d at 1315.

Funding the Contras

Beginning in 1982, Congress adopted a variety of statutory directives to restrict the Reagan administration's assistance to the Contra forces, which executive officials hoped would overthrow the Sandinista government in Nicaragua. Over the years, Congress learned that the administration continued to pursue its policy in Central America.[111] Finally, on October 12, 1984, Congress adopted strict language intended to prohibit all executive assistance of any kind to support the Contras. The all-embracing language of the Boland Amendment appeared to prevent further circumventions by executive officials:

> During fiscal year 1985, no funds available to the Central Intelligence Agency, the Department of Defense, or any other agency or entity of the United States involved in intelligence activities may be obligated or expended for the purpose or which would have the effect of supporting, directly or indirectly, military or paramilitary operations in Nicaragua by any nation, group, organization, movement, or individual.[112]

Congress constructed this tortured language because the administration had demonstrated a willingness to exploit every possible loophole. It was the intention of Congress in 1984 to close them all. Once the Iran-Contra scandal became public in 1986, some executive officials used the excuse that they found the statutory restrictions too confusing or inconsistent. Senator Christopher Dodd (D-Conn.) suspected early in 1985 that the administration might seek ways of continuing assistance to the Contras. During Senate hearings, he said there had been rumors or newspaper stories that the administration might try to fund the Contras "through private parties or through funneling funds through friendly third nations, or possibly through a new category of assistance and asking the Congress to fund the program openly."[113] Ambassador Langhorne Motley, appearing as the administration's spokesman, assured Dodd that the executive branch understood the meaning of the Boland Amendment and had no intention of trying to evade it with tricks: "Nobody is trying to play games with you or any other Member of Congress. That res-

---

111. Louis Fisher, "How Tightly Can Congress Draw the Purse Strings?," 83 Am. J. Int'l L. 758 (1989).
112. 98 Stat. 1837, 1935, §8066(a) (1984).
113. "Security and Development Assistance," hearings before the Senate Committee on Foreign Relations, 99th Cong., 1st Sess. 908 (1985).

olution stands, and it will continue to stand; and it says no direct or indirect. And that is pretty plain English; it does not have to be written by any bright, young lawyers. And we are going to continue to comply with that."[114]

Motley provided similar assurances to the House Committee on Appropriations on April 18, 1985, testifying that the administration would not attempt to solicit funds from outside sources to assist the Contras.[115] When President Ronald Reagan signed the continuing resolution that contained the strict language of the Boland Amendment, he did not issue a statement claiming that Congress had overstepped its powers and that the administration would pursue its course in Nicaragua. The Attorney General did not challenge the constitutionality of the Boland Amendment. The Office of Legal Counsel in the Justice Department did not conclude in any internal memorandum that the amendment was invalid or nonbinding.

Nevertheless, at the very moment that Motley testified before two congressional committees and offered his assurances, executive officials were actively soliciting funds from private parties and from foreign governments to assist the Contras. Instead of overthrowing the Sandinista regime, the administration almost overthrew itself. As explained in the next chapter, President Reagan waived all claims to executive privilege to avoid the risk of impeachment.

Legislative Vetoes

When executive agencies are required to submit certain programs or policies to designated committees for approval, the committees have strong grounds for insisting on documents. These committee vetoes date back to the period just after the Civil War. Legislation in 1867 placed the following restriction on appropriations for public buildings and grounds: "To pay for completing the repairs and furnishing the executive mansion, thirty-five thousand dollars: *Provided*, That no further payments shall be made on any accounts for repairs and furnishing the executive mansion until such accounts shall have been submitted to a joint committee of Congress, and approved by such committee."[116]

At various times, Presidents challenged the constitutionality of these committee vetoes. In 1920, President Woodrow Wilson vetoed a bill because it provided that no government publication could be printed, issued, or discontin-

---

114. Id. at 910.
115. "Department of Defense Appropriations for 1986 (Part 2)," hearings before the House Committee on Appropriations, 99th Cong., 1st Sess. 1092 (1985).
116. 14 Stat. 469 (1867).

ued unless authorized under regulations prescribed by the Joint Committee on Printing. Wilson said that Congress had no right to endow a joint committee or a committee of either House "with power to prescribe 'regulations' under which executive departments may operate."[117] In 1933, Attorney General William Mitchell regarded as unconstitutional a bill that authorized the Joint Committee on Internal Revenue Taxation to make the final decision on any tax refund in excess of $20,000."[118] The joint committee presently conducts a review (in effect a veto) of tax refunds that exceed $2,000,000.[119]

During World War II, a number of committee vetoes emerged to take care of emergency conditions. Because of the volume of wartime construction it became impractical to follow the customary practice of having Congress authorize each defense installation or public works project. Beginning with an informal system in 1942, all proposals for acquisition of land and leases were submitted in advance to the Naval Affairs Committees for their approval. On the basis of that informal understanding, Congress agreed to pass general authorization statutes in lump sum without specifying the particular projects. Two years later Congress converted that informal practice to a statutory requirement. Additional "coming into agreement" provisions were added in 1949 and 1951, requiring the approval of the Armed Services Committees for acquisition of land and real estate transactions.[120]

Beginning with President Truman, the executive branch began to object to these committee vetoes, often threatening not to abide by them. In 1955, Attorney General Herbert Brownell protested that the committee veto represented an unconstitutional infringement of executive duties.[121] Congress turned to other procedures that yielded precisely the same control. A bill was drafted to prohibit appropriations for certain real estate transactions unless the Public Works Committees first approved the contracts. President Dwight D. Eisenhower signed the bill after Brownell assured him that this procedure—based on the authorization-appropriation distinction within the legislative process—was within Congress's power.[122] The form had changed; the committee veto remained.

---

117. H. Doc. No. 764, 66th Cong., 2d Sess. 2 (1920).
118. 37 Op. Att'y Gen. 56 (1933).
119. 26 U.S.C. §6405(a) (2000).
120. Virginia A. McMurtry, "Legislative Vetoes Relating to Public Works and Buildings," in "Studies on the Legislative Veto," House Committee on Rules, 96th Cong., 2d Sess. 432–514 (1980).
121. 41 Op. Att'y Gen. 230 (1955), reprinted in 60 Dick. L. Rev. See also 41 Op. Att'y Gen. 300 (1957).
122. Joseph P. Harris, Congressional Control of Administration 230–31 (1964).

In *INS* v. *Chadha* (1983), the Supreme Court supposedly struck down all legislative vetoes as unconstitutional. The Court declared that legislative vetoes—committee vetoes, one-House vetoes, or two-House vetoes—were invalid because Congress could control the executive branch only by respecting two constitutional principles: bicameralism (action by both chambers) and the Presentation Clause (submitting all legislative measures to the President for his signature or veto).[123] Three years later, in the Gramm-Rudman case, the Court again insisted that Congress could not intrude upon executive powers: "once Congress makes its choice in enacting legislation, its participation ends. Congress can thereafter control the execution of its enactment only indirectly—by passing new legislation."[124]

The Court's static theory of government was too much at odds with the practices developed over a period of decades by the political branches. Neither agency officials nor lawmakers wanted the stilted model announced by the Court. Congress continued to enact committee vetoes in the years following *Chadha*, and agencies continued to comply with requirements to seek the approval of legislative panels, usually the Appropriations Committees. Agencies tolerate this procedure because with it they receive the flexibility and discretion they need to make adjustments in the middle of a fiscal year.[125]

The foothold given to Congress through the appropriations power to seek and obtain agency documents applies also to two other central powers assigned to the legislative branch: the impeachment power and the power over appointments. Those powers, discussed in the next two chapters, offer multiple opportunities for Congress to gain access to sensitive documents from the President and executive agencies.

---

123. 462 U.S. 919 (1983).
124. Bowsher v. Synar, 478 U.S. 714, 733–34 (1986).
125. For the continuation of committee vetoes after *Chadha*, see Louis Fisher, "The Legislative Veto: Invalidated, It Survives," 56 Law and Contemp. Prob. 273 (1993).

3

THE IMPEACHMENT POWER

In the struggle over information and documents, Congress has especially strong leverage when it unleashes the impeachment process. Presidents concede that when interbranch conflicts reach that level, traditional arguments used to deny lawmakers information have no credibility. Congressional access is compelling not only when a President is personally accused of an action that may merit removal from office, but extends more broadly to malfeasance in the administration, including corruption, criminal activity, unethical conduct, and personal wrongdoing by agency officials. Although impeachment was used once against a Cabinet official—Secretary of War William Belknap in 1876—it is reserved now for the President and federal judges. To sanction departmental heads and other executive officials who withhold documents or refuse to testify, Congress relies on the powers of subpoena and contempt.

Presidential Policies

When President Washington denied the House the papers it requested on the Jay Treaty, he said that the only ground on which the House might have legitimately requested the documents was impeachment, "which the resolution has not expressed."[1] Presumably, if Congress had requested the documents on that basis, Washington would have acquiesced. In the midst of the debate over the Jay Treaty, Rep. William Lyman said that the impeachment power "certainly implied the right to inspect every paper and transaction in any department, otherwise the power of impeachment could never be exercised with any effect."[2] The power of impeachment, said President James Polk, gives to the House of Representatives

---

1. Annals of Cong., 4th Cong., 1st Sess. 759 (1796).
2. Id. at 601.

the right to investigate the conduct of all public officers under the Government. This is cheerfully admitted. In such a case the safety of the Republic would be the supreme law, and the power of the House in the pursuit of this object would penetrate into the most secret recesses of the Executive Department. It could command the attendance of any and every agent of the Government, and compel them to produce all papers, public or private, official or unofficial, and to testify on oath to all facts within their knowledge.[3]

President Ulysses S. Grant advanced a peculiar theory in 1876, after the House adopted a resolution requesting information on how many times he had been out of the nation's capital conducting official business. The resolution permitted him to withhold the information if he considered it "incompatible with the public interest," but he chose to cite constitutional reasons for withholding the information. One reason, poorly considered, was that if the House sought the information with impeachment in mind, the Constitution recognized a guaranty that "protects every citizen, the President as well as the humblest in the land, from being made a witness against himself."[4] Other Presidents, facing possible impeachment, have not sought refuge behind the Self-Incrimination Clause. It's a theoretical possibility, but politically unappealing.

Even short of impeachment, reliance on executive privilege is likely to be impolitic when lawmakers make serious charges of administrative malfeasance. The Supreme Court has noted that the power of Congress to conduct investigations "comprehends probes into departments of the Federal Government to expose corruption, inefficiency or waste."[5] Attorney General William Rogers told a Senate committee in 1958 that the withholding of documents from Congress "can never be justified as a means of covering mistakes, avoiding embarrassment, or for political, personal, or pecuniary reasons."[6] In 1982, Attorney General William French Smith said that he would not try "to shield [from Congress] documents which contain evidence of criminal or unethical conduct by agency officials from proper review."[7] During a news conference

---

3. 5 Richardson 2284 (April 20, 1846).
4. 9 Richardson 4316 (May 4, 1876).
5. Watkins v. United States, 354 U.S. 178, 187 (1957).
6. "Freedom of Information and Secrecy in Government," hearing before the Subcommittee on Constitutional Rights of the Senate Committee on the Judiciary, 85th Cong., 2d Sess. 5 (1958).
7. Letter of November 30, 1982, to Congressman John Dingell, reprinted in H. Rept. No. 968, 97th Cong., 2d Sess. 41 (1982).

in 1983, President Reagan remarked: "We will never invoke executive privilege to cover up wrongdoing."[8]

White House Counsel Lloyd Cutler, in a memo of September 28, 1994, provided guidance for congressional requests to departments and agencies for documents. Congressional requests would be complied with "to the fullest extent consistent with the constitutional and statutory obligations of the Executive Branch."[9] Although the doctrine of executive privilege would be asserted to protect "the confidentiality of deliberations within the White House," in circumstances that involve communications "relating to investigations of personal wrongdoing by government officials, it is our practice not to assert executive privilege, either in judicial proceedings or in congressional investigations and hearings."[10]

Andrew Jackson Fights Back

President Andrew Jackson, a jealous defender of executive prerogatives, found himself at times assailed by both Houses. He was censured by the Senate in 1834 on the ground that he had violated the Constitution, and was charged three years later with possible corruption by a special committee of the House. Both chambers seemed to imply that he might have committed impeachable offenses. In each case, to prevent legislative encroachment and a narrowing of presidential power, Jackson had to define and defend the rights of his office.

The Senate Resolution

The first dispute turned largely on the issue of whether the Secretary of the Treasury functioned as an executive officer or a legislative agent. Could Congress delegate to the Secretary, rather than the President, the duty of placing government money either in the U.S. Bank or in state banks? President Jackson removed the Secretary of the Treasury in order to find someone willing to follow his instructions, not those of Congress. The Senate responded by passing a resolution of censure: "*Resolved*, That the President, in the late Execu-

---

8. Public Papers of the Presidents, 1983, I, at 239.
9. Memorandum for all Executive Department and Agency General Counsels from Lloyd N. Cutler, Special Counsel to the President, "Congressional Requests to Departments and Agencies for Documents Protected by Executive Privilege," September 28, 1994, at 1.
10. Id.

tive proceedings in relation to the public revenue, has assumed upon himself authority and power not conferred by the Constitution and laws, but in derogation of both."[11]

Essentially, the Senate charged Jackson with committing an impeachable act. In a lengthy and impassioned defense, Jackson insisted that the Secretary of the Treasury was "wholly an executive officer" and could be removed at will by the President.[12] He was outraged that the Senate could censure him on the basis of unspecified charges and without an opportunity to be heard: "Without notice, unheard and untried, I thus find myself charged on the records of the Senate and in a form hitherto unknown in our history, with the high crime of violating the laws and Constitution of my country."[13] He advised the Senate to follow constitutional procedures. If Senators thought he had violated the Constitution, they had to first wait for the House to impeach, after which the Senate could vote to convict. There was no constitutional warrant, he said, for the Senate to hide behind a resolution of censure. Three years later the Senate ordered its resolution of censure expunged from the record.[14] As discussed later in this chapter, both the House and the Senate considered censure resolutions against President Clinton in the midst of impeachment proceedings, but dismissed the resolutions as inappropriate.

The House Investigation

The second dispute came toward the end of Jackson's second term in office. What seemed to kick off the controversy was a presidential compliment to executive agencies. In his eighth annual message of December 5, 1836, Jackson said that it was "due to the various Executive Departments to bear testimony to their prosperous condition and to the ability and integrity with which they have been conducted." It had been his aim "to enforce in all of them a vigilant and faithful discharge of the public business, and it is gratifying to me to believe that there is no just cause of complaint from any quarter at the manner in which they have fulfilled the objects of their creation."[15]

Such sentiments seem innocent, even innocuous, but Jackson's enemies in Congress seized the moment to turn presidential flattery into an open-ended legislative search for agency wrongdoing. Rep. Henry A. Wise, a Jackson De-

---

11. S. Journal, 24th Cong., 2d Sess. 123–24 (April 14, 1834).
12. 3 Richardson 1301.
13. Id. at 1289.
14. Cong. Debates, 24th Cong., 2d Sess. 379–418, 427–506 (1837).
15. 4 Richardson 1478.

mocrat about to turn Whig, took sharp offense at Jackson's message. He was convinced that all of the executive departments had become "hideously corrupt, disordered, and dangerous."[16] On December 13, 1836, Wise offered a resolution to create a select committee to investigate the truthfulness of Jackson's appraisal of the agencies. Wise spoke with heavy sarcasm, explaining how Jackson had earned the "title of Hero" with his military victories. "Hail, second Savior!," Wise said, was "shouted from the lips of every grateful heart."[17] Once elected to the White House, Jackson became "the favorite pet of the people, who was to scourge bribery and corruption, whose name was to be the terror of all evil-doers, whose policy was to be retrenchment and reform, by whom the independence of Congress of executive patronage was to be maintained."[18]

Jackson's use of patronage stoked Wise's ire: "His ruthless proscription for opinion's sake turned faithful public servants out of their employment, and snatched from the mouths of their families their bread."[19] Wise charged that congressional independence had "been totally destroyed by corrupt bribes and the power of appointing members to office." Nothing mattered but "the will of the President." Hundreds of thousands of dollars had been lavished on the White House, producing "all the regalia of a palace."[20] Was Wise hurling invective at the President? Perish the thought. He dismissed such speculation: "let no one infer that I am indulging in any tirade against the President, or that I am venting any spleen whatever." He wished Jackson a long life, "to witness the effects of his errors, if errors he has committed, to acknowledge and repent of them."[21]

Wise insisted that Congress investigate the truth of Jackson's claim that "the various executive departments have been conducted with ability and integrity, and that they are in a prosperous condition."[22] He wanted a committee of nine members,

> with power to send for persons and papers, and with instructions to inquire into the condition of the various executive departments, the ability and integrity with which they have been conducted, into the manner in which the public business has been discharged in all of them, and into all causes of complaint, from any quarter, at the man-

---

16. Henry A. Wise, Seven Decades of the Union 155 (1871).
17. Cong. Debates, 24th Cong., 2d Sess. 1058 (1836).
18. Id.
19. Id. at 1059.
20. Id. at 1060.
21. Id.
22. Id. at 1065.

ner in which said Departments, or their business or offices, or any of their officers or agents, of every description whatever, directly or indirectly connected with them in any manner, officially or unofficially, in duties pertaining to the public interest, have fulfilled or failed to accomplish the objects of their creation, or have violated their duties, or have injured or impaired the public service and interest;....[23]

Wise's resolution was adopted by the Committee of the Whole, 86 to 78.[24] Considering that Jacksonian Democrats controlled the House by a large margin, 145 to 98, the vote here is surprising. However, Wise directed some of his venom not at Jackson but at his successor, Martin Van Buren: "I hold Mr. Van Buren responsible for most mischief that has been done, and most that is now doing:..."[25] Democratic control of the House would virtually disappear under Van Buren, dropping to a margin of only 108 to 107.

Having passed the Committee of the Whole—an intermediate stage—the Wise resolution now had to be accepted by the full House. The House agreed to most of the resolutions that allocated parts of Jackson's annual message to different committees, but continued to debate the Wise resolution.[26] Rep. Dutee Pearce, a Democrat from Rhode Island, opposed the resolution, partly on the ground that all of the substantive parts of Jackson's message had already been assigned to standing committees fully capable of evaluating how well the agencies had conducted their business.[27] In a position later adopted by Jackson, Pearce challenged Wise or any other member to come forward with specific—not general—charges.[28] His amendment, requiring the select committee "to inquire into any specific causes of complaint which may be alleged against the integrity of the administration of any of the departments or their bureaus," and giving the committee power to send for persons and papers,[29] was never acted on. Weeks of debate dragged on. Finally, on January 17, 1837, the House went directly to the Wise amendment and it passed by the remarkable margin of 165 to 9.[30]

Yet it was scarcely a victory for Wise. With the House consuming a month in debating his resolution, only six weeks remained in the Congress to conduct the inquiry. Named chairman of the select committee, Wise complained that

---

23. Id. at 1057.
24. Id. at 1067.
25. Id. at 1066.
26. Id. at 1068.
27. Id. at 1082.
28. Id. at 1083–84.
29. Id. at 1084.
30. Id. at 1410–11.

his colleagues "now propose to give me this Herculean task" and that it was "too late for any investigation."[31] On January 24, Wise wrote to Jackson, requesting the departments to furnish the committee with a list of all officers or agents, or deputies, who had been appointed during Jackson's two terms in office. The committee wanted to know from those individuals of "any innovations, not authorized by law, (if such exist,)," and when and why the changes originated.[32]

Within two days, Jacked penned a stinging reply. He first noted that Wise, in his speech to the House, "preferred many severe but vague charges of corruption and abuse in the executive departments." Under the resolution, Jackson said, the President and departmental heads were not expected "to answer to any specific charge; not to explain any alleged abuse; not to give information as to any particular transaction; but, assuming that they have been guilty of the charges alleged, calls upon them to furnish evidence against themselves!"[33] Jackson advised Wise to reduce his general charges to specifications, allowing the committee to investigate agency wrongdoing, if it existed. Instead, what Wise had done was to ask Jackson and his Cabinet "to become our own accusers, and to furnish the evidence to convict ourselves; and this call purports to be founded on the authority of that body in which alone, by the constitution, the power of impeaching us is vested!" Jackson vowed to repel such legislative inquiries "as an invasion of the principles of justice, as well as of the constitution; and I shall esteem it my sacred duty to the people of the United States to resist them as I would the establishment of a Spanish inquisition."[34]

Jackson now turned the tables on Wise. If Wise, after issuing accusations against the administration, was unwilling to bring specific charges, the committee should call him and any other member who claimed that corruption existed, and ask them under oath "whether you or they know of any specific corruption or abuse of trust in the executive departments; and, if so, what it is." Jackson said that if any member could "point to any case where there is the slightest reason to suspect corruption or abuse of trust, no obstacle which I can remove shall be interposed to prevent the fullest scrutiny by all legal means. The offices of all the departments will be opened to you, and every proper facility furnished for this purpose."[35] The gauntlet had been thrown at Wise: either come up with something specific or shut up.

---

31. Id. at 1409, 1410.
32. Cong. Debates, 24th Cong., 2d Sess., vol. 13, part 2, Appendix, at 201; also at H. Rept. No. 194, 24th Cong., 2d Sess. 29 (1837).
33. Cong. Debates, 24th Cong., 2d Sess., vol. 13, part 2, Appendix, at 202.
34. Id.
35. Id.

Jackson closed by expressing "astonishment" that Congress would have authorized the Wise inquiry. Under House rules "there are six standing committees...whose special duties are to examine annually into all the details of those expenditures in each of the executive departments."[36] Investigations of that nature need time and attention. What could possibly be achieved, Jackson implied, from a rushed investigation by a newly established select committee in the closing weeks of a Congress?

The select committee asked Senator Hugh Lawson White to testify. However, he advised the committee that he would hold himself "disgraced" by sharing "intimate and confidential" conversations and correspondence he had with Jackson. Upon hearing of White's dilemma, Jackson wrote to the select committee on January 31, 1837, stating that he absolved White "from all obligations of confidence in regard to any thing that has passed between us." Jackson wanted every conversation with White, "on all and every subject, faithfully disclosed, with the time when, and the place where; and I hope the committee will interrogate him as to every point or matter of confidence that ever existed between us."[37]

Wise issued the report of his committee on the last day of the 24th Congress, March 3, 1837. The committee called 28 witnesses.[38] As to its task, the committee majority viewed its inquiry "in no other light than a preliminary measure to ascertain whether there were sufficient grounds to justify a process of impeachment."[39] To engage in an investigation of this nature, they said, could be justified only under the constitutional clause that gave the House "the sole power of impeachment." The majority asserted: "It follows, therefore, that the only constitutional power under which the House of Representatives, as a co-ordinate branch of the Government, could constitute a committee to inquire into alleged 'corrupt violations of duty' by another co-ordinate branch of the Government, (the Executive,) is the 'power of impeachment.'"[40]

Following Jackson's suggestion, the committee called Wise and asked him, under oath, if he knew of any executive act that was either corrupt or a violation of duty. Wise supplied no evidence. When the committee asked for the names of those who had informed him of executive abuse or corruption, Wise refused to respond.[41] Under these conditions, the majority recommended language that repudiated Wise:

---

36. Id.
37. Id. at 208.
38. Id. at 189.
39. Id.
40. Id. at 190.
41. Id. at 195.

Resolved, That, so far as has come to the knowledge of the committee from the results of this investigation, the condition of the various executive departments is prosperous, and that they have been conducted with ability and integrity; that the President has aimed to enforce, in all of them, a vigilant and faithful discharge of the public business; and that there is no just cause of complaint, from any quarter, at the manner in which they have fulfilled the objects of their creation.[42]

The members of the minority on the committee simply noted that Jackson had declined to give the committee the documents and papers it had requested, and that in the absence of information the committee had no way of determining the truth or falsehood of allegations that had been made of abuses and neglect of duty in the executive departments.[43] On that note the House investigation ended with a whimper.

Impeaching Andrew Johnson

Unlike the impeachments of Richard Nixon and Bill Clinton, both involving charges of cover-up and obstruction of justice, the impeachment of Andrew Johnson did not raise any issue of access to executive branch documents. Republicans in Congress, locked in a battle with Johnson over Reconstruction policies, had been looking for a way to impeach him. The opportunity came with the Tenure of Office Act of 1867, which gave the Senate a role in the suspension and removal of federal officers. If the Senate refused to concur in the President's decision to suspend an official, including a member of his own Cabinet, the suspended officer would resume the functions of his office. Johnson vetoed the bill, claiming that it violated the Constitution and the construction placed upon it by the First Congress.[44] Both Houses promptly overrode the veto and the bill became law on March 2, 1867.[45]

Johnson hoped that the thorn in his Cabinet, Secretary of War Edwin Stanton, would resign. No such luck. Unwilling to wait any longer, Johnson wrote to Stanton on August 5, 1867 to say that "your resignation as Secretary of War will be accepted."[46] Stanton didn't take the hint. A day later he replied that he would not resign. Johnson suspended Stanton on August 12 and replaced him

---

42. Id. at 198.
43. Id. (third point under "Views of the Minority").
44. 8 Richardson 3690–96.
45. 14 Stat. 430 (1867).
46. 8 Richardson 3782.

with Ulysses S. Grant, to serve as Secretary of War ad interim.[47] Johnson thought that the constitutionality of the Tenure of Office Act would be taken to the Supreme Court, where it would be struck down. No such luck again.

On January 13, 1868, the Senate refused to concur in the suspension.[48] At that point Grant resigned, locked his office, and left the key with a military aide. Stanton walked over, picked up the key, and reentered his old office.[49] On February 21, Johnson removed Stanton and replaced him with Lorenzo Thomas.[50] Those actions led directly to impeachment proceedings.

The House charged Johnson with many offenses, ranging from usurpation of power to corrupt interference in elections.[51] Members of the House first took aim at "the special acts of mal-administration" involving Johnson's "great overshadowing purpose of reconstructing the shattered governments of the rebel States in accordance with his own will."[52] The House had no problem in gaining access to documents and hearing testimony from administration officials.[53] When the House on February 10 requested extensive correspondence between Johnson and Grant, Johnson supplied it the next day.[54] By the time the House agreed to articles of impeachment, most related to Stanton and the Tenure of Office Act.[55] In the Senate, the effort to remove Johnson fell one vote short of the two-thirds majority needed.

Watergate

During his impeachment proceedings, Richard Nixon insisted on the right to withhold information from a congressional inquiry if he determined that the release of such documents would violate the constitutional doctrine of executive privilege. Faced with subpoenas from the House Judiciary Committee, Nixon argued that the release of presidential conversations to Congress would undermine the independence of the executive branch and jeopardize

---

47. Id. at 3754.
48. 16 Senate Executive Journal 130 (1887).
49. Albert Castel, The Presidency of Andrew Johnson 159 (1979).
50. 8 Richardson 3861.
51. H. Rept. No. 7, 40th Cong., 1st Sess. 1 (1867).
52. Id. at 2.
53. Impeachment Investigation: Testimony taken before the Judiciary Committee of the House of Representatives in the Investigation of the Charges Against Andrew Johnson, 39th Cong., 2d Sess. and 40th Cong., 1st Sess. (1867).
54. 8 Richardson 3800–18.
55. Id. at 3907–12.

the operations of the White House. A line had to be drawn somewhere, he told the committee, and he would be the one to do it. The committee would get some documents, but not all, and Nixon would decide whether the documents needed to be edited before release.[56] The committee denied that a President had any authority to determine what kind of evidence to share with a Congress conducting an impeachment inquiry.[57]

In June 1972, five people were arrested while trying to burglarize the headquarters of the National Democratic Committee at the Watergate complex. It was quickly established that others were involved and they could be traced to the Republican Committee to Re-elect the President (CRP). In August, President Richard Nixon offered advice that would later come back to haunt him: "What really hurts in matters of this sort is not the fact that they occur, because overzealous people in campaigns do things that are wrong. What really hurts is if you try to cover it up."[58]

When Congress started to investigate, Nixon issued a statement on March 2, 1973, objecting to the appearance of White House Counsel John Dean at congressional hearings. Nixon said that "no President could ever agree to allow the Counsel to the President to go down and testify before a committee."[59] He later elaborated on the reasons for refusing to allow White House aides to testify: "Under the doctrine of separation of powers, the manner in which the President personally exercises his assigned powers is not subject to questioning by another branch of Government. If the President is not subject to such questioning, it is equally appropriate that members of his staff not be so questioned, for their roles are in effect an extension of the Presidency."[60] As explained in Chapter 10, White House aides often testify before congressional committees.

In a statement on March 15, Nixon offered other reasons for denying Congress the right to question Dean at legislative hearings: "Mr. Dean is Counsel to the White House. He is also one who was counsel to a number of people on the White House Staff. He had, in effect, what I would call a double privilege, the lawyer-client relationship, as well as the Presidential privilege."[61] Nixon reiterated that members of the White House staff "will not appear before a committee of Congress in any formal session."[62]

---

56. John R. Labovitz, Presidential Impeachment 201–06 (1978).
57. Id. at 205.
58. Public Papers of the Presidents, 1972, at 828.
59. Public Papers of the Presidents, 1973, at 160.
60. Id. at 185.
61. Id. at 203.
62. Id. at 211.

Political pressures made it impossible for Nixon to adhere to those legal doctrines. On April 17, he agreed to allow White House aides to testify before the Senate Select Committee on Presidential Campaign Activities, provided they followed four ground rules: White House aides would appear, in the first instance, in executive session, if appropriate; executive privilege would be expressly reserved and could be asserted during the course of the hearing to any question; the proceedings could be televised; and all members of the White House staff would appear "voluntarily" and testify under oath to "answer fully all proper questions."[63] Reference to the voluntary appearance enabled Nixon to retain some semblance of his separation of power theory, but basically the White House capitulated while insisting that it didn't have to.

On July 7, Nixon further relaxed the guidelines. He directed that the right of executive privilege concerning possible criminal conduct "no longer be invoked for present or former members of the White House staff."[64] He also agreed to permit "the unrestricted testimony of present and former White House staff members" before the committee.[65] Beginning on May 17 and continuing until September 23, 1975, a number of White House aides testified before the committee, including John Dean, Jeb Magruder, Alexander Butterfield, Herbert Kalmbach, John Ehrlichman, H.R. Haldeman, Patrick Buchanan, Leonard Garment, and Gen. Alexander M. Haig, Jr.[66]

Special Prosecutor Archibald Cox urged Sam Ervin, chairman of the Senate Watergate Committee, not to hold televised hearings. Cox feared that the pretrial publicity would jeopardize his prosecution efforts and that the committee would grant immunity to key witnesses. Undeterred, Ervin went ahead. Cox later conceded that the hearings "certainly were a contribution to the public good as it turned out. None of them did interfere in any way with prosecution, and they may have produced some evidence...that might not otherwise have come out."[67] The hearings disclosed to the public a remarkable fact about White House operations. Alexander Butterfield, administrator of the Federal Aviation Administration, told committee staff about the existence of listening and recording devices in the Oval Office.

---

63. Id. at 299.
64. Id. at 636–37.
65. Id. at 637.
66. The complete list appears in Louis Fisher, "White House Aides Testifying Before Congress," 27 Pres. Stud. Q. 139, 141–42 (1997), and is discussed in Chapter 10 of this book.
67. Ken Gormley, Archibald Cox: Conscience of a Nation 270–73 (1997).

After much legal maneuvering, some of these tapes wound up in the hands of Judge John Sirica. They revealed unmistakable evidence of a cover-up, such as Nixon's remark at a March 22, 1973 meeting: "And, uh, for that reason, I am perfectly willing to—I don't give a shit what happens. I want you to stonewall it, let them plead the Fifth Amendment, cover-up or anything else, if it'll save the plan."[68] Other tapes, released as a result of the Supreme Court's decision in *United States v. Nixon* (1974), demonstrated that Nixon had agreed that the CIA should put a halt to the FBI investigation.[69] With the release of the tapes, Nixon recognized that a House vote of impeachment "is, as a practical matter, virtually a foregone conclusion."[70] He announced his resignation on August 8, 1974, effective the next day.

The House Judiciary Committee prepared three articles of impeachment. The first charged that Nixon "prevented, obstructed, and impeded the administration of justice." Article I included "withholding relevant and material evidence or information from lawfully authorized investigative officers." Article II focused on Nixon's abuse of the IRS, the FBI, and the CIA to violate the constitutional rights of citizens. In Article III, the committee stated that Nixon had failed to produce "papers and things as directed by duly authorized subpoenas" issued by the committee, and that he had "willfully disobeyed such subpoenas."[71]

In elaborating on Article III, the committee explained that eight subpoenas sought tape recordings, notes and other writings relating to 147 conversations, a list of Nixon's meetings and phone conversations for five specified periods, papers and memos relating to the Watergate break-in, and copies of Nixon's daily news summaries for a 3½ month period in 1972. The committee informed Nixon that those materials were necessary for the committee to investigate the Watergate matter, domestic surveillance, possible connections between campaign contributions from certain diary cooperatives and governmental decisions on price supports, the conduct of ITT antitrust litigation, and the alleged abuse of the IRS. In response to the subpoenas, Nixon produced edited transcripts of all or part of 33 subpoenaed conversations and six conversations that had not been subpoenaed, edited copies of notes taken by Ehrlichman during meetings with Nixon, and copies of certain White House news summaries. The committee received no handwritten notes by Nixon and none of the tapes of 147 subpoenaed conversations. Article III passed the

---

68. John J. Sirica, To Set the Record Straight 162 (1979).
69. H. Rept. No. 93-1305, 93d Cong., 2d Sess. 53 (1974).
70. Public Papers of the Presidents, 1974, at 622.
71. H. Rept. No. 93-1305, 93d Cong., 2d Sess. 1–4 (1974).

committee by a vote of 21 to 17.[72] Nixon's refusal to comply with the subpoenas, said the committee, "is a grave interference with the efforts of the Committee and the House to fulfill their constitutional responsibilities...."[73]

The committee concluded that the edited transcripts of 33 conversations, provided by Nixon, were untrustworthy and unreliable. In comparing the edited transcripts with recordings it had it found omissions, material added, attributions of statements by one speaker when they were made by another, statements the White House called unintelligible when the committee could hear the words, and statements that "were inaccurately transcribed, some in a manner that seriously misrepresented the substance and tone of the actual conversation."[74] After the Supreme Court decision, the White House informed Judge John Sirica that the tape of an April 17, 1973 conversation between Nixon, Haldeman and Ehrlichman contained a gap of approximately five minutes. The edited transcript given to the committee did not indicate any gap.[75] These and other disclosures convinced the committee that not only had Nixon failed to comply with the terms of the subpoenas, the edited transcripts "do not accurately and completely reflect the conversations that they purport to transcribe."[76]

Iran-Contra

The Iran-Contra story broke to a startled nation in November 1986, revealing that the Reagan administration had sold arms to Iran and had sent funds to the Contra rebels in Nicaragua in violation of statutory restrictions. White House officials learned from Watergate that worse than the deed was the cover-up. Attorney General Edwin Meese, III, thought that the merging of assistance to the Contras with the sale of arms to Iran could cause the possible "toppling" of Reagan, unless the administration made facts publicly available and got them "out the door first."[77] Presidential aides worried about the vulnerability of President Reagan to impeachment.[78] Getting facts out quickly would prevent opponents from charging a cover-up.[79] Because Reagan made

---

72. Id. at 187–88.
73. Id. at 188–89.
74. Id. at 203.
75. Id. at 204.
76. Id. at 205.
77. Theodore Draper, A Very Thin Line: The Iran-Contra Affairs 521 (1991).
78. Lawrence B. Walsh, Firewall: The Iran-Contra Conspiracy and Cover-up 9, 355, 358–59, 360 (1997).
79. Id. at 189, 379.

documents and executive officials available to Congress and waived executive privilege, members of Congress never took seriously the thought of impeaching Reagan.[80]

President Reagan permitted his two former National Security Advisers, Robert McFarlane and John Poindexter, to testify before Congress,[81] allowed his Cabinet officials, including Secretary of State George Shultz and Secretary of Defense Caspar Weinberger, to discuss with Congress their conversations with the President,[82] and made available to Congress thousands of sensitive, classified documents.[83] Shultz told the Iran-Contra committee that, as instructed by President Reagan, he had made available to the committee and other investigative groups "my records, cables, memoranda, my notes of my personal recollections made contemporaneously with events, all of the material that I have has been made available and you have it."[84] In his previous 10½ years as a Cabinet officer, he had always taken the position that his conversations with the President were "privileged, and I would not discuss them. This is an exception, and I have made this material available at the President's instruction...."[85] Similarly, Weinberger testified that he would never discuss "any conversations, any advice, any opinions, any meetings that I have had with the President. I have never done that until early this year, I guess it was. When—at the President's directions, I spoke very fully and very frankly of all the statements made in meetings with the President in connection with this special matter...."[86]

Through his cooperation with Congress, Reagan hoped to avoid any risk of impeachment. He also directed Attorney General Meese to go the special panel and request an independent counsel. The panel appointed Lawrence Walsh, whose efforts to uncover the full scope of the scandal were regularly thwarted by the administration's strategy of withholding information, denying the release of classified documents, and issuing presidential pardons.

---

80. William S. Cohen and George J. Mitchell, Men of Zeal: A Candid Inside Story of the Iran-Contra Hearings 45–50 (1988).
81. Draper, A Very Thin Line, at 498.
82. Id. at 540.
83. Report of the Congressional Committees Investigating the Iran-Contra Affair, H. Rept. No. 100-43 and S. Rept. No. 100-216, 100th Cong., 1st Sess. xvi (1987).
84. "Iran-Contra Investigation," Joint Hearings before the Senate Select Committee on Secret Military Assistance to Iran and the Nicaraguan Opposition and the House Select Committee to Investigate Covert Arms Transactions with Iran (Part 100-9), 100th Cong., 1st Sess. 1–2 (1987).
85. Id. at 2.
86. Id. (Part 100-10), at 132.

As part of the investigation, Walsh looked into the activities of Joseph Fernandez, the CIA station chief in Costa Rica who helped Col. Oliver North supply the Contras in violation of the Boland Amendment. On June 20, 1988, a grand jury indicted Fernandez for false statements and obstruction and for conspiring with North and others to carry out the covert action. The conspiracy count was later dropped. Nevertheless, the pursuit of Fernandez would illuminate the CIA's role and probably lead to others in the administration who worked with Fernandez. However, that line of inquiry was snuffed out when Attorney General Richard Thornburgh refused to release classified information needed for the trial.[87]

On June 16, 1992, a grand jury indicted Weinberger for five felonies, including one count of obstructing a congressional investigation, two counts of making false statements, and two charges of perjury. Here was an opportunity to learn about the involvement of a Cabinet officer. Moreover, President George Bush was likely to be called to Weinberger's trial to testify. Although Bush had denied knowing that Weinberger and Shultz had opposed the sale of arms to Iran, a supplemental indictment of Weinberger revealed that Bush, as Vice President, had attended the White House meeting where Reagan overrode Weinberger and Shultz.[88]

Once again Walsh hit a stone wall. On December 24, 1992, President Bush pardoned six people involved in the Iran-Contra affair. Heading the list was Weinberger, but the pardon order also covered three member of the CIA involved in Iran-Contra: Duane Clarridge, Alan Fiers, and Clair George. Clarridge had been indicted on seven felony counts; Fiers, facing indictment for a felony count, had agreed to plead guilty to two misdemeanors and cooperate with Walsh; George was charged with lying to three congressional panels and a federal judge. George's case ended in a mistrial, but a retrial found him guilty of two felony counts of lying to Congress.[89] The pardons wiped out the last chance to learn the extent of CIA involvement.

Clinton's Impeachment

President Clinton was investigated by two outside counsel. After the independent counsel statute expired in 1992, Attorney General Janet Reno invoked her own authority a year later to appoint Robert Fiske as special prosecutor to

---

87. Walsh, Firewall, at 210–11, 218–19.
88. Id. at 415, 419.
89. Id. at 285–86, 313, 423, 446.

investigate several issues, including the involvement of Bill and Hillary Clinton in a real estate investment that became known as Whitewater. When Congress reauthorized the independent counsel statute in 1994, Reno asked the special panel of three judges to appoint an independent counsel. They selected Kenneth Starr.

Starr inherited some of the issues that Fiske had explored, including Whitewater and the death of White House aide Vincent Foster. Starr's jurisdiction expanded in 1996 to include the firing of staff from the White House Travel Office and charges that the White House had misused confidential FBI files. In 1998, Starr was assigned the task of investigating allegations of subornation of perjury, obstruction of justice, and intimidation of witnesses surrounding the affair between Clinton and White House intern Monica Lewinsky.

Starr managed to prevail on a series of legal disputes after the White House had placed one hurdle after another in his path. Presidential aides insisted that they could not be compelled to testify at the grand jury. Hillary Clinton believed that her discussions with a government attorney were privileged. The Secret Service argued that the agents responsible for protecting the President should not be forced to testify about matters of Clinton's conduct. On all those matters and others, Starr won at every level: from the district court through appellate courts. Efforts by the administration to take the issues to the Supreme Court were unsuccessful. These court victories for Starr came at substantial cost, however, for the investigation dragged on and gave some the impression that Starr was out to "get the President."

On September 11, 1998, Starr forwarded to the House of Representatives a report on the Lewinsky matter, concluding that Clinton may have committed impeachable offenses, including lying under oath at a deposition, lying under oath to a grand jury, and obstruction of justice. Starr also found "substantial and credible" information that Clinton's actions since January 17, 1998, regarding his relationship with Lewinsky, "have been inconsistent with the President's constitutional duty to faithfully execute the laws."[90]

This latter charge had several parts, including Starr's conclusion that Clinton had "repeatedly and unlawfully invoked the executive privilege to conceal evidence of his personal misconduct from the grand jury."[91] Starr drew attention to the 1994 opinion by White House Counsel Lloyd Cutler that executive privilege would not be invoked for cases involving personal wrongdoing by an

---

90. The Starr Report 244 (New York: Public Affairs, 1998).
91. Id. at 247.

executive official.[92] Yet Clinton invoked executive privilege to cover the testimony of five witnesses (Bruce Lindsey, Cheryl Mills, Nancy Hernreich, Sidney Blumenthal, and Lanny Breuer) and acquiesced in the Secret Service's attempt to create a new protection function privilege, to prevent Secret Service officers from testifying. All such efforts by Clinton failed.[93]

The House Judiciary Committee considered Starr's recommendations and reported four articles of impeachment: perjury in the grand jury, perjury in the civil case, obstruction of justice, and abuse of power. The latter two did not repeat Starr's claim that Clinton had unlawfully invoked executive privilege. Instead, the committee in Article III charged that Clinton had "prevented, obstructed, and impeded the administration of justice" and had engaged in a "course of conduct or scheme designed to delay, impede, cover up, and conceal the existence of evidence and testimony" related to the Paula Jones suit.

Article IV charged that Clinton had engaged in conduct that resulted in "misuse and abuse of his high office," impaired the conduct of lawful inquiries, and "refused and failed" to respond to written questions submitted to him by the committee.[94] On November 5, 1998, the committee presented Clinton with 81 requests for admission, allowing him to dispute or affirm sworn evidence held by the committee. Clinton responded on November 27. Similar to the judgment of the House Judiciary Committee in 1974 regarding Nixon's response, the committee concluded that several of Clinton's answers were "clearly perjurious, false, and misleading." In responding in that manner, the committee said, Clinton "exhibited contempt for the constitutional prerogative of Congress to conduct an impeachment inquiry."[95] The committee found that his answers were "a continuation of a pattern of deceit and obstruction of duly authorized investigations."[96]

Article IV originally included a paragraph charging that Clinton had "frivolously and corruptly asserted executive privilege…for the purpose of delaying and obstructing a Federal criminal investigation and the proceedings of a Federal grand jury."[97] Rep. George Gekas (R-Pa.) offered an amendment to strike three paragraphs from Article IV, including the one on executive privilege. His amendment was adopted 29 to 5. Rep. Bob Goodlatte (R-Va.) explained the purpose of the Gekas amendment. While those voting in favor of the amendment believed that Clinton had "improperly exercised executive

---

92. Id.
93. Id. at 248–50.
94. H. Rept. No. 105-830, 105th Cong., 2d Sess. 4 (1998).
95. Id. at 77.
96. Id.
97. Id. at 85.

privilege," they didn't believe this conduct by Clinton represented an impeachable offense.[98]

The House impeached Clinton on the articles dealing with perjury and obstruction, not on abuse of power. The Senate declined to remove Clinton from office, voting 50 to 50 for the obstruction article and 45 to 55 for the perjury article, far short of the necessary two-thirds majority. However, several Senators who voted "not guilty" explained in their floor statements that Clinton was actually guilty of one or both counts. For example, Senator Robert C. Byrd (D-W.Va.) voted "not guilty" on both articles although he thought that Clinton's behavior constituted "an impeachable offense, a political high crime or high misdemeanor against the state."[99] Not wanting to remove Clinton, Byrd voted "not guilty." Other Senators, including Susan Collins (R-Me.), Olympia Snowe (R-Me.), James Jeffords (R-Vt.), Fred Thompson (R-Tenn.), Ted Stevens (R-Alas.), and Slade Gorton (R-Wash.), concluded that Clinton was guilty on one or both articles but voted "not guilty" because they thought removal was unwarranted.[100] Senator Snowe put it his way; "Acquittal is not exoneration."[101] John Breaux, a Democrat from Louisiana, voted against the articles but cautioned that his vote "is not a vote on the innocence of this President. He is not innocent."[102] Bob Kerrey, Democrat from Nebraska, added: "While there is plenty of blame to go around in this case, the person responsible for it going this far is the President of the United States."[103]

Is Censure an Option?

As an alternative to impeachment, the House considered and rejected a motion to censure Clinton, raising some of the same issues faced by the Senate in 1834 when it censured President Andrew Jackson. Draft language by House Democrats stated it to be the sense of Congress that Clinton had "violated the trust of the American people, lessened their esteem for the office of President and dishonored the office which they have entrusted to him." Staying away from the explosive charges of perjury and obstruction of justice, the draft censure resolution nevertheless came close by charging that Clinton had "made

---

98. Id. at 84.
99. 145 Cong. Rec. S1636 (daily ed. February 12, 1999).
100. Id. at S1568, S1546–47, S1669–71, S1595, S1554–55, S1559, and S1462–64.
101. Id. at S1546.
102. Id. at S1501.
103. Id. at S1505.

false statements concerning his reprehensible conduct with a subordinate" and "wrongly took steps to delay discovery of the truth." Clinton, "by his conduct has brought upon himself and fully deserves the censure and condemnation of the American people and the Congress; and by his signature on this joint resolution, the President acknowledges this censure."[104]

Clinton was ready to sign the resolution if presented to him: "Should they determine that my errors of word and deed require their rebuke and censure, I am ready to accept that."[105] However, the Republicans on the House Judiciary Committee concluded that the Constitution "contains a single procedure for Congress to address the fitness for office of the President of the United States—impeachment by the House, and subsequent trial by the Senate."[106] The framers, by requiring a majority vote in the House and a two-thirds vote in the Senate, intended to make impeachment "into such an awesome power that Congress could not use it to harass executive officials or otherwise interfere with operations of coordinate branches."[107]

The Republicans on the Judiciary Committee also decided that a censure resolution would violate the Constitution's prohibition on bills of attainder, which the British Parliament had used to punish individuals. By prohibiting that procedure, the framers intended to prevent "legislative exercise of the judicial function, or more simply trial by legislature."[108] Would Clinton's agreement to sign the censure resolution erase its punitive nature? The Republicans said it would not, pointing to legislative history that a resolution of censure is either an action to punish the President or not, and if it is intended to punish, it is a bill of attainder. If it does not punish the President, "it is meaningless."[109]

When the resolution containing the articles of impeachment reached the House floor, Rep. Rick Boucher (D-Va.) offered a motion to recommit the resolution to House Judiciary with instructions to report it back with a resolution of censure. The chair held that the motion to recommit with instructions was not germane. When a member attempted to appeal the chair's ruling, the House voted 230 to 204 to lay the appeal on the table.[110]

Senate Democrats drafted a censure resolution as a way of expressing bipartisan rebuke to Clinton. His "inappropriate relationship with a subordi-

---

104. Washington Post, December 13, 1998, at A28.
105. Public Papers of the Presidents, 1998, II, at 2158.
106. H. Rept. No. 105-830, at 137.
107. Id.
108. Id. at 138 (citing United States v. Brown, 381 U.S. 437, 442 (1965)).
109. Id. at 138–39 (citing Rep. Edward Pease (R-Ind.)).
110. 144 Cong. Rec. H12031-39 (daily ed. December 19, 1998).

nate in the White House…was shameless, reckless, and indefensible." He "deliberately misled and deceived the American people and officials in all branches of the United States Government." The reference to all branches meant that he misled and deceived the courts, a point made explicit by stating that he "gave false or misleading testimony and impeded discovery of evidence in judicial proceedings." Senate Democrats were much more blunt here than House Democrats. Impeding discovery of evidence in a judicial proceedings seems indistinguishable from obstruction of justice. Other portions of the censure resolution stated that Clinton had brought "shame and dishonor to himself and to the Office of the President" and had "violated the trust of the American people."[111] Facing a possible filibuster, the Senate put the censure resolution aside.[112]

Other than President Grant's curious comment in 1876, Presidents and their administrations recognize that when the impeachment machinery starts up, arguments about executive privilege, confidential communications, and other traditional arguments for withholding information from Congress look too much like obstruction of justice to seriously entertain. Of course, a President's assurance that he will "fully cooperate" with the inquiry does not mean that he and the White House will not try every conceivable roadblock. In the end, the House will get the information it needs to pursue impeachment and it can expect support from the courts if an administration decides to block legislative access.

Whether an impeachment of a President will succeed depends on the emergence of bipartisan support. In the case of Nixon, a number of Republicans on the House Judiciary Committee joined with Democrats in agreeing that impeachment was justified. That development, along with the Supreme Court's opinion in *United States* v. *Nixon* (1974), was sufficient ground for Nixon to resign. With Clinton, the committee broke along party lines. Just as one can accuse the Republicans on the committee for voting in partisan manner, so one can make the same argument about the Democrats who defended Clinton. Either way, the lack of bipartisan support in the House doomed any prospect of removal by the Senate.

---

111. New York Times, February 6, 1999, at A8.
112. Eric Schmitt, "In the End, Senate Passes No Harsh Judgment on Clinton," New York Times, February 13, 1999, at A8; Edward Walsh, "Senate Puts Censure Resolution on Hold—Indefinitely," Washington Post, February 13, 1999, at A32; Eric Schmitt, "Threat of Filibuster Makes a Vote on Censure Nearly Impossible," New York Times, February 12, 1999, at A16.

4

THE APPOINTMENT POWER

Until the President submits the name of a nominee to the Senate, Congress has no grounds for gaining access to the files relating to the individual's past employment or experience. Matters change fundamentally when the President nominates the person to public office and needs the cooperation and approval of the Senate. At that point he may be forced to surrender documents that could otherwise be withheld under the doctrine of executive privilege. The President might face two options, neither one attractive. One is to surrender sensitive documents to Congress and agree to have executive officials testify before congressional committees. If that choice is unacceptable, the other option is to abandon the nominee. Precisely those conditions emerged with regard to the appointment of Richard Kleindienst in 1972 to be Attorney General and William H. Rehnquist in 1986 to be Chief Justice. At any time in the appointment process, Senate "holds" and the threat of a filibuster can force the release of executive branch documents.

Kleindienst Nomination

President Nixon's nomination of Richard G. Kleindienst in 1972 to be Attorney General precipitated lengthy hearings by the Senate Judiciary Committee, eventually forcing the administration to allow a White House aide to testify. The nomination seemed to go smoothly at first. The committee voted unanimously on February 24 to approve Kleindeinst, who had served as Deputy Attorney General.[1] The administration expected the nomination to come to the floor for easy confirmation.

---

1. CQ Weekly Report, February 26, 1972, at 452.

Before that could happen, Jack Anderson published several explosive columns charging that the administration had entered into a corrupt deal with the International Telephone and Telegraph Corp. (ITT). A column published on February 29 claimed to have evidence that Attorney General John Mitchell agreed to drop an antitrust case against the company in return for a pledge of $400,000 to help finance the 1972 Republican National Convention in San Diego.[2] A March 1 column accused Kleindienst of telling "an outright lie" by denying any connection between the settlement and the cash and by disclaiming any role in the department's out-of-court settlement.[3]

The previous year, Kleindienst had been pressured by the White House to drop the antitrust action against ITT. White House aide John Ehrlichman called Kleindienst on April 19, 1971, telling him not to appeal one of the ITT cases. Kleindienst replied that the department would proceed with the appeal as planned. Within a few minutes, President Nixon was on the phone, directing Kleindienst "to drop the goddamn thing. Is that clear?"[4] Kleindienst told Attorney General Mitchell about the call, explaining that if the President's order prevailed he would have to resign and so would two others: Richard McLaren, head of the Antitrust Division, and Solicitor General Erwin Griswold. A few days later Mitchell told Kliendienst to proceed with the appeal.[5]

Faced with the sensational allegations in the Jack Anderson columns, Senate Judiciary opened a special hearing on March 2 to have Kleindienst explain his role in the department's decision to settle the case.[6] Senate hearings had produced conflicting statements as to whether ITT President Harold S. Geneen had discussed antitrust policy with White House aide Peter M. Flanigan.[7] Some Senators wanted Flanigan to testify, but White House Counsel John Dean wrote to the committee on April 12, stating that the doctrine of executive privilege protected Flanigan and other White House aides from testifying before congressional committees: "Under the doctrine of separation of powers, and long-established historical precedents, the principle that members of the President's

---

2. Jack Anderson, "Secret Memo Bares Mitchell-ITT Move," Washington Post, February 29, 1972, at B11.
3. Jack Anderson, "Kleindienst Accused in ITT Case," Washington Post, March 1, 1972, at B15. A third column summarized the first two; Jack Anderson, "Contradictions Cited in ITT Case," Washington Post, March 3, 1972.
4. Richard Kleindienst, Justice: The Memoirs of an Attorney General 91 (1985).
5. Id. at 92–93.
6. CQ Weekly Report, March 4, 1972, at 510.
7. 1972 CQ Almanac 218–19.

immediate staff not appear and testify before congressional committees with respect to the performance of their duties is firmly established."[8]

Firmly established? That overstates both principle and practice within the executive branch, and certainly a number of Senators refused to accept such a doctrine. By party-line votes of 6 to 6, the committee rejected three motions to subpoena White House aides to testify.[9] Senator Charles McC. Mathias, Jr. (R-Md.) attempted to arrange a private, informal meeting between Flanigan and the committee, but that never materialized.[10] Senator Sam Ervin insisted that the Senate should not vote on Kleindienst "so long as those fellows aren't coming up here and the White House is withholding information."[11] Ervin made it clear that if the nomination cleared the committee, he might filibuster it during floor action.[12] Senator John Tunney (D-Cal.) called Ervin a "master of the filibuster."[13] Ervin added: "If the President wants to make his nominee for Attorney General a sacrificial lamb on the altar of executive privilege, that will be his responsibility and not mine."[14]

With a filibuster looming, the White House within a few days abandoned Dean's legal theory. Flanigan advised the committee that he would testify if the questions were limited to his role in hiring Richard J. Ramsden, a financial analyst, and meeting with Geneen. By a 12 to 1 vote the committee accepted those conditions.[15] Flanigan appeared at the hearings on April 20 to discuss the two issues he identified and to respond to some other matters. He later responded to written questions submitted by the committee.[16] Following committee action, the Senate confirmed Kleindienst by a vote of 64 to 19.

As part of Nixon's efforts to save his presidency, he asked Kleindienst and several others to resign to give an appearance of housecleaning. Kleindienst wanted his name announced separately from the planned resignations of

---

8. "Sen. Ervin Hints Filbuster on Kleindienst After Panel Rejects Calling of Nixon Aide," Wall Street Journal, April 13, 1972, at 4.
9. 1972 CQ Almanac 221.
10. Id.
11. "Panel Votes Not to Subpoena Nixon Aides on I.T.T.," New York Times, April 13, 1972, at 8.
12. "Sen. Ervin Hints Filbuster on Kleindeinst After Panel Rejects Calling of Nixon Aide," Wall Street Journal, April 13, 1972, at 4.
13. Id.
14. Sanford G. Ungar, "GOP Move Imperils Kleindienst," Washington Post, April 13, 1972, at A24.
15. 1972 CQ Almanac 221.
16. Id. at 223; "Richard G. Kleindienst — Resumed" (Part 3), hearings before the Senate Committee on the Judiciary, 92d Cong., 2d Sess. 1585 (1972).

Dean, Ehrlichman, and Bob Haldeman, but the names were announced together.[17] Kleindienst later pled guilty to a misdemeanor for not telling the truth at his confirmation hearing about Nixon's intervention in the ITT case. He could have been sentenced to a year in jail and fined $1,000. Instead, Judge George L. Hart, Jr. sentenced him to one month in prison and fined him $100. He then suspended both the sentence and the fine, placing Kleindienst on one month's unsupervised probation.[18]

L. Patrick Gray III

On February 17, 1973, President Nixon announced the selection of L. Patrick Gray III to be the new FBI Director. Gray had been serving as acting director since May 3, 1972, following the death of J. Edgar Hoover. When Gray's name was announced, his support in the Senate for confirmation seemed fairly strong.[19] During hearings by the Senate Judiciary Committee on February 28 and March 1, Senators began to express concern about Gray's political background and his performance as acting director on such issues as the Watergate break-in, alleged wiretaps on newsmen, and leaks of FBI documents. To alleviate the concerns of the Senate, Gray offered to open FBI files with regard to the Watergate case and allow Senators to look through them.[20] He estimated that it would take a Senator about forty hours to review the files, prompting Senator Robert C. Byrd to dismiss the offer as "not worth a hill of beans" unless Senate staff members were given access. Gray rejected that proposal, except for the staff of the select Senate committee that was investigating Watergate.[21]

To clear up some of the issues that had been raised, Senator Tunney said he planned to ask the Senate Judiciary Committee to issue a subpoena to White House Counsel John Dean.[22] Some Senators were concerned that Dean had been present during every FBI interview of a White House staff member, and also had access to FBI documents on the Watergate investigation.[23] At a

---

17. Public Papers of the Presidents, 1973, at 326–28; Kleindienst, Justice, at 168.
18. Kleindienst, Justice, at 175–76.
19. "FBI Chief: L. Patrick Gray III," CQ Weekly Report, February 24, 1973, at 378.
20. "Patrick Gray: Senators Worry About FBI in Politics," March 3, 1973, at 479.
21. "FBI Director: Watergate Linked to Gray Nomination," CQ Weekly Report, March 10, 1973, at 551.
22. "A Subpoena to White House," CQ Weekly Report, March 10, 1973, at 557.
23. "The White House and Watergate," CQ Weekly Report, March 10, 1973, at 557.

news conference the following day, March 2, President Nixon objected to Dean's appearance: "no President could ever agree to allow the Counsel to the President to go down and testify before a committee."[24] At the same time, Nixon said that if the committee asked for information "that a member of the White House Staff may have, we will make arrangements to provide that information."[25]

On March 13, all nine Democrats and all seven Republicans on the Senate Judiciary Committee invited Dean to appear and testify concerning his relationship to Gray, the FBI investigation of Watergate, and the use of FBI information about that inquiry. Dean declined to come, but offered to provide written responses to questions submitted by the committee. Senator Ervin objected that it was impossible to cross-examine a written response.[26] At a news conference on March 15, Nixon was asked if he intended to prohibit Dean from testifying if it meant the defeat of Gray's nomination. Nixon responded that he could not believe the Senate "might hold Mr. Gray as hostage to a decision on Mr. Dean."[27] When asked whether he would allow Dean to sit down informally with Senators and respond to questions, Nixon rejected that compromise.[28]

The deadlock over Dean's appearance before the committee became a major factor in the Senate's decision not to confirm Gray. On April 5, Nixon announced his intention to withdraw Gray's nomination to be FBI Director. He explained that he had asked Dean to conduct "a thorough investigation of alleged involvement in the Watergate episode," and directed Gray "to make FBI reports available to Mr. Dean." Gray's compliance with his order, Nixon said, "exposed Mr. Gray to totally unfair innuendo and suspicion, and therefore seriously tarnished his fine record as Acting Director and promising future at the Bureau."[29]

With this announcement, Nixon released Gray gently and with respect. Privately, Nixon and his top aides decided that Gray's testimony had threatened the administration and his nomination would have to be abandoned. The press learned that Gray, under White House pressure, had destroyed some Watergate documents. Gray's status within the White House is reflected in Ehrlichman's remark that he should be left to "hang there; let him twist slowly,

---

24. Public Papers of the Presidents, 1973, at 160.
25. Id. at 160–61.
26. "Nixon, the Senate, the FBI: To the Battle Stations," CQ Weekly Report, March 17, 1973, at 630.
27. Public Papers of the Presidents, 1973, at 203.
28. Id. at 205.
29. Id. at 257.

slowly in the wind."[30] Afterwards, FBI agents found in Gray's safe some Watergate documents, given him by the CIA, that Gray had never shared with FBI investigators.[31]

Judicial Nominations

In recent decades, a number of nominations for judgeships have been delayed while the Senate waits for documents that the White House refuses, initially, to release. The congressional leverage is such that continued refusal would mean the loss of the candidate. The pressure builds until the White House offers some sort of accommodation to satisfy the needs of the Senate Judiciary Committee. An alternative is for the White House to hold firm, hoping that the next election will produce a Senate more supportive of presidential nominations. An administration strategy of delay is more attractive for lower court nominees than for openings that appear on the Supreme Court.

Rehnquist for Chief Justice

On July 31, 1986, President Reagan refused to give the Senate Judiciary Committee certain internal memos that his nominee for Chief Justice, William Rehnquist, had written while serving in the Justice Department as head of the Office of Legal Counsel (OLC) from 1969 to 1971. The reason for invoking executive privilege was familiar: to protect the confidentiality and candor of the legal advice submitted to Presidents and their assistants.[32] At least with regard to OLC memos, this position is strained. Unlike many legal memos produced within the executive branch, OLC memos are regularly published.

Rehnquist agreed to the release of the documents, but the White House did not.[33] Whatever the merits of the administration's legal theory, the political setting was not favorable. With Democrats on the committee rounding up votes to subpoena the papers,[34] the dispute threatened to prevent action not only on Rehnquist but also on the nomination of Antonin Scalia to be Associate Justice. The Senate planned to vote on both Rehnquist and Scalia on Au-

---

30. Fred Emery, Watergate 247 (1995); John Ehrlichman, Witness to Power 374 (1982).
31. Emery, Watergate, at 349.
32. Al Kamen and Ruth Marcus, "Reagan Uses Executive Privilege to Keep Rehnquist Memos Secret," Washington Post, August 1, 1986, at A1.
33. Id.
34. Howard Kurtz and Ruth Marcus, "Democrats Seek to Subpoena Papers," Washington Post, August 2, 1986, at A1.

gust 14.[35] Scalia had headed the OLC office under President Ford, from 1974 to 1977. Senator Paul Laxalt (R-Nev.) negotiated with the administration to see whether a compromise could be reached.[36]

In an op-ed piece for the *Los Angeles Times*, Senator Ted Kennedy put the matter succinctly: "Rehnquist: No Documents, No Senate Confirmation."[37] Kennedy said the committee needed to review Rehnquist's OLC memos in such areas as domestic surveillance of the military, wiretapping of journalists, mass arrests of anti-war demonstrators, reform of the classification system, investigation of security leaks, and the part he played in the nomination and confirmation of federal judges. Kennedy agreed with the position advanced by Senator Ervin some years back that Presidents have no right to demand confirmation of a nominee while withholding information that Senators need to perform their constitutional role.

In an effort to move the Rehnquist and Scalia nominations, President Reagan agreed to allow the committee access to some of Rehnquist's OLC memos. Instead of the original request for all of his memos on such broad issues as "civil rights" and "civil liberties," the list was narrowed to about 25 to 30 documents.[38] A bipartisan majority of the committee—eight Democrats and two Republicans—had lined up in support of a subpoena. Under the agreement, six Senators and six staff members were allowed to read the OLC memos.[39] Later, the committee requested and received additional documents prepared by Rehnquist while in the Justice Department.[40] Having satisfied its needs for information within the executive branch, the Senate then confirmed Rehnquist and Scalia on September 17.

Robert Bork

In 1987, President Reagan nominated Robert Bork to be Associate Justice of the Supreme Court. As part of committee preparation, Senator Joe Biden

---

35. George Lardner, Jr. and Al Kamen, "Senators to Push for Rehnquist Memos," Washington Post, August 5, 1986, at A4.
36. Kurtz and Marcus, "Democrats Seek to Subpoena Papers," at A1.
37. Edward M. Kennedy, "Rehnquist: No Documents, No Senate Confirmation," Los Angeles Times, August 5, 1986, Part II, at 5.
38. Al Kamen and Howard Kurtz, "Rehnquist Told in 1974 of Restriction in Deed," Washington Post, August 6, 1986, at A1.
39. Howard Kurtz and Al Kamen, "Rehnquist Not in Danger Over Papers," Washington Post, August 7, 1986, at A1, A14.
40. "Senators Are Given More Rehnquist Data," Washington Post, August 8, 1986, at A3.

of the Judiciary Committee wrote to Attorney General Meese for "certain material in the possession of the Justice Department and the Executive Office of the President." The list of documents included written products by Bork while he was Solicitor General. For example, the committee wanted all documents from 1973 through 1977 regarding Bork's views on the constitutionality of the President's "pocket veto" power. Among the documents requested: the decision not to petition for certiorari in the case of *Kennedy v. Sampson*, 511 F.2d 430 (D.C. Cir. 1977), the entry of the judgment in *Kennedy v. Jones*, 412 F.Supp. 353 (D.D.C. 1976), and the policy regarding pocket vetoes publicly adopted by President Ford in April 1976. Additional documents covered Bork's role during the Watergate investigation, especially his dismissal of Archibald Cox as Special Prosecutor and communications that Bork had with President Nixon, Alexander Haig, Leonard Garment, Fred Buzhardt, Elliot Richardson, and William Ruckelshaus. The committee request also dealt with Bork's participation as Solicitor General in seven cases decided by the Supreme Court.[41]

The Justice Department gave Biden the documents. Some were forwarded, such as memos from the Solicitor General's office on the pocket veto issue. Others, under seal by order of a federal district court, had to be unsealed and supplied to the committee. A few were converted to redacted versions (deleting a few sentences of classified material) or in unclassified form. The department explained that "the vast majority of the documents you have requested reflect or disclose purely internal deliberations within the Executive Branch, the work product of attorneys in connection with government litigation or confidential legal advice received from or provided to client agencies within the Executive Branch." Releasing such materials "seriously impairs the deliberative process within the Executive Branch, our ability to represent the government in litigation and our relationship with other entities." Yet the department waived those considerations "to cooperate to the fullest extent possible with the Committee and to expedite Judge Bork's confirmation process."[42]

When the Senate Judiciary Committee issued its report on Judge Bork's nomination, it included a fifteen-page memo that he wrote as Solicitor General on the constitutionality and policy considerations of the President's pocket veto power.[43] In the end, after a tumultuous confirmation hearing, the Senate rejected Bork 58 to 42. During the administration of George W. Bush, this

---

41. 149 Cong. Rec. S2886–88 (daily ed. February 27, 2003).
42. Id. at S2888 (letter of August 24, 1987 from Laura Wilson, for Assistant Attorney General John R. Bolton, to Senator Joseph R. Biden, Jr.).
43. S. Exec. Rept. No. 100-7, 100th Cong., 1st Sess. 313 (1987).

type of document from the Solicitor General's office would be withheld from the Senate regarding the nomination of Miguel Estrada.

Stephen Trott

The nomination of Stephen S. Trott for Ninth Circuit judge was held up for four months in 1988 because Senators Ted Kennedy and Howard Metzenbaum wanted internal documents from the Justice Department. Trott had been Assistant Attorney General of the Criminal Division. Kennedy and Metzenbaum used his nomination to gain access to a report by the department's Public Integrity Section, which sources claimed contained a recommendation to Attorney General Meese to seek the appointment of an independent counsel to probe Faith Ryan Whittlesey, former ambassador to Switzerland. Meese later decided against an independent counsel. Justice Department officials argued that the confidentiality of the report was protected by statute.[44]

Refusing to release the report, the department explained: "As you know, it is a longstanding policy of the Department not to provide copies of internal, deliberative memoranda to persons outside the Department."[45] That may have been "longstanding policy," but the Trott nomination was not going to move unless and until the department yielded, which it did. Internal departmental documents about its investigation into Whittlesey were turned over to the Senate Judiciary Committee. Senators on the committee, and three staff aides from each side, were allowed to look at three "decisional memoranda."[46] Having received the documents they wanted, Kennedy and Metzenbaum released their hold on the nomination.[47]

Miguel Estrada

In a replay of earlier fights over nominees to federal courts, President George W. Bush's nomination of Miguel Estrada to the D.C. Circuit in 2002 sparked requests by Senate Democrats for memoranda he wrote while a

---

44. "Justice Aide Kept on Hold," Washington Post, March 23, 1988.
45. Ruth Marcus, "Impasse Over Justice Department Ends," Washington Post, March 25, 1988, at A23 (quoting Assistant Attorney General John R. Bolton).
46. Id.
47. "After 4-Month Hold, Senate OKs Trott to U.S. Appeals Court," Los Angeles Times, March 25, 1988, Part I, p. 15.

lawyer in the Office of Solicitor General from 1992 to 1997. Unlike Bork, who wrote many decisions while on the D.C. Circuit and published widely in law reviews and other outlets, Estrada had much less of a written record to guide the judgment of Senators. The nomination was significant because the D.C. Circuit is often viewed as a stepping-stone to the Supreme Court, and it appeared likely that Bush would want to name the first Hispanic to the Court.

The White House, pointing to a letter from several former Solicitors General, refused to release the documents, arguing that to do so would inhibit lawyers from offering candid advice.[48] As with Rehnquist, Estrada said he had no objection to sharing the documents with the Senate Judiciary Committee: "If it were up to me, I would be more than proud to have you look at everything that I have done as a lawyer."[49]

Why would release of Estrada's memos chill the willingness of government lawyers to provide frank advice? Paul Wolfson, who worked as an assistant to the Solicitor General from 1994 to 2002, explains that it is in the SG's office that "DOJ's litigation and policy decisions come together."[50] That, by itself, shouldn't shield agency documents. Wolfson offers other reasons for keeping these memos private: "Sometimes they contain unflattering descriptions of the reasoning of a judge, or a federal agency's rationale for a regulation, or Congress' wording of a statute."[51] This remark seems to call attention to a writing style that can be disparaging or derisive toward other agencies and branches. Such language might be very illuminating and useful for Senators who need to judge the qualifications, temperament, and maturity of a judicial nominee.

In the past, Congress had access to internal deliberative documents in the Justice Department, including the conduct of open and closed cases. Those precedents were detailed during a hearing before the House Government Reform Committee on February 6, 2002, regarding FBI corruption in its Boston office. After a confrontation with the Bush administration and the first invocation of executive privilege by President Bush, the documents were released. That dispute is discussed in the next chapter.

---

48. Neil A. Lewis, "Fight Brews Over a Judicial Nominee," New York Times, September 24, 2002, at A21.

49. Neil A. Lewis, "Bush Judicial Choice Imperiled by Refusal to Release Papers," New York Times, September 27, 2002, at A26.

50. Paul Wolfson, "Looking for a Paper Trail," National Law Journal, October 21, 2002, at A20.

51. Id.

No committee action was taken on Estrada in 2002, when Democrats controlled the Senate Judiciary committee 10 to 9. After the fall elections gave the Republicans control of the Senate and a 10-9 edge on the committee, they approved Estrada's nomination by a party-line vote. Minority Leader Tom Daschle announced that the Democrats might pursue a filibuster to block Estrada's confirmation.[52] When the filibuster began, Daschle remarked that until Estrada's SG opinions were made available, "we will not be in a position to allow a vote to come to the Senate floor."[53] The White House continued to withhold Estrada's memos.[54] To break the deadlock, Senate Majority Leader Bill Frist offered to make Estrada available for a second hearing, on the condition that the Democrats would allow a vote after that.[55] The Democrats turned down the offer, insisting that the administration release the memos and other work papers from Estrada's tenure in the Office of Solicitor General.[56]

Ambassador to Guyana

In 1991, the appointment of George Fleming Jones to be U.S. Ambassador to Guyana was delayed 17 months until Senator Jesse Helms received documents he wanted from the State Department.[57] During a visit by Helms to Chile in 1986, one of his aides was accused of leaking U.S. intelligence information to the government of former Chilean President Augusto Pinochet. At that time, Jones was deputy chief of mission in the U.S. Embassy. Helms insisted that the State Department show him secret cable traffic regarding the visit. The department shared with him a number of documents but refused to turn over two cables, which they called internal memoranda.[58]

---

52. Helen Dewar, "Filibuster Over Estrada Considered," Washington Post, February 6, 2003, at A4.
53. Neil A. Lewis, "Filibuster on Judgeship Halts Business in the Senate," New York Times, February 12, 2003, at A18.
54. Helen Dewar, "Deadlock Over Estrada Deepens," Washington Post, February 13, 2003, at A4.
55. Helen Dewar, "Bush Calls for Limit to Senate Debates," Washington Post, March 12, 2003, at A4.
56. Jennifer A. Dlouhy, "Democrats Snub Frist's Compromise Offer to Hold New Estrada Hearing," CQ Today, March 12, 2003, at 3.
57. Al Kamen, "Ambassador to Guyana is Appointed After 17-Month Standoff," Washington Post, November 29, 1991, at A40.
58. Id.

For the next few years, Helms bided his time, waiting for the appropriate moment to strike. The opportunity came in June 1990, when Jones was nominated for the position of ambassador to Chile. Helms now had the necessary leverage. After Helms renewed his request for the cables and the State Department again refused, he blocked the nomination. As the months rolled by and Helms held firm, Deputy Secretary of State Lawrence Eagleburger took a drive to Capitol Hill and stopped by Helms' office to show him the cables, which had been critical of both Helms and his aide. The memos had not been written by Jones. The State Department had merely decided to withhold from Helms documents that he might find offensive. After looking at the cables, Helms released his hold and Jones's nomination went forward.[59]

Environmental Crimes Section (DOJ)

In the early 1990s, the Subcommittee on Oversight and Investigations of the House Energy and Commerce Committee began an investigation into the work of the Environmental Crimes Section (ECS) within the Justice Department, particularly the shift of prosecution responsibilities from U.S. Attorneys in the field to Washington officials. By 1994, this investigation had become entangled with the nomination of Lois Schiffer to be Assistant Attorney General of the Environment and Natural Resources Division.

Subcommittee hearings in September 1992 reviewed the concern of Congress over the past decade in inadequate criminal investigative resources at the Environmental Protection Agency. Chairman John D. Dingell (D-Mich.) said that EPA's criminal enforcement record, under legislative prodding, "has come a long way—only to be stifled by the activities of the Department of Justice."[60] He charged that ECS had acquired a veto power over environmental prosecutions nationwide, and that local U.S. attorney's offices and "even the line attorneys" in ECS objected to DOJ's decisions in Washington, D.C.[61] Focusing on six cases, Dingell criticized the department for failing to prosecute responsible corporate officials or for entering into plea bargains that collected only modest monetary fines.[62]

---

59. Id.
60. "EPA's Criminal Enforcement Program," hearing before the Subcommittee on Oversight and Investigations, House Committee on Energy and Commerce, 102d Cong., 2d Sess. 1 (1992).
61. Id. at 1–2.
62. Id. at 2.

Dingell wrote to the Justice Department on June 2, 1993, requesting copies of specific documents on six closed cases, communications to and from the six companies, calendars and daily diaries of certain departmental officials, and other documents.[63] Responding by letter on June 17, the department agreed to allow the subcommittee to interview nine departmental officials in connection with the environmental crimes program. The interviews could begin before the document request had been responded to.[64] The department advised the DOJ attorneys that "the subcommittee may be empowered to subpoena you if you choose not to be interviewed...."[65] President Clinton did not intervene in this subcommittee-department dispute. White House Communications Director Mark Gearan announced: "We will not assert any privilege or waiver."[66]

In March 1994, the subcommittee subpoenaed the records of six cases handled by the Environment and Natural Resources Division. In addition to sending the subpoenas, Dingell and ranking minority member Dan Schaefer (R-Colo.) released letters to the Senate Judiciary Committee, asking that the confirmation of Lois Schiffer be delayed.[67] She had been serving as Acting Attorney General of the Environment and Natural Resources Division and had been nominated for the permanent position on February 2, 1994. Schaefer expressed his concern about her confirmation because of what he described as "obstruction of the subcommittee's work on oversight of the nation's environmental laws."[68] The correspondence from Dingell and Schaefer to Senate Judiciary carried extra punch because of its bipartisan stature.

As the dispute deepened, ECS chief Neil S. Cartusciello announced his resignation.[69] By that time, the subcommittee had begun receiving some of the documents it had subpoenaed.[70] After Schiffer moved to find a replacement for Cartusciello, the hearing on her nomination tentatively was scheduled.[71] Further delays set in, but after the subcommittee was satisfied with the coop-

---

63. Letter from Dingell to Associate Attorney General Webster L. Hubbell, June 2, 1993.
64. Letter from Hubbell to Dingell, June 17, 1993.
65. Form letter from Anthony C. Moscato to the nine attorneys, June 28, 1993.
66. Jim McGee, "House Panel Subpoenas Justice," Washington Post, March 12, 1994, at A4.
67. Id.
68. Id.
69. Jim McGee, "Chief of Environmental Crimes Section Quits," Washington Post, April 2, 1994, at A4.
70. Id.
71. Al Kamen, "Teaming Up," Washington Post, July 13, 1994, at A15.

eration it had received from the Justice Department, Schiffer was confirmed by the Senate on October 6, 1994.[72]

This type of executive-legislative dispute illustrates that Congress has sufficient tools at its command to wrest from the administration the documents it needs to fulfill congressional duties. The question is whether lawmakers will press their advantage. As noted by Neal Devins, the issue is "not the adequacy of congressional power to obtain information, *but* the willingness of committee chairs and staffers to aggressively pursue information."[73]

Senate "Holds"

The informal practice of imposing "holds" allows any Senator to request that floor action on a bill or nomination be deferred. The Senate Majority Leader may then decide whether to honor the request. Although there have been objections to "secret holds"—holds that are not identified with a particular Senator—holds are frequently a legitimate means of pursuing legislative interests. Efforts to place limits on holds, such as requiring Senators to make their actions known to the sponsor of a bill, have been extremely difficult to enforce.

There are many reasons for placing a hold, but often it is to obtain information that the executive branch has refused to release to Congress. A typical power struggle occurred in the Senate in 1989, when two Democratic committee chairmen, Donald W. Riegle, Jr. of Michigan and Alan Cranston of California, advised the White House that their committees would not schedule confirmation hearings on nominees until the administration provided FBI reports on the nominees to the majority and minority staff directors. Riegle's committee had jurisdiction over the nomination of more than two dozen officials of the Department of Housing and Urban Development, as well as nominees for the Securities and Exchange Commission, the Council of Economic Advisers, and other executive agencies. Cranston's committee had ju-

---

72. See 140 Cong. Rec. 28360 (1994). For further details on this controversy, see "Damaging Disarray: Organization Breakdown and Reform in the Justice Department's Environmental Crimes Program," 103-T, Staff of Subcommittee on Oversight and Investigations of the House Committee on Energy and Commerce, 103d Cong. (Comm. Print 1994); Neal Devins, "Congressional-Executive Information Access Disputes: A Modest Proposal—Do Nothing," 48 Admin. L. Rev. 109, 123–25 (1996).

73. Devins, "Congressional-Executive Information Access Disputes," at 133 (emphasis in original).

risdiction over the Department of Veterans Affairs and the Court of Veterans Appeals. White House Counsel C. Boyden Gray offered to allow the committee chairman and ranking minority members access to the FBI reports.[74] On an impasse like this, a Senate threat carries high credibility.

Senator John Warner announced in 1993 that he would release his hold on the intelligence authorization bill after receiving assurance from the CIA that it would search its files for information on Defense Department nominee Morton Halperin. The CIA had previously said that it could not find the documents requested by Republican members of the Senate Armed Services Committee. CIA Director James Woolsey promised to search agency files and provide a timely response. He had planned to brief committee Republicans on this issue but apparently was ordered not to do so by White House Counsel Bernard Nussbaum.[75]

In 1997, Senator Charles Grassley used holds to force the State Department to comply with a statutory procedure that required the administration to submit to Congress on November 1 of each year the names of countries that the administration would certify as cooperating on drug control. After the administration had missed several deadlines and extended deadlines in submitting the list, he put a hold on nominations for ambassadors to Bolivia, Haiti, Jamaica, and Belize. As Senator Grassley said: "we need to get the administration's attention so that they will abide by the law."[76] No doubt this tactic prompts the administration to order agency compliance with statutory requirements.

In 1999, several Senators wrote to the State Department, expressing their concern about the department's treatment of Linda Shenwick, who worked at the U.S. mission to the United Nations. After providing Congress information on mismanagement at the UN, she was threatened with a suspension and transfer to another job. Senator Grassley charged that Shenwick "is guilty of committing the crime of telling the truth. And when you commit truth, you're history in the State Department."[77] As a way of getting the department's attention, Grassley placed a hold on the nomination of Richard Holbrooke to be U.S. ambassador to the UN. He explained that if lawmakers did not pro-

---

74. Ann Devroy, "White House, Senators Feud on FBI Data," Washington Post, May 19, 1989, at A1.
75. Bill Gertz, "CIA Offer of Help on Nominee Frees Up Authorization Bill," Washington Times, November 5, 1993, at A5.
76. 143 Cong. Rec. S11632 (daily ed. November 4, 1997).
77. Statement by Senator Grassley, 145 Cong. Rec. S7587 (daily ed. June 24, 1999); "Sen Grassley's 'hold,'" Editorial, The Hill, August 11, 1999, at 10.

tect agency whistleblowers, "a valuable source of information to Congress will likely dry up."[78] After being reassured that Shenwick would not be punished by the State Department, Grassley lifted his objections to Holbrooke, who was confirmed. However, Grassley blocked approval of three other ambassadorial nominees to underscore his intention to protect Shenwick.[79]

Reform proposals to regulate and restrict holds in the Senate have been unsuccessful. Senators are jealous of their ability to act independently and are unlikely to see that capacity diminished. In 1993, Senator Majority Leader George Mitchell announced some general guidelines on the use of holds. He denied that Senators have the right to "indefinitely postpone and, therefore, defeat outright nominations or legislation in the Senate."[80] He summarized the policy followed by Democratic and Republican leaders over the years, requiring Senators to notify their leaders about any need to consult with them about a bill or nomination. Before the scheduling of a bill or nomination, Senators had an obligation to discuss the issue with the committee chairman and/or the ranking member or sponsor. If Senators planned to object to a unanimous consent request, they should be on the floor at the announced time for the legislation or nomination.[81]

It is precisely this procedure for unanimous consent motions that gives great power to an individual Senator and makes it so difficult to regulate the use of holds. The House of Representatives has a Rules Committee that determines how much time shall be allowed to debate a bill, and what kind of amendments are to be allowed. In the Senate, such matters are handled by the Democratic and Republican leaders who draft a unanimous consent request. To do that, they need to touch base with every Senator to make sure that their needs are accommodated. Otherwise, when the majority leader comes to the floor and announces "I ask unanimous consent…," an individual Senator can object, forcing the party leaders to hammer out another unanimous consent agreement.

Mitchell explained his policy on the use of holds. He pledged to respect requests by Senators for advance notifications of actions on a bill or nominee:

---

78. Sen. Chuck Grassley, "Holds Practice Needs Big Changes," Letter to the Editor, Roll Call, August 2, 1999, at 4.

79. George Archibald, "Grassley Shifts Tack; Holbrooke Path Clear," Washington Times, August 5, 1999, at A6; Helen Dewar, "Holbrooke Nomination Clears Hurdle," Washington Post, August 5, 1999, at A4. For Senate debate on Grassley's hold on Holbrooke, see 145 Cong. Rec. S10216–17, S10268–74 (daily ed. August 4–5, 1999).

80. 139 Cong. Rec. 10202 (1993).

81. Id. at 10202–03.

"I believe this is a reasonable procedure and I think a Senator is entitled to a reasonable period of time to prepare for legislation or to consult with a nominee."[82] He then stated:

> So I do believe that Senators have the right, as a part of this process, to raise policy concerns with the administration. But it should be clear that no Senator has the right to insist that the administration agree with his or her position on a policy or on a project, as a specific price to be paid for action on a nominee or on legislation.
>
> That is to say, a Senator cannot reasonably expect that a hold can be used as a way of indefinitely postponing or killing outright a bill or nomination, simply because the administration does not agree with the Senator's position on a particular policy or a project.[83]

Mitchell told Senators what they could "reasonably expect." As one reporter put it, his policy could be translated as "No more hostage-taking."[84] However, not every Senator will agree to be "reasonable" when the stakes are high, either in terms of needs back home or larger questions of national and international policy. In such cases, a Senator may decide to impose a hold for a long period of time until the administration takes certain actions, which may be the release of agency documents or an agreement not to take sanctions against a whistleblower who a Senator believes is being unjustifiably punished for telling the truth.

Objections are raised to "secret" holds: where a Senator blocks action without being named. Critics of this process insist that all holds "should be announced publicly—what or whom is being held, and who is doing it—and should not apply for more than two weeks."[85] Some Senators have pushed this reform proposal, but with little success. In 1997, Senator Ron Wyden offered an amendment to make it a standing order of the Senate that a Senator who notifies the leadership of his or her intention to object to proceeding to a motion or matter "shall disclose the objection (hold) in the Congressional Record not later than 2 session days after the date of said notice."[86] Wyden objected not to holds but to anonymous holds: "I think when one Member of the U.S.

---

82. Id. at 10203.
83. Id.
84. Helen Dewar, "Impasse on Clinton Nominees Eases," Washington Post, May 19, 1993, at A13.
85. Norman Ornstein, "Senatorial Choke Hold," New York Times, May 18, 1993, at A21.
86. 143 Cong. Rec. S9872 (daily ed. September 24, 1997).

Senate moves to effectively block the consideration of a bill or a nomination, they ought to make it clear to their constituents that they are the individual blocking this matter."[87] Ironically, when Wyden asked unanimous consent to speak on his amendment the following day for ten minutes, objection was heard.[88] Four years later, in 2001, a reporter observed that the effort in the Senate to eliminate secret holds "seems to be a dead letter."[89] Toward the end of 2001, Senator Patrick Leahy objected that "one or more Republicans Senators"—he didn't know who—had held up final passage of the 21st Century Department of Justice Appropriations Authorization Act.[90]

Must the Senate Always Act?

The Senate filibuster of Miguel Estrada in 2003 led to proposals to force the Senate to vote on nominees, either up or down. On May 9, 2003, Senate Majority Leader Bill Frist introduced S. Res. 138, designed to gradually reduce the number of votes needed to close debate: from its present 60 votes to 57, after the second cloture motion, and "by 3 additional votes on each succeeding motion, until the affirmative vote is reduced to a number equal to or less than an affirmative vote of a majority of the Senators duly chosen and sworn. The required vote shall then be a simple majority."[91]

Majority rule is an important principle in democratic government, but it is not an overriding or preeminent value. If it were, minority rights could be given short shrift, the President would be elected by the majority vote of the people rather than through the Electoral College, and there would be no reason for the supermajorities that govern constitutional amendments, impeachment, veto overrides, treaties, and expelling members of Congress. The fact that the Constitution expressly provides for these supermajorities does not make additional supermajorities unconstitutional. In a 1971 opinion decided by a unanimous Court, Chief Justice Warren Burger remarked: "Certainly any departure from strict majority rule gives disproportionate power to the minority. But there is nothing in the language of the Constitution, our

---

87. Id.
88. Id. at S9874.
89. Helen Dewar, "Senate Pact on 'Holds' Seems to Be a Dead Letter," Washington Post, November 12, 2001, at A23; Helen Dewar, "Senator Seeks to Stamp Out Secretive 'Holds,'" Washington Post, November 17, 2001, at A4.
90. 147 Cong. Rec. S13290 (daily ed. December 14, 2001).
91. S. Res. 138, 108th Cong., 1st Sess. 4 (2003).

history, or our cases that requires that a majority always prevail on every issue."[92]

To equate the congressional process with majority rule does not reflect legislative practice. Under Section 5 of Article I, each House of Congress "may determine the Rules of its Proceedings." Both chambers have adopted rules that require a supermajority for certain legislative actions. Political power is deliberately parceled out to small groups, such as committees and subcommittees, often making it difficult for a majority to prevail, or at least quickly. In committee, a small number of Senators decide whether to act at all on a presidential proposal.

Nothing in the U.S. Constitution compels Congress to act on a presidential proposal, whether for legislation, a treaty, or a nomination. The deliberative process implies legislative choice, including the freedom to do nothing. Of course Congress must as a practical matter act on certain measures, such as appropriations bills and nominations to federal office. Otherwise, government could not function. However, there is no legal obligation on the part of the Senate to act on a particular nominee, whether for an executive agency or the federal courts.

Not only is there no constitutional requirement to take a floor vote for or against a nominee, there is no requirement for a committee to act. There is no offense to constitutional requirements if a committee receives a nominee and concludes that the qualifications of the individual do not warrant a committee hearing or committee action. Perhaps the committee learns of defects in the nominee that would needlessly embarrass the individual or the administration through a public hearing. The committee may postpone action for any number of reasons, including the administration's decision not to release documents that the committee believes are necessary to give full consideration to the nominee's qualifications. If the Senate as a whole decides that the committee has unfairly blocked action that deserves a floor vote, procedures are available to discharge the committee. Otherwise, it is the committee's call. The full Senate generally defers to committee actions not to act on a nominee.

Senate action or inaction depends on how the President nominates a judge. It is possible to read the constitutional text as granting the President the exclusive role in nomination: "he shall nominate, and by and with the Advice and Consent of the Senate, shall appoint...." Presidents, however, consult with Senators during the nomination phase to facilitate confirmation. If the President builds an interbranch consensus, he more easily secures the Senate's con-

---

92. Gordon v. Lance, 403 U.S. 1, 6 (1971).

sent. If the President excludes the Senate from offering advice on the nomination and submits a controversial choice, the Senate will be more inclined to take no action at all, either in committee or on the floor. For controversial nominees that are reported out of committee, one would expect lengthy debate on the floor and possibly a filibuster. If a President wants to be assured of a floor vote—up or down—on a nominee, the answer lies not in a change in Senate rules but in the President's willingness to consult closely and meaningfully with Senators.

Senate control over nominations gives it a decided edge in demanding information from the executive branch. The message from a committee of jurisdiction is quite blunt: "To evaluate this nominee, we need the following documents." In the case of Rehnquist and other nominees, an administration may decide to abandon cherished, "long-standing" doctrines of executive privilege in order to move a nomination out of committee and onto the floor. This type of Senate threat is not always effective. An administration may prefer to keep the documents and drop the nominee, or perhaps wait for the next election to produce a Senate more supportive of presidential choices.

5

Congressional Subpoenas

The Supreme Court has described the congressional power of inquiry as "an essential and appropriate auxiliary to the legislative function."[1] The issuance of a subpoena pursuant to an authorized investigation is "an indispensable ingredient of lawmaking."[2] To be legitimate, a congressional inquiry need not produce a bill or legislative measure. "The very nature of the investigative function—like any research—is that it takes the searchers up some 'blind alleys' and into nonproductive enterprises. To be a valid legislative inquiry there need be no predictable end result."[3]

This chapter describes how committee subpoenas are used to force testimony and the release of documents. For witnesses who invoke their Fifth Amendment privilege against self-incrimination, Congress can grant them immunity from prosecution. Five examples of subpoena power are examined: Rep. John Moss arrayed against the Federal Trade Commission, a House subcommittee requesting a Justice Department legal opinion on seizing suspects abroad, a conflict between a House committee and the Justice Department involving the Inslaw affair, a Senate committee seeking documents on Whitewater, and a House investigation into FBI corruption.

Issuing a Subpoena

Lawmakers and their committees usually obtain the information they need for legislation or oversight without threats of subpoenas. They understand that committee investigations have to satisfy certain standards. Legislative in-

---

1. McGrain v. Daugherty, 272 U.S. 135, 174 (1927).
2. Eastland v. United States Servicemen's Fund, 421 U.S. 491, 505 (1975).
3. Id. at 509.

quiries must be authorized by Congress, pursue a valid legislative purpose, raise questions relevant to the issue being investigated, and inform witnesses why questions put to them are pertinent.[4] Congressional inquiries may not interfere with the independence of decisionmakers in adjudicatory proceedings before a department or agency.[5] However, lawmakers may still use oversight powers to monitor the adjudicatory process.[6] Other arguments may be offered to resist a subcommittee subpoena, such as the need to protect confidential trade secrets or to protect information within the Justice Department,[7] but those justifications can be overridden by legislative needs.

Federal courts give great deference to congressional subpoenas. If the investigative effort falls within the "legitimate legislative sphere," the congressional activity—including subpoenas—is protected by the absolute prohibition of the Speech or Debate Clause, which prevents members of Congress from being "questioned in any other place." In a 1975 case, the Supreme Court ruled that such investigative activities are immune from judicial interference.[8] A concurrence by Justices Marshall, Brennan, and Stewart did not agree that "the constitutionality of a congressional subpoena is always shielded from more searching judicial inquiry."[9] In a dissent, Justice Douglas rejected the majority's position regarding broad legislative immunity from judicial review.[10]

As a tool of legislative inquiries, both Houses of Congress authorize their committees and subcommittees to issue subpoenas to require the production of documents and the attendance of witnesses regarding matters within the committee's jurisdiction. Committee subpoenas "have the same authority as if they were issued by the entire House of Congress from which the committee is drawn."[11] If a witness refuses to testify or produce papers in re-

---

4. Wilkinson v. United States, 365 U.S. 399, 408–09 (1961); Ashland Oil, Inc. v. FTC, 409 F.Supp. 297, 305 (1976).
5. Pillsbury Co. v. FTC, 354 F.2d 952, 963 (5th Cir. 1966).
6. ATX, Inc. v. U.S. Department of Transportation, 41 F.3d 1522 (D.C. Cir. 1994); State of California v. FERC, 966 F.2d 1541 (9th Cir. 1992); Power Authority of the State of New York v. FERC, 743 F.2d 93 (2d Cir. 1984); Peter Kiewit Sons' Co. v. U.S. Army Corps of Engineers, 714 F.2d 163 (D.C. Cir. 1983).
7. See John C. Grabow, Congressional Investigations: Law and Practice 79–85 (1988); James Hamilton & John C. Grabow, "A Legislative Proposal for Resolving Executive Privilege Disputes Precipitated by Congressional Subpoenas," 21 Harv. J. Legis. 145 (1984); James Hamilton, The Power to Probe 57–78 (1977); and Raoul Berger, "Congressional Subpoenas to Executive Officials," 75 Colum. L. Rev. 865 (1975).
8. Eastland v. United States Servicemen's Fund, 421 U.S. at 501.
9. Id. at 515.
10. Id. at 518.
11. Exxon Corp. v. FTC, 589 F.2d 582, 592 (1978), cert. denied, 441 U.S. 943 (1979).

sponse to a committee subpoena, and the committee votes to report a resolution of contempt to the floor, the full House or Senate may vote in support of the contempt citation. The contempt power is covered in detail in the next chapter.

Committees and subcommittees are authorized to request, by subpoena, "the attendance and testimony of such witnesses and the production of such books, records, correspondence, memoranda, papers, and documents as it considers necessary." For a committee or subcommittee to issue a subpoena, a majority must be present, although the power to authorize and issue subpoenas may be delegated to the committee chairman.[12] Committee rules can vary the procedures for issuing subpoenas.

A congressional subpoena identifies the name of the committee or subcommittee; the date, time, and place of the hearing a witness is to attend; and the particular kind of documents sought. A subpoena may state that if the documents are delivered by a particular date, the person who has custody over the documents need not appear. Congressional subpoenas are typically served by the U.S. Marshall's office or by committee staff. The Senate has statutory authority to seek civil enforcement of its subpoenas over private individuals.[13] The House relies on its rules and criminal contempt statutes.[14]

It is rare for an executive official to wholly sidestep a congressional subpoena. In 1989, a House subcommittee issued a subpoena to former Housing and Urban Development Secretary Samuel Pierce. He appeared, but invoked his constitutional right not to incriminate himself. He became the first former or current Cabinet official to invoke the Fifth Amendment since the Teapot Dome scandal of 1923.[15] In 1991, Secretary of Commerce Robert Mosbacher became the first sitting Cabinet officer to refuse to appear before a congressional committee to explain why he would not comply with a subpoena.[16]

In 1981, Attorney General William French Smith issued an opinion that analyzed how the administration should respond to a congressional subpoena.

---

12. House Rule XI(2)(m). See also Senate Rule XXVI(1).
13. 2 U.S.C. §§ 288b(b), 288d (2000); 28 U.S.C. § 1365 (2000).
14. 2 U.S.C. §§ 192–194 (2000).
15. Valerie Richardson and Jerry Seper, "House Committee Subpoenas Pierce," Washington Times, September 21, 1989, at A5; Gwen Ifill, "Pierce Invokes Fifth Amendment," Washington Post, September 27, 1989, at A1; Haynes Johnson, "Teapot Dome of the '80s," Washington Post, September 29, 1989, at A2.
16. Susan B. Glasser, "Secretary Spurns Census Subpoena," Roll Call, December 12, 1991, at 1.

He concluded that when Congress issues a subpoena as part of a "legislative oversight inquiry," access by Congress has less justification than when it seeks information for legislative purposes.[17] He acknowledged that Congress "does have a legitimate interest in obtaining information to assist it in enacting, amending, or repealing legislation." Yet "the interest of Congress in obtaining information for oversight purposes is, I believe, considerably weaker than its interest when specific legislative proposals are in question."[18] This distinction between legislation and oversight is strained and unconvincing. Congress has as much constitutional right to oversee the execution of laws as it does to pass them. Moreover, even if such a distinction could be drawn, Congress could easily erase it by introducing a bill to "justify" every oversight proceeding.

Immunity

Private citizens, more so than agency officers, may invoke certain constitutional protections, such as the First Amendment rights of free association and free speech. Witnesses may claim the Fifth Amendment privilege against self-incrimination.[19] A witness before a congressional committee has a constitutional right not "to be a witness against himself."[20] If a witness refuses to testify by invoking the Fifth Amendment, Congress can vote to force testimony by granting the witness either partial or full immunity.

By majority vote of either House or a two-thirds vote of a committee, Congress may request a federal court to issue an order that compels a witness to testify, giving the witness either partial immunity or full immunity. Partial immunity ("use immunity") means that the person's testimony may not be used against him in a criminal case, although the person might be prosecuted on the basis of other information, including information gathered and sequestered before the immunized testimony is delivered. Full immunity ("transactional immunity") offers absolute protection against prosecution for the offense.

During the Iran-Contra investigation in 1987, Congress offered partial immunity to several witnesses, including Col. Oliver North. He was later convicted of three felonies, but those charges were subsequently dismissed be-

---

17. 5 Op. O.L.C. 27, 29–30 (1981).
18. Id. at 30.
19. Wilkinson v. United States, 365 U.S. at 409.
20. U.S. Const., amend. 5 ("No person...shall be compelled in any criminal case to be a witness against himself").

cause of his immunized testimony. Under standards imposed by the D.C. Circuit, prosecutors must show that a defendant's testimony could have had no influence on the witnesses called to a trial. Otherwise, the remarks of the witnesses are "tainted" and may not be used to convict.[21]

In such situations Congress decides whether it is more important to inform itself and the public rather than have a successful prosecution. Lawrence Walsh, the independent counsel for Iran-Contra, described this setting of national priorities: "If the Congress decides to grant immunity, there is no way that it can be avoided. They have the last word and that is a proper distribution of power.... The legislative branch has the power to decide whether it is more important perhaps even to destroy a prosecution than to hold back testimony they need."[22]

The *Ashland* Case

A dispute between a House subcommittee and the Federal Trade Commission (FTC) began on April 16, 1975, when the commission issued an order requiring Ashland Oil, Inc. to submit information on Ashland's estimates of natural gas reserves on various leases. Ashland submitted the information on August 27, stating that the information was confidential and of a proprietary nature, and that disclosure to competitors would cause injury to Ashland.[23]

On October 6, in his capacity as a member of Congress, John Moss asked the commission to make available to him data gathered by the commission relating to lease extensions on federal lands. FTC denied the request for the reason that the data sought constituted "trade secrets and commercial or financial information [and] geological and geophysical information and data, including maps, concerning wells," and that such materials were exempt from mandatory disclosure under subsections (b)(4) and (b)(9) of the Freedom of

---

21. United States v. North, 910 F.2d 843 (D.C. Cir. 1990), cert. denied, 500 U.S. 941 (1991). See also United States v. Poindexter, 951 F.2d 369 (D.C. Cir. 1991), cert. denied, 506 U.S. 1021 (1992).

22. Lawrence E. Walsh, "The Independent Counsel and the Separation of Powers," 25 Houston L. Rev. 1, 9 (1988). For proposals to change the immunity statute to make congressional grants of immunity less costly to prosecutors and to Congress, see Ronald F. Wright, "Congressional Use of Immunity Grants After Iran-Contra," 80 Minn. L. Rev. 407 (1995).

23. H. Rept. No. 94-756, 94th Cong., 1st Sess. 6–7 (1975).

Information Act (FOIA).[24] The agency's position was remarkably lame. Moss had to point out that FOIA specifically provides that the statutory procedure for withholding certain information from the public has nothing to do with Congress. The procedure "is not authority to withhold information from Congress."[25] Moss proceeded to make a second request for the material, this time as chairman of the Subcommittee on Oversight and Investigation (of House Committee on Interstate and Foreign Commerce).

After the commission agreed to furnish Moss with the information, Ashland Oil, Inc., went to court to enjoin the FTC from releasing the data. At that point the subcommittee issued a subpoena on December 2, ordering the FTC chairman to appear the following day with the requested documents.[26] On the deadline day, the commission wrote to Moss, advising him that on November 24 a district judge had issued a temporary restraining order enjoining the commission "from disclosing the documents to any third party, including Congress...."[27] With the matter tied up in court, the Committee on House Administration reported a resolution on December 17, providing for the appointment of a special counsel to represent the House and the Committee on Interstate and Foreign Commerce in judicial proceedings related to the subpoena. The committee vote for the resolution was strongly bipartisan, 17 to 2.[28]

The full House passed the resolution on December 18, authorizing Moss to intervene and appear in the case in order to secure the information needed for his subcommittee. Wayne Hays, chairman of the Committee on House Administration, objected that the judicial proceedings "infringe upon the rights of the House of Representatives or...could infringe upon the rights of the House of Representatives."[29] In a bipartisan display of the House protecting its institutional interests, the resolution passed without a dissent.

A federal district court agreed that the data at issue constituted "trade secret" information within the purview of Section 6(f) of the Federal Trade Commission Act.[30] However, the court noted that the exemptions in FOIA do

---

24. Ashland Oil, Inc. v. F.T.C., 409 F.Supp. 297, 300 (D.D.C. 1976). Subsection (b)(4) covers "trade secrets and commercial or financial information obtained from a person and privileged or confidential"; subsection (b)(9) covers "geological and geophysical information and data, including maps, concerning wells."
25. 5 U.S.C. §552(d) (2000).
26. H. Rept. No. 94-756, at 3.
27. Id. at 4.
28. Id. at 1.
29. 121 Cong. Rec. 41707 (1975).
30. Ashland Oil, Inc., 409 F.Supp. 297, 303–04 (D.D.C. 1976).

not apply to Congress,[31] and that the information sought in the subpoena was properly within the subcommittee's jurisdiction.[32] Finally, the court ruled that Ashland Oil had failed to show that release of the material to the subcommittee would irreparably injure the company. The court rejected the argument that the transfer of the data from the FTC to the subcommittee would lead "inexorably to either public dissemination or disclosure to Ashland's competitors." An abstract, unsubstantiated charge that a committee might leak sensitive materials is no ground for withholding documents from Congress. Courts must assume that congressional committees "will exercise their powers responsibly and with due regard for the rights of affected parties."[33]

That decision was affirmed by the D.C. Circuit.[34] A dissenting judge concluded that the subpoena was invalid, but the majority noted that FTC's decision to turn over the materials to the subcommittee "was not based on — and in fact predated — issuance of the subpoena."[35] The commission had agreed to provide Moss with the material after receiving the letter in his capacity as subcommittee chairman. The majority pointed out that the dissent's discussion of the subpoena "rests solely on an interpretation of statements made by the Government counsel during oral argument."[36]

DOJ Opinion: Seizing Suspects Abroad

Beginning in 1989, Congress held hearings on whether the FBI could seize a suspect in a foreign country without the cooperation and consent of that nation. On November 8, a subcommittee of the House Judiciary Committee received testimony from William P. Barr, head of the Office of Legal Counsel (OLC) in the Justice Department, State Department Legal Adviser Abraham D. Sofaer, and Oliver B. Revell, Associate Deputy Director of Investigations in the FBI.[37] Although OLC concluded in 1980 that the FBI had no authority

---

31. Id. at 302.
32. Id. at 305–06.
33. Id. at 308.
34. Ashland Oil, Inc. v. F.T.C., 548 F.2d 977 (D.C. Cir. 1976).
35. Id. at 979. For additional analysis of *Ashland*, see Paul C. Rosenthal and Robert S. Grossman, "Congressional Access to Confidential Information Collected by Federal Agencies," 15 Harv. J. Legis. 74 (1977).
36. Id. at 980.
37. "FBI Authority to Seize Suspects Abroad," hearing before a subcommittee of the House Committee on the Judiciary, 101st Cong., 1st Sess. (1991).

to make such arrests,[38] Barr explained that OLC had reexamined its position and issued an opinion on June 21, 1989, partially reversing the 1980 opinion.[39] Notwithstanding publication of the first opinion, Barr insisted that the second "must remain confidential."[40] Although he refused to release the 1989 opinion, he offered to explain "our conclusions and our reasoning to the committee."[41] He gave reasons why he regarded the 1980 opinion "flawed."[42]

Sofaer noted that Barr had restricted his analysis to the application of domestic legal authority to kidnappings abroad. Under international law, Sofaer said, such kidnappings are a violation. He continued: "While Congress and the President have the power to depart from international law, the courts have in effect insisted that they do so unambiguously and deliberately. This doctrine reflects how our Nation's respect for international law is built into our domestic legal system, and the high value accorded that law in theory and practice."[43]

The administration decided to withhold the 1989 document. Attorney General Dick Thornburgh wrote to the subcommittee on November 28, 1989, explaining why it could not have the OLC opinion: "Apart from classified information, there is no category of documents in the Department's possession that I consider more confidential than legal opinions to me from the Office of Legal Counsel."[44] Subcommittee chair Don Edwards replied that OLC opinions had been made available to Congress in previous years.[45] In a letter on January 24, 1990, Edwards provided Thornburgh with other examples of OLC opinions being released to Congress.[46]

On January 31, 1990, the chairman of House Judiciary, Jack Brooks, wrote to Thornburgh about a number of difficulties that Congress had experienced in receiving executive branch documents. With regard to the OLC opinion on extraterritorial arrests, Brooks said:

> There should be no question that this is a matter involving an extremely serious national policy to which both the Congress and the Executive Branch should give extremely careful consideration. No

---

38. 4B Op. O.L.C. 543 (1980).
39. "FBI Authority to Seize Suspects Abroad," at 3.
40. Id. at 4.
41. Id. at 5.
42. Id.
43. Id. at 23.
44. Id. at 92.
45. Id. at 94.
46. Id. at 96–98.

purpose is served by denying Congress access to all of the legal thought and analysis that have been directed to this issue, including that upon which the Justice Department relied in reaching its decision. I do not believe that it is either legally supportable or in the nation's best interests for the Justice Department to pick and choose which opinions of the Office of Legal Counsel are made available to the Congress. Indeed, it is my understanding that these opinions are published periodically. There is no justification for shielding them from Congressional access at the precise moment that critical decisions are being made.[47]

Responding on February 20, 1990, Thornburgh suggested to Brooks a possible accommodation. As a substitute for the OLC opinion, the Justice Department would prepare "a comprehensive written statement of the Department's legal position on these issues."[48] Thornburgh concluded that he was "not sure it is useful for us to exchange volleys over competing legal theories on this issue. No concrete dispute over national security information is before us. What is important is that on a practical, day-to-day basis we are able to work out our differences in this sensitive area in good faith."[49]

The two sides, however, were unable to reach an acceptable accommodation, resulting in a subcommittee subpoena on July 25, 1991. The subcommittee argued that it needed the 1989 memo to determine whether it was necessary for Congress to legislate in this area. Unless Thornburgh turned over the document by 9 A.M. on July 31, the committee would vote to hold him in contempt.[50] The administration decided not to comply with the subpoena, threatening to assert executive privilege. Some administration officials argued that release of the document might jeopardize the criminal prosecution of such defendants as General Manuel Antonio Noriega, who was arrested in Panama in January 1990, after the U.S. invasion. Brooks denied this line of reasoning: "This committee's request will in no way expose sensitive information to the public nor will it in any way deter or slow criminal prosecutions in these matters."[51]

---

47. Id. at 102.
48. Id. at 119.
49. Id. at 120–21.
50. Joan Biskupic, "Panel Challenges Thornburgh Over Right to Documents," CQ Weekly Report, July 27, 1991, at 2080.
51. David Johnston, "Administration to Fight House Panel's Subpoena," New York Times, July 30, 1991, at A12.

As the interbranch collision neared, the two sides were able to find some common ground. In a letter to Brooks on July 30, 1991, Assistant Attorney General W. Lee Rawls stated that in return for President Bush not asserting executive privilege, the subcommittee and the department agreed that the subcommittee "will suspend, but not dissolve, the subpoena until further notice," to permit further negotiations toward an accommodation.[52] Bush decided not to invoke executive privilege, and the Justice Department agreed to allow one or more committee members to review the legal memo if the subcommittee would suspend the subpoena and remove the threat of a contempt vote.[53]

During this period, the Bush administration leaked the 29-page opinion to the *Washington Post*.[54] In 1993, the department decided to publish the memo in its regular series of OLC opinions. Although the cloth edition of *Opinions of the Office of Legal Counsel* suggests it was printed in 1989, the preliminary print (paper) was not released until 1993.[55]

DOJ Documents: The Inslaw Affair

During the same time period as the confrontation over the kidnapping memo, the House and the Justice Department engaged in another showdown. On December 5, 1990, Chairman Brooks convened a hearing of the Judiciary Committee to review the refusal of Attorney General Thornburgh to provide the committee with access to all documents regarding a civil dispute brought by Inslaw, Inc., a computer company. Inslaw charged that high-level officials in the Justice Department conspired to force Inslaw into bankruptcy and have its computer software program, called PROMIS, transferred or bought by a rival company to help the department keep track of civil and criminal cases. Federal Bankruptcy Judge George Bason had already ruled that the Justice Department "took, converted, and stole" Inslaw's proprietary software, using "trickery, fraud, and deceit."[56]

---

52. Letter from Rawls to Brooks, July 30, 1991.

53. David Johnston, "Both Sides Softening Stance on Documents on Foreign Arrests," New York Times, August 1, 1991, at B7; "Justice Yields to House, Averting Showdown," CQ Weekly Report, August 3, 1991, at 2179.

54. Michael Isikoff, "U.S. 'Power' on Abductions Detailed," Washington Post, August 14, 1991, at A14.

55. 13 Op. O.L.C. 163 (1989).

56. "The Attorney General's Refusal to Provide Congressional Access to 'Privileged' Inslaw Documents," hearing before a subcommittee of the House Committee on the Judiciary, 101st Cong., 2d Sess. 1 (1990).

The Justice Department denied those charges, claiming that what was at stake was a contract dispute. Brooks said that the controversy reached the highest levels of the department, including at least two Assistant Attorneys General, a Deputy Attorney General, and Attorney General Meese. Because House and Senate investigating committees had been denied access to documents needed to establish the department's guilt or innocence, Brooks concluded that he was "even more convinced that the allegations concerning INSLAW must be fully and independently investigated by the committee."[57]

Although the committee and the Justice Department disagreed over access to particular documents, the ranking member of the committee, Hamilton Fish (R-N.Y.), pointed out that the department had given considerable assistance to the legislative investigation, arranging for over fifty interviews with departmental employees, handing over "voluminous written materials," and providing space for congressional staff.[58] In a letter to Fish, Assistant Attorney General W. Lee Rawls noted that in an accommodation with House Judiciary, "the Department did not insist on its usual practice of having a Department representative at these interviews."[59] Committee staff also had access, pursuant to a confidentiality agreement, "to the files reflecting investigations by the Office of Professional Responsibility, and we have provided documents generated during investigations by the Criminal Division into allegations of wrongdoing relating to Inslaw."[60] Committee staff were allowed to depose departmental employees "without the presence of Department counsel," and were given access to the Civil Division's files on the Inslaw litigation. Out of tens of thousands of documents, the department "withheld only a minute fraction, which are privileged attorney work product that would not be available to a party in litigation with the United States."[61]

At the hearing, the committee heard testimony from Steven R. Ross, House General Counsel, who analyzed the Attorney General's decision to withhold documents because of pending civil litigation and the need for the department to protect litigation strategy and agency work products.[62] Ross took exception to the position advanced by Rawls in his letter to Rep. Fish that congressional investigations "are justifiable only as a means of facilitating the task of passing legislation." Such a standard, Ross said, would "eradicate the time-hon-

---

57. Id. at 2.
58. Id. at 3.
59. Id. at 163.
60. Id. at 164.
61. Id.
62. Id. at 77.

ored role of Congress of providing oversight, which is a means that has been upheld by the Supreme Court on a number of occasions, by which the Congress can assure itself that previously passed laws are being properly implemented."[63] Fish interrupted at that point to agree that the sentence by Rawls was "not a technically correct statement of the power of the Congress" and was "far too narrow."[64]

Ross also challenged the claim by the Justice Department that it could deny Congress documents to protect pending litigation. Ross reviewed previous decisions by the Supreme Court to demonstrate that information could not be withheld from Congress simply because of "the pendency of lawsuits."[65] The congressional investigation of Anne Gorsuch, discussed in the next chapter, was cited by Ross as another example of the Justice Department labeling documents as "enforcement sensitive" or "litigation sensitive" to keep materials from Congress.[66]

The media monitored the collision between Brooks and the Justice Department.[67] Finally, on July 25, 1991, a subcommittee of House Judiciary issued a subpoena to Thornburgh. A newspaper story said that the night before the subcommittee was scheduled to vote on the subpoena, the Justice Department indicated that it was willing to turn over the Inslaw documents. Brooks, given recent departmental promises, said he was too skeptical to accept the offer.[68] He wanted access to the documents to decide whether the department had acted illegally by engaging in criminal conspiracy. When the committee failed to receive the materials, Brooks said that the committee would consider contempt of Congress proceedings against the department.[69]

At that point several hundred documents were delivered to the committee, which later released a formal investigative report on the Inslaw affair.[70] The committee gained access to sensitive files of the Office of Professional Re-

---

63. Id. at 78.
64. Id.
65. Id. at 79.
66. Id. at 80–81.
67. Mary McGrory, "Nixon's Shadow Lengthens," Washington Post, December 6, 1990, at A2; Paul M. Barrett, "Thornburgh, Brooks Clash Over Charge of Wrongdoing at Justice Department," Wall Street Journal, December 10, 1990, at B7A.
68. Joan Biskupic, "Panel Challenges Thornburgh Over Right to Documents," CQ Weekly Report, July 27, 1991, at 2080. See also David Johnston, "Administration to Fight House Panel's Subpoena," New York Times, July 30, 1991, at A12.
69. Susan B. Glasser, "Deadline Passes, But Justice Dept. Still Hasn't Given Papers to Brooks," Roll Call, September 19, 1991, at 12.
70. H. Rept. No. 857, 102d Cong., 2d Sess. (1992).

sponsibility (OPR) in the Justice Department and received more than 400 documents that the department had described as related to "ongoing litigation and other highly sensitive matters and 'protected' under the claims of attorney-client and attorney work product privileges."[71]

Whitewater Notes

On December 8, 1995, the Special Senate Committee to Investigate Whitewater Development Corporation and Related Matters (the Senate Whitewater Committee) issued a subpoena for certain documents. The White House announced that it would withhold material concerning a November 5, 1993, meeting at the law offices of Williams & Connolly, which had been retained by President Clinton and First Lady Hillary Clinton to provide personal counsel for Whitewater-related matters. Senior presidential aides and private lawyers discussed whether documents sought by Congress could be withheld on the ground that they were protected by the lawyer-client privilege and executive privilege. Present at the meeting: White House Counsel Bernard Nussbaum, White House aides Neil Eggleston and Bruce Lindsey, three private attorneys (David Kennedy, Stephen Engstrom, and James Lyon), and Associate White House Counsel William Kennedy, who took extensive notes at the meeting.[72]

President Clinton said that he believed the President "ought to have a right to have a confidential conversation with his minister, his doctor, his lawyer."[73] That argument would carry weight if Clinton had met solely with private attorneys, but his claim was undermined by the presence of four government lawyers at the meeting. Government lawyers are not expected to provide advice to Presidents on private financial and legal matters and certainly not on the same confidential basis as a private attorney. Lloyd Cutler, when he was appointed special counsel to President Clinton, explained: "When it comes to a President's private affairs, particularly private affairs that occurred before he

---

71. Id. at 92–93.
72. S. Rept. No. 104-191, 104th Cong., 1st Sess. 3 (1995); Stephen Labaton, "White House Gives Rationale for Balking at a Subpoena," New York Times, December 13, 1995, at B14; Susan Schmidt, "White House Rejects Subpoena," Washington Post, December 13, 1995, at A1.
73. Ruth Marcus and Susan Schmidt, "Legal Experts Uncertain on Prospects of Clinton Privilege Claim," Washington Post, December 14, 1995, at A14.

took office, those should be handled by his own personal private counsel, and in my view not by the White House Counsel."[74]

Moreover, communications between a government attorney and an executive official lack the confidentiality that exists between a private attorney and an executive official. Under law, any government attorney who learns of "[a]ny information, allegation, or complaint" involving government officers and employees shall report such matter to the Attorney General, with certain exceptions.[75] Aware of that statute, government attorneys should alert officials in the government, "even the President,...not to expect counsel to keep confidential what a private counsel would in such a situation."[76]

Within a few days, the White House offered to turn over the Kennedy notes if the committee agreed that the meeting was privileged. The committee refused because it learned of other meetings attended by White House officials and private attorneys. As part of the effort at compromise, the White House told the committee that it could assume that whatever material White House officials had obtained about Whitewater—including confidential documents from the Resolution Trust Corporation (RTC)—had been turned over to Clinton's private lawyers during the meeting. Some Republicans regarded it as improper for the White House to pass along confidential RTC or any other law enforcement documents to the President's private lawyers. Unable to reach an acceptable compromise, the committee voted to send the issue to the Senate floor and from there to federal district court.[77] Clinton objected that he should not be "the first president in history" to give up his right to attorney-client confidentiality.[78]

By December 15, the White House had indicated its willingness to drop most of the conditions it had established for turning over the Kennedy notes to the committee. The change in White House policy occurred hours after the committee voted to ask the full Senate to go to court to enforce the subpoena.[79]

---

74. S. Rept. No. 104-191, at 13.

75. 28 U.S.C. §538(b) (2000). The information is reported "unless (1) the responsibility to perform an investigation with respect thereto is specifically assigned otherwise by another provision of law; or (2) as to any department or agency of the Government, the Attorney General directs otherwise with respect to a specified class of information, allegation, or complaint."

76. Charles Tiefer, "The Specially Investigated President," 5 U. Chi. Roundtable 143, 191 n.212 (1998).

77. Susan Schmidt, "Compromise on Notes Rejected," Washington Post, December 15, 1995, at A2.

78. Id.

79. Susan Schmidt, "White House Eases Stance on Notes," Washington Post, December 16, 1995, at A19.

As a step toward an accommodation, the chairman of the Senate committee said he would be willing "to send a letter saying we do not feel that there would be any waiver of any privilege, that the administration's turning over the notes would not be deemed a waiver in our eyes."[80]

On December 20, the Senate debated a resolution that directed the Senate Legal Counsel to bring a civil action to enforce the subpoena. The resolution invoked a special statute regarding the authority of the Senate Legal Counsel.[81] In a letter on that same day to the committee, White House Special Counsel Jane Sherburne described various options, stating: "We have said all along that we are prepared to make the notes public; that all we need is an assurance that other investigative bodies will not use this as an excuse to deny the President the right to lawyer confidentiality that all Americans enjoy."[82] That was a red herring. No one denied Clinton the right to confidentiality with a *private* attorney, the same right that all Americans enjoy. She said that Independent Counsel Kenneth Starr had agreed that he would not argue that turning over the Kennedy notes constituted a waiver of the attorney-client privilege claimed by President Clinton. The White House sought a similar understanding from two House committees with jurisdiction over Whitewater matters. Sherburne asked the Senate for assistance in obtaining from the House the same understanding reached with Starr.[83]

The resolution passed the Senate by a vote of 51 to 45.[84] On the following day, the White House agreed to give the Kennedy notes to the Senate Whitewater Committee. Rep. Jim Leach, chairman of the House Banking and Financial Services Committee, objected to the "apparently unprecedented circumstance of a request by the White House that information not be conveyed to one legislative body without the procedural concurrence of the other."[85] Leach also expressed concern that government attorneys working in the White House might have given confidential law enforcement information to the Clintons' private attorney.[86] Further, Leach noted that Congress throughout its his-

---

80. John Solomon, "D'Amato Yields on Some Terms Set by Clinton," Washington Post, December 17, 1995, at A13.
81. 141 Cong. Rec. 37705 (1995); Charles Tiefer, "The Senate and House Counsel Offices: Dilemmas of Representing in Court the Institutional Congressional Client," 61 Law & Contemp. Prob. 47, 56–57 (1998).
82. 141 Cong. Rec. at 37730.
83. Id.
84. Id. at 37761.
85. Letter from Leach to Speaker Newt Gingrich, December 21, 1995, at 1.
86. Id. at 2.

tory has maintained that the attorney-client privilege "cannot be claimed as a matter of right before a legislative committee,"[87] and stated that the attorney-client privilege did not apply to the November 5, 1993 meeting because government attorneys were present. To Leach, "one cannot waive a privilege that never came into being in the first place."[88]

Having discussed these fundamental principles, Leach stated this position for the House: "(1) It is well-established by congressional precedent and practice that acceptance of a claim of attorney-client privilege rests in the sole and sound discretion of Congress, and cannot be asserted as a matter of right; (2) It is the opinion of the House that no valid claim of attorney-client privilege has been asserted by the President, rendering unnecessary any exercise of congressional discretion to recognize a privilege in this instance; (3) Even if the document in question qualified for the attorney-client privilege, its disclosure to Congress would not constitute a waiver of the privilege as to third parties, under well-settled House and judicial precedents; and (4) The House accordingly will not assert that any such waiver has occurred."[89] Under these cross-pressures, the Kennedy notes were released to Congress.[90] White House spokesman Mark Fabiani put a positive spin on the long-simmering dispute: "We're eager to release these notes to the public."[91]

FBI Corruption in Boston

Toward the end of 2001, President George W. Bush invoked executive privilege for the first time. He acted in response to subpoenas issued by the House Government Reform Committee covering two issues: campaign finance and FBI corruption in Boston. He advised Attorney General John Ashcroft not to release the documents to the committee because disclosure "would inhibit the candor necessary to the effectiveness of the deliberative processes by which the Department makes prosecutorial decisions." He argued that giving the committee access to the documents "threatens to politicize the criminal justice process" and undermine the fundamental purpose of the separation of powers doctrine, which "was to protect individual liberty."[92]

---

87. Id. at 3.
88. Id. at 3–4.
89. Id. at 4–5.
90. Susan Schmidt, "Whitewater Notes Being Surrendered," Washington Post, December 22, 1995, at A1. See Tiefer, "The Specially Investigated President," at 189–93.
91. Schmidt, "Whitewater Notes Being Surrendered," at A11.
92. 37 Weekly Comp. Pres. Doc. 1783 (2001).

This kind of sweeping language, grounded in fundamental constitutional principles, appeared to shut the door in the face of the committee. In fact, Bush's statement made it clear he was ready to negotiate. He advised the Justice Department to "remain willing to work informally with the Committee to provide such information as it can, consistent with these instructions and without violating the constitutional doctrine of separation of powers."[93] In the end, Bush succeeded in withholding the campaign finance documents but folded on the Boston materials.

There could hardly be a subject area less attractive for Bush's first use of executive privilege than FBI's conduct in Boston. During hearings on May 3, 2001, the House Government Reform Committee laid out the basic facts. It wanted documents concerning the FBI's role in a 30-year-old scandal in Boston that sent innocent people to prison for decades and allowed mobsters to commit murder. The FBI tolerated this injustice because it wanted to preserve its access to informers, while at the same time knowing that the individuals imprisoned were innocent of the charges. During this crime spree, some FBI agents took cash from the mobsters.[94] This sordid record prompted the committee investigation, and it was on such a dispute that Bush decided to invoke executive privilege.

On December 13, 2001, the day following Bush's decision to assert executive privilege, the committee held further hearings on the Boston matter. Michael Horowitz, appearing on behalf of the Justice Department, defended the use of executive privilege to keep from the committee documents regarding the department's decision to prosecute or decline to prosecute. The reason for withholding these pre-decisional documents was "to protect the integrity of Federal prosecutive decisions" and to make sure that such decisions are based on "evidence and the law, free from political and other improper influences."[95] Releasing such documents to the committee, he said, "would undermine the integrity of the core executive branch decisionmaking function."[96]

This testimony was far too rigid to survive as departmental doctrine. Six days after the hearings, the department wrote a much more conciliatory letter to the committee chairman. It now stated "that the Department and the

---

93. Id.
94. "Investigation Into Allegations of Justice Department Misconduct in New England—Volume 1," hearings before the House Committee on Government Reform, 107th Cong., 1st–2d Sess. 1–4 (2001–02).
95. Id. at 379.
96. Id. at 380.

Committee can work together to provide the Committee additional information without compromising the principles maintained by the executive branch. We will be prepared to make a proposal as to how further to accommodate the Committee's needs as soon as you inform us in writing of the specific needs the Committee has for additional information."[97]

On January 10, 2002, White House Counsel Alberto R. Gonzales wrote to the committee, noting that it was a "misimpression" that congressional committees could never receive deliberative documents from a criminal investigation or prosecution. "There is no such bright-line policy, nor did we intend to articulate any such policy." Instead, the department would treat such documents "through a process of appropriate accommodation and negotiation to preserve the respective constitutional roles of the two Branches." The committee's subpoenas "sought a very narrow and particularly sensitive category of deliberative matters—prosecution and declination memoranda—as well as the closely related category of memoranda to the Attorney General regarding the appointment of a special prosecutor" for the campaign finance investigation. Yet Gonzales signaled that such materials, under certain conditions, might be shared with the committee: "Absent unusual circumstances, the Executive Branch has traditionally protected those highly sensitive deliberative documents against public or congressional disclosure."[98]

The dispute had clearly moved away from fixed departmental principles to the specific question of whether "unusual circumstances" were absent or present. Clearly it was the latter. Gonzales said that the administration "recognizes that in unusual circumstances like those present here, where the Executive Branch has filed criminal charges alleging corruption in the FBI investigative process, even the core principle of confidentiality applicable to prosecution and declination memoranda may appropriately give way, to the extent permitted by law, if Congress demonstrates a compelling and specific need for the memoranda."[99] The White House was now "prepared to accommodate the Committee's interest in a manner that should both satisfy the Committee's legitimate needs and protect the principles of prosecutorial candor and confidentiality."[100]

---

97. Letter from Assistant Attorney General Daniel J. Bryant to Rep. Dan Burton, chairman of the House Committee on Government Reform, December 19, 2001, at 2.
98. Letter from Alberto R. Gonzales, Counsel to the President, to Rep. Dan Burton, January 10, 2002, at 1.
99. Id. at 2.
100. Id. at 3.

The committee held hearings a third time, on February 6, 2002, to hear testimony from experts who cited specific instances of the executive branch giving congressional committees access to prosecutorial memoranda for both open and closed investigations.[101] Under these multiple pressures, the Bush administration agreed to give the Government Reform Committee prosecutorial memos on FBI conduct in Boston. Some of the documents were released within a hour of the committee's decision to hold President Bush in contempt.[102]

Congressional subpoenas represent the first volley from a committee that has decided that executive branch documents are necessary to fulfill legislative responsibilities, and that informal negotiations between the two branches have failed. Issuance of a subpoena is usually successful in dislodging the documents, particularly when the committee request enjoys broad bipartisan support, as was the case with the probe into FBI operations in Boston. If that step is ineffective, the committee can deliberate on the necessity of going the next step by holding an executive official in contempt.

---

101. "Investigation Into Allegations of Justice Department Misconduct in New England—Volume 1," at 520–604 (testimony by Charles Tiefer and Morton Rosenberg).
102. Vanessa Blum, "White House Caves On Privilege Claim," Legal Times, March 18, 2002, at 1. See Charles Tiefer, "President Bush's First Executive Privilege Claim: The FBI/Boston Investigation," 33 Pres. Stud. Q. 201 (2003).

6

The Contempt Power

When the executive branch refuses to release information or allow officials to testify, Congress may decide to invoke its contempt power. Although the legislative power of contempt is not expressly provided for in the Constitution and exists as an implied power, as early as 1821 the Supreme Court recognized that without this power the legislative branch would be "exposed to every indignity and interruption that rudeness, caprice, or even conspiracy, may mediate against it."[1] If either House votes for a contempt citation, the President of the Senate or the Speaker of the House shall certify the facts to the appropriate U.S. Attorney, "whose duty it shall be to bring the matter before the grand jury for its action."[2] Individuals who refuse to testify or produce papers are subject to criminal contempt, leading to fines of not more than $100,000 and imprisonment up to one year.[3]

This chapter begins by covering contempt actions, from 1975 to 1981, against six Cabinet officers who refused to surrender documents to Congress: Secretary of Commerce Rogers C. B. Morton, HEW Secretary F. David Mathews, Secretary of State Henry Kissinger, HEW Secretary Joseph A. Califano, Jr., Secretary of Energy Charles W. Duncan, Jr., and Secretary of Energy James B. Edwards. With contempt citations looming, the two branches reached a compromise settlement that gave Congress access to the documents. The remainder of the chapter focuses on more recent contempt actions, including Secretary of the Interior James Watt, Administrator of the Environmental Pro-

---

1. Anderson v. Dunn, 6 Wheat. (19 U.S.) 204, 228 (1821).
2. 2 U.S.C. § 194 (2000).
3. Id., § 192. As a result of sentencing classification of offenses, the original $1,000 maximum in § 192 has been increased to $100,000 as a Class A misdemeanor. See also Todd D. Peterson, "Prosecuting Executive Branch Officials for Contempt of Congress," 66 N.Y.U. L. Rev. 563 (1991), and John C. Grabow, Congressional Investigations: Law and Practice 86–99 (1988).

tection Agency Anne Gorsuch, White House Counsel Jack Quinn, and Attorney General Janet Reno.

The contempt action against Gorsuch revealed a weakness in the statutory procedures that Congress relies on for contempt, especially when the interests of the Justice Department are directly at stake. Citing an executive official for contempt requires the executive branch—through a U.S. Attorney—to bring the action. In the Gorsuch case, which challenged executive privilege doctrines developed by the Justice Department, action was not taken by the executive branch until a federal judge nudged the two parties toward an accommodation.

Actions from 1975 to 1981

From 1975 to the start of the Reagan administration, Congress several times threatened to hold executive officials in contempt for refusing to cooperate with congressional committees. In the face of statutory and constitutional reasons offered by the administration for withholding information from Congress, in the end the committees persisted and gained access to the requested documents. To minimize some of these disputes in the future, Congress amended statutory language to clarify the right of legislative committees to agency information.

Rogers C. B. Morton

A 1975 tug of war between the branches, with Congress the eventual victor, concerned reports compiled by the Department of Commerce identifying the U.S. companies that had been asked to join a boycott—organized by Arab nations—of companies doing business with Israel. Secretary of Commerce Rogers Morton refused to release the documents to a House Interstate and Foreign Commerce subcommittee, citing the following language from Section 7(c) of the Export Administration Act of 1969: "No department, agency, or official exercising any functions under this Act shall publish or disclose information obtained hereunder which is deemed confidential or with reference to which a request for confidential treatment is made by the person furnishing such information, unless the head of such department or agency determines that the withholding thereof is contrary to the national interest."[4]

---

4. Letter of July 24, 1975, from Secretary Morton to John E. Moss, chairman of the Subcommittee on Oversight and Investigations, House Committee on Interstate and Foreign Relations, reprinted, "Contempt Proceedings Against Secretary of Commerce, Rogers

In his letter of July 24, 1975, to the subcommittee, Morton said he understood the need to provide Congress "with adequate information on which to legislate," but concluded that "disclosing the identity of reporting firms would accomplish little other than to expose such firms to possible economic retaliation by certain private groups merely because they *reported* a boycott request, whether or not they complied with that request."[5] Morton's response implied that whatever he gave the subcommittee would be shared with the public.

On July 28, the subcommittee issued a subpoena. In a letter to the committee on August 22, Morton again reiterated his refusal to release the documents, explaining that his decision was not based "on any claim of executive privilege, but rather on the exercise of the statutory discretion conferred upon me by the Congress."[6] In other words, based on discretionary authority granted him by Congress, he would deny information to a legislative committee. He said he was prepared to make copies of the documents available, "subject only to deletion of any information which would disclose the identity of the firms reporting, and the details of the commercial transactions involved."[7]

At subcommittee hearings on September 22, Chairman John Moss told Secretary Morton that Section 7(c) did not "in any way refer to the Congress nor does the Chair believe that any acceptable interpretation of that section could reach the result that Congress by implication had surrendered its legislative and oversight authority under Article I and the Rules of the House of Representatives."[8]

Morton told Moss that he had been advised by Attorney General Edward Levi not to make the documents available to the committee.[9] In a letter dated September 4, 1975, Levi had advised Morton that the subpoena did not override the confidentiality requirement of Section 7(c), and that the committee was not entitled to receive the information "unless, in exercising the discretion granted by §7(c), you determine that withholding them would be 'contrary to the national interest.'"[10] Levi cited some earlier opinions by Attorneys

---

C. B. Morton," hearings before the Subcommittee on Oversight and Investigations of the House Committee on Interstate and Foreign Commerce, 94th Cong., 1st Sess. 153 (1975).
  5. Id. at 153–54 (emphasis in original).
  6. Id. at 158.
  7. Id.
  8. Id. at 4.
  9. Id. at 6.
  10. "Contempt Proceedings Against Secretary of Commerce, Rogers C. B. Morton," at 173. Levi's opinion is also reprinted at 43 Op. Att'y Gen. 29 (1975).

General that "proceeded under the general assumption—which I share—that statutory restrictions upon executive branch disclosure of information are presumptively binding even with respect to requests or demands of congressional committees."[11] An argument of that nature will almost always lead to trouble for an executive official.

On November 11, the subcommittee voted 10 to 5 to find Morton in contempt for failure to comply with the subpoena of July 28.[12] The prospect of contempt proceedings provided sufficient incentive for Morton to release the material to the subcommittee.[13] To avoid this problem in the future, Congress passed legislation in 1977 to specify that Section 7(c) does not authorize the withholding of information from Congress, and that any information obtained under the Export Administration Act "shall be made available upon request to any committee or subcommittee of Congress of appropriate jurisdiction. No such committee or subcommittee shall disclose any information obtained under this Act which is submitted on a confidential basis unless the full committee determines that the withholding thereof is contrary to the national interest."[14]

David Mathews

On the same day that the House Subcommittee on Oversight and Investigation decided to cite Morton for contempt, it met to consider a separate contempt citation against F. David Mathews, Secretary of the Department of Health, Education, and Welfare (HEW).[15] The subcommittee, concerned that some hospitals were receiving Medicare payments automatically without meeting federal standards for the Medicare program, wanted letters Mathews had received from the Joint Commission on Accreditation of Hospitals (JCAH).[16]

Turning first to his agency general counsel for legal advice, Mathews was told not to release the documents to the subcommittee. In a letter of October

---

11. "Contempt Proceedings Against Secretary of Commerce, Rogers C. B. Morton," at 173–74.

12. Id. at 137.

13. 1975 CQ Almanac, at 343–44. See also 121 Cong. Rec. 3872–76, 36038–39, 40230, 40768–69 (1975).

14. 91 Stat. 241, §113 (1977), amending 83 Stat. 845, §7(c) (1969). Contempt actions against Morton, Duncan, Watt, and Gorsuch are also explored by Peter M. Shane, "Negotiating for Knowledge: Administrative Responses to Congressional Demands for Information," 44 Adm. L. Rev. 197, 202–12 (1992).

15. "Contempt Proceedings Against Secretary of HEW Joseph A. Califano, Jr.," 95th Cong., 2d Sess. 55 (Comm. Print No. 95-76, 1978).

16. "Mathews Subpoena," CQ Weekly Report, November 22, 1975, at 2527.

17, 1975, the general counsel limited his analysis to statutory construction. He interpreted a confidentiality section in the Social Security Act as "on its face an absolute pledge of confidentiality" because it contained no exceptions, either for Congress or the judiciary.[17] On the same day that Mathews received this legal guidance, he wrote to the subcommittee that he had been advised that "it would be a violation of the law for me to furnish you these JCAH documents given in confidence."[18]

The subcommittee subpoenaed the material, setting a deadline of 10 A.M. on November 12. On the day of the deadline, Attorney General Levi advised Mathews to produce the documents to the subcommittee. Levi read the statutory language "on a confidential basis" as placing in the HEW Secretary a discretionary authority to assure that the information is "not to be made public but may be conveyed to the Congress on proper request."[19] Levi's analysis of the statutory provision "on its face" differed fundamentally from Mathew's general counsel. Levi said this about the reliance on the confidentiality provision:

> It seems to me unlikely that reliance included some belief that the information could be kept out of the hands of the Congress, since it was apparent upon the face of the statute, that Congress knew the existence of these documents and the identity of their sole possessor. It was obvious that the Congress could as easily subpoena the information from JCAH itself as from HEW. Or, to place the matter in its present context: It is apparent that if we now find, by reason of the statute, the Committee on Interstate and Foreign Commerce cannot obtain the information from HEW, they can immediately subpoena it from JCAH itself. There hardly seems any purpose to be served by such a circuitous procedure, and I think it would be unreasonable to assume that in enacting the vague and weak confidentiality provision of this statute, and referring specifically to JCAH, the Congress intended it.[20]

Mathews, by making the information available to the subcommittee, removed the threat of a House vote on the contempt citation.[21]

---

17. Id. at 60–61 (letter of October 17, 1975, from Acting General Counsel John Barrett to Secretary Mathews).
18. Id. at 59–60 (letter of October 17, 1975, from Mathews to Rep. John E. Moss, Chairman of the Oversight and Investigations Subcommittee).
19. Id. at 56 (letter of November 12, 1975, from Levi to Mathews).
20. Id.
21. "Mathews Subpoena," CQ Weekly Report, November 22, 1975, at 2527.

Henry Kissinger

On November 6, 1975, the House Select Committee on Intelligence issued a subpoena to Secretary of State Henry Kissinger, directing him to provide: "All documents relating to State Department recommending covert action made to the National Security Council and the Forty Committee and its predecessor committees from January 20, 1961 to the present." The Forty Committee made recommendations to the President on specific covert actions.[22]

The subpoenaed documents were referred to the White House for review. Attorney General Levi examined the documents and recommended that executive privilege be invoked. A letter to Kissinger on November 14 from White House Counsel Philip Buchan confirmed in writing the President's instruction to Kissinger to decline compliance with the subpoena.[23] At stake were ten documents, dating from 1962 through 1972, consisting of recommendations from State Department officials to the Forty Committee, its predecessor (the 303 Committee), or to the President.[24]

When Kissinger failed to provide the documents by the deadline established in the subpoena (November 11), the committee met in open session on November 14 to determine what action to take against him. By a vote of 10 to 2, the committee recommended that the Speaker certify the committee report regarding Kissinger's contumacious conduct and proceed to a contempt citation.[25] Kissinger objected that the subpoena raised "serious questions all over the world of what this country is doing to itself and what the necessity is to torment ourselves like this month after month."[26]

Acting on the advice of the Justice Department, President Gerald Ford invoked executive privilege on November 14 to keep the material from the committee. In a letter to the committee dated November 19 and released November 20, he said that release of the documents, which included "recommendations from previous Secretaries of State to previous Presidents," would jeopardize the internal decisionmaking process.[27] A few days later, in a letter to the committee, Ford cautioned that the dispute "involves grave mat-

---

22. H. Rept. No. 94-693, 94th Cong. 4–5 (1975).
23. "Kissinger's Tenure, U.S. Foreign Policy Are Clouded by House Panel's Citations," Wall Street Journal, November 17, 1975, at 5.
24. H. Rept. No. 94-693, at 13.
25. Id. at 2. See "Kissinger Contempt Citation," CQ Weekly Report, November 15, 1975, at 2506.
26. George Lardner, Jr., "Committee Votes Contempt Action for Kissinger," Washington Post, November 15, 1975, at A6.
27. Public Papers of the Presidents, 1975, II, at 1867.

ters affecting our conduct of foreign policy and raises questions which go to the ability of our Republic to govern itself effectively."[28] Recognizing that Congress had constitutional responsibilities "to investigate fully matters relating to contemplated legislation,"[29] Ford told the committee that he directed Kissinger not to comply with the subpoena on the grounds of executive privilege because the documents "revealed to an unacceptable degree the consultation process involving advice and recommendations to Presidents Kennedy, Johnson, and Nixon."[30] Ford pointed out that some of the documents concerned the National Security Council (NSC) and that, as of November 3, Kissinger was no longer his National Security Adviser.[31] As to those materials, "there has been a substantial effort by the NSC staff to provide these documents."[32]

Kissinger dismissed the contempt proceeding "an absurdity"[33] and "frivolous," warning that it would have adverse effects worldwide: "I profoundly regret that the committee saw fit to cite in contempt a secretary of state, raising serious questions all over the world what this country is doing to itself."[34] On December 9, three committee members and two staff members visited the White House to determine which documents would be made available.[35] The next day, they received an oral briefing on the information that had been the target of the subpoena and an NSC aide read verbatim from documents concerning the covert actions.[36] On December 10, the committee chairman announced that the White House was in "substantial compliance" with the subpoena and that the contempt action was "moot."[37]

---

28. Id. at 1887.
29. Id.
30. Id. at 1889.
31. Id. at 1889–90.
32. Id. at 1890.
33. John M. Crewdson, "Three-Count Contempt Citation of Kissinger Defended in House," New York Times, November 18, 1975, at 15.
34. Judy Gardner, "Pike Pushes Kissinger Contempt Citations," CQ Weekly Report, November 22, 1975, at 2572.
35. "Contempt Vote on Kissinger is Linked to Data Ford Gives," New York Times, December 10, 1975, at 12.
36. Pat Towell, "Contempt Action Against Kissinger Dropped," CQ Weekly Report, December 13, 1975, at 2712.
37. Id. at 2711.

Joseph A. Califano, Jr.

In 1978, a subcommittee of the House Committee on Interstate and Foreign Commerce began an investigation into the manufacturing process used by drug companies to make generic drugs and to price brand-name drugs. The panel examined charges that drug companies merely put trade names on drugs manufactured by generic drug firms and sold them at much higher prices. One way to claim manufacturing responsibility was for a trade name company to put an employee in a generic drug house while the product was being manufactured. Rep. Al Gore explained the subcommittee's interest: "What we are seeking to do is to determine whether or not the public is being fleeced by a process whereby brand name drug companies are getting generic drugs and calling them special brand name drugs simply because they resort to the rule of having one of their employees stationed at the generic drug plant as the drugs are being made."[38]

In order to learn more about this "man-in-the-plant" strategy, the subcommittee requested documents from the Department of Health, Education, and Welfare (HEW). The subcommittee had both oversight and legislative interests. A bill (H.R. 12980) had been introduced to limit or eliminate the man-in-the-plant practice.[39] In July, subcommittee chairman John Moss sent several letters to HEW Secretary Joseph A. Califano, Jr. for the documents. Califano's involvement added a rich irony. A few years earlier, when Moss sought trade secret data from the FTC, the dispute eventually went to court in the case of *Ashland Oil, Inc.* v. *FTC*, discussed in Chapter 5. The private attorney the subcommittee hired to represent its interest in court was Califano. He and Moss now found themselves on opposite sides of a similar dispute.

Failing to receive the material, the subcommittee agreed on July 27 to subpoena Califano. The full committee issued a subpoena dated August 4. In a memo of August 9, the Justice Department advised HEW that language in the Food, Drug, and Cosmetic Act, prohibiting FDA employees from disclosing trade secret information, justified the withholding of the material from the subcommittee. Section 301(j) of that statute prohibited the "using by any person to his own advantage, or revealing, other than to the Secretary or officers or employees of the Department, or to the courts when relevant in any judicial proceeding under this chapter, any information acquired under authority [of

---

38. "Contempt Proceedings Against Secretary of HEW Joseph A. Califano, Jr.," 95th Cong., 2d Sess. 42 (Comm. Print No. 95-76, 1978).

39. Id. at 1–2.

specified sections] of this title concerning any method or process which as a trade secret is entitled to protection."[40] The Justice Department memo argued:

> Where an agency is barred by statute from disclosing certain information, congressional committees have no right to that information unless there is a clearly expressed congressional intent to exclude committee access from the general restriction on disclosure....
>
> ...Indeed, it is significant that section 301(j) explicitly provides for disclosure to one of the coordinate branches of government, *i.e.*, the courts, but makes no comparable provision for disclosure to committees of the Congress.[41]

This memo relied in part on Attorney General Levi's memo in 1975 on the Rogers Morton contempt action. If that position were to stand, Congress would lose access to documents covered by many other statutes. At that time, about a hundred statutory sections contained confidentiality provisions that could be interpreted by the executive branch to deny committees information they needed for legislation and oversight.[42] The subcommittee therefore felt an obligation to challenge the Justice Department analysis. As Gore put it to Califano:

> Mr. Secretary, in our society, laws, principles, and rights are often in conflict. We have two in conflict in this instance.
>
> On the one hand we have article I of the U.S. Constitution. On the other we have section 301(j) of the Federal Food and Drug Cosmetic Act.
>
> You have chosen to place more importance on section 301(j) of the Federal Food and Drug Cosmetic Act than on article I of the U.S. Constitution.[43]

The purpose of Section 301(j), Gore said, was to prevent FDA employees from giving confidential trade secrets to competitor drug companies, not to keep from Congress information that is readily available to the HEW Secretary.[44] At a meeting with the subcommittee on August 16, Califano produced

---

40. 21 U.S.C. §331(j) (1976).
41. Id. at 7, 10 (letter from Acting Attorney General Michael J. Egan to HEW Under Secretary Hale Champion).
42. Id. at 13 (memorandum of August 7, 1978 from Morton Rosenberg, Legislative Attorney for the Congressional Research Service, to Rep. John Moss).
43. Id. at 43.
44. Id.

some material but also stated that any documents relating to trade secret information and the manufacturing process would be blackened out because of the Justice Department legal analysis.[45] Chairman Moss made it clear that the blackened-out material did not comply with the subpoena.[46] Califano explained that his refusal to release the unredacted material had nothing to do with separation of powers or executive privilege, but rather with the statutory language that prohibited the release of trade secret information. Congress, he said, "has the power to change that statute."[47] Califano said he had no question about the committee keeping information confidential: "Your record is impeccable."[48]

During the discussion with Califano, one subcommittee member asked whether the confrontation between the two branches could be averted if the subcommittee subpoenaed the companies directly for the manufacturing process information. Subcommittee counsel John McElroy Atkisson answered that it would be possible, and that the companies would have no legal ground for defying such subpoenas, but said it "flies in the teeth of the idea…that the Congress would exclude itself from the very same information conveniently in the hands of the Secretary which is only down the block here."[49] Chairman Moss added that the Justice Department analysis opened "a pandora's box" to a hundred similar statutes that could be used to deny information to Congress. Moreover, accepting Califano's suggestion to rewrite the statute would take the committee from an option that enjoys privileged status in the House (a contempt citation) to the process of amending a statute, which is not privileged and could take a year or two.[50]

Moss told Califano that he was "without legal justification in your refusal to comply with the subcommittee's subpena."[51] Califano persisted in his refusal, stating that he was "bound to follow the opinion of the Attorney General."[52] The subcommittee then voted 9 to 8 to find Califano in contempt for failing to comply with the subpoena.[53] A month later, the subcommittee

---

45. Id. at 4.
46. Id. at 5.
47. Id. at 18.
48. Id. at 48.
49. Id. at 49.
50. Id. at 49, 51.
51. Id. at 19.
52. Id.
53. Id. at 87. See "House Panel Votes Contempt Citation Against Califano," Wall Street Journal, August 17, 1978, at 5; Mary Russell, "House Panel Backs Contempt Citation After Califano Refuses to Yield Data," Washington Post, August 17, 1978, at A2; "Moss v. Califano" (editorial), Washington Post, August 18, 1978, at A18.

dropped the contempt action after Califano turned over the materials that had been subpoenaed. Califano explained that a further review by the department of the withheld material disclosed that some information had been "inappropriately deleted" from documents given to the panel.[54]

On August 17, the day after the subcommittee voted for contempt, Califano asked the Justice Department to further consider its interpretation of Section 301(j). On September 8, Attorney General Griffin Bell cited additional legislative history in affirming the position of Acting Attorney General Michael J. Egan that the section prohibited Califano from furnishing trade secret data to Congress or its committees.[55] Notwithstanding that legal analysis, Califano gave the disputed material to the subcommittee.

Charles W. Duncan, Jr.

On April 2, 1980, President Carter imposed a fee on imported oil and gasoline in an effort to reduce domestic consumption. A subcommittee of the House Government Operations Committee requested in writing, on April 8, certain categories of material from the Department of Energy (DOE). With no documents delivered, the subcommittee held a hearing on April 16 to investigate the delay. Thomas Newkirk, the department's Deputy General Counsel for Regulation, told the subcommittee that he was "not prepared to submit the documents at this time" because White House Counsel Lloyd Cutler was reviewing a pile of documents "between a foot and 18 inches high."[56] Newkirk thought the documents might be subject to the claim of executive privilege because they revealed the "deliberative process underlying the President's decision to impose the gasoline conservation fee."[57] The subcommittee voted unanimously to instruct Newkirk to deliver the documents by 5 o'clock that evening.[58]

After the department let the deadline slip, the subcommittee voted unanimously on April 22 to subpoena the materials from Energy Secretary Charles W. Duncan, Jr. On the following day, the subcommittee received 28 docu-

---

54. "House Unit Ends Bid To Cite for Contempt HEW Chief Califano," Wall Street Journal, September 22, 1978, at 10.
55. 43 Op. Att'y Gen. 116 (1978).
56. "The Petroleum Import Fee: Department of Energy Oversight," hearings before a Subcommittee of the House Government Operations Committee, 96th Cong., 2d Sess. 3, 27 (1980).
57. Id. at 5.
58. Id. at 35. See Richard L. Lyons, "On Capitol Hill," Washington Post, April 18, 1980, at A5.

ments but also a letter from Duncan explaining that to the extent the subcommittee request involved "deliberative materials underlying a major Presidential decision," it would "seriously undermine the ability of the Chief Executive and his Cabinet Officers to obtain frank legal and policy advice from their advisors."[59] Newkirk appeared before the subcommittee on April 24 to state that the department would not comply in full with the subcommittee's request of April 8, but did not rest his case on executive privilege.[60] By a vote of 9-0, the subcommittee subpoenaed Duncan to appear before the subcommittee on April 29 and bring the requested documents.[61]

In the face of these bipartisan, unanimous subcommittee votes, Duncan appeared at the April 29 hearing to tell the subcommittee: "I must decline to turn over the documents and I do not have them with me at this time."[62] However, he also offered to allow the subcommittee chairman and the ranking minority member to review the documents "in confidence to assist in defining that request."[63] Rep. Paul McCloskey (the ranking minority member) objected that "the idea that two members of a nine-member committee should be trusted and some should not be is repugnant to the rules of the House."[64] After further efforts to reach an accommodation collapsed, the subcommittee voted 8 to 0 to hold Duncan in contempt for not complying with the April 24 subpoena.[65]

The subcommittee held another hearing on May 14, with Secretary Duncan again in attendance. Subcommittee chairman Toby Moffett announced that "at long last the subcommittee has been provided with every document it feels it needs to conduct its inquiry. Subcommittee members and staff have seen every document specifically demanded under the subpena we issued April 24, and any document we deemed useful to this investigation has now been produced."[66] On the previous day, a federal district court had struck down Carter's April 2 proclamation as invalid, either under the President's inherent

---

59. "The Petroleum Import Fee," hearings, at 100.
60. Id. at 98–100.
61. Id. at 116–17; Richard D. Lyons, "House Unit Subpoenas Duncan," New York Times, April 25, 1980, at D3.
62. "The Petroleum Import Fee," hearings, at 122.
63. Id. at 123.
64. Id.
65. Id. at 139. See "House Unit Cites Duncan For Gas-Tax Contempt," New York Times, April 30, 1980, at D18.
66. "The Petroleum Import Fee," hearings, at 142. See also Dale Tate, "President's Oil Import Fee Assailed in Congress, Court," CQ Weekly Report, May 17, 1980, at 1308; Elder Witt, "Carter Foiled in First Tilt With Executive Privilege," CQ Weekly Report., May 17, 1980, at 1352.

power or under statutory authority.[67] A White House spokesman said that he didn't think executive privilege was ever formally asserted, either by President Carter or Secretary Duncan, although there was consideration of doing so.[68] In any event, the subcommittee received the material it requested.[69]

James B. Edwards

The following year, at the start of the Reagan administration, Secretary of Energy James B. Edwards narrowly avoided a contempt citation from the House Government Operations Committee. The dispute involved legislative access to documents regarding contract negotiations between the Energy Department and the Union Oil Company to build an oil shale plant in Colorado. Committee members were concerned that the department was moving too hastily in awarding billions of dollars in federal subsidies to major oil companies, particularly prior to the Reagan administration's plans to create a Synthetic Fuels Corporation.[70] Failing to obtain the requested materials, the Environment, Energy and Natural Resources Subcommittee voted 6 to 4 on July 23 to hold Edwards in contempt.

The dispute was not merely executive-legislative. The administration was also split. Edwards wanted to sign the contract, but OMB Director David Stockman opposed federal subsidies to the synthetic fuels program and had taken steps to block the contract with Union Oil.[71] The full committee was scheduled to vote on the contempt citation on the morning of July 30, 1981. Edwards said he would not produce the documents until the contract between the Energy Department and Union Oil had been signed. President Reagan agreed to the project and officials from the Energy Department and Union signed the contract. At that point, thirteen boxes of documents on the contract negotiations were delivered to the committee.[72]

---

67. Independent Gasoline Marketers Council v. Duncan, 492 F.Supp. 614 (D.D.C. 1980).
68. "Executive Privilege, Revisited," CQ Weekly Report, June 21, 1980, at 1753.
69. The subcommittee's confrontation with Secretary Duncan, including correspondence, is discussed in H. Rept. No. 96-1099, 96th Cong., 2d Sess. 18–30, 33–56 (1980).
70. "DOE's Enforcement of Alleged Pricing Violations by the Nation's Major Oil Companies," hearing before a Subcommittee of the House Committee on Government Operations, 97th Cong., 1st Sess. 2, 57–60 (1981).
71. Martin Schram, "Reagan Overrides Stockman, Backs Edwards on Synfuel," Washington Post, July 30, 1981, at A2.
72. Andy Plattner, "Edwards' Contempt Citation Headed Off by Approval of Synthetic Fuel Contract," CQ Weekly Report, August 1, 1981, at 1425.

James Watt

In 1981, Interior Secretary James Watt refused to give a House subcommittee 31 documents relating to a reciprocity provision in the Mineral Lands Leasing Act. The reciprocity provision involved Canada. Watt based his refusal on the judgment of Attorney General William French Smith that the documents were "either necessary and fundamental to the deliberative process presently ongoing in the Executive Branch or relate to sensitive foreign policy considerations."[73] Smith's decision led to President Reagan's first claim of executive privilege.[74] The confrontation escalated to a recommendation by the House Committee on Energy and Commerce to cite Watt for contempt.

Attorney General Smith insisted that "the interest of Congress in obtaining information for oversight purposes is, I believe, considerably weaker than its interests when specific legislative proposals are in question."[75] Congressional oversight, he said, "is justifiable only as a means of facilitating the legislative task of enacting, amending, or repealing laws."[76] That argument lacked historical and legal support. The first major investigation by Congress—of General St. Clair's defeat—was not conducted for the purpose of legislation. The Supreme Court recognizes that the power of Congress to conduct investigations "comprehends probes into departments of the Federal Government to expose corruption, inefficiency, or waste."[77] Courts have consistently held that the investigative power is available not merely to legislate or when a "potential" for legislation exists, but even for pursuits down blind alleys.[78] Moreover, Congress could easily neutralize Smith's argument by introducing a bill whenever it wanted to conduct oversight.

Smith's second major argument for withholding the documents was based on the need to protect the deliberative process, especially "predecisional, de-

---

73. 43 Op. Att'y Gen. 327, 328 (1981). See also "Executive Privilege: Legal Opinions Regarding Claim of President Ronald Reagan in Response to a Subpoena Issued to James G. Watt, Secretary of the Interior," prepared for the use of the Subcommittee on Oversight and Investigations of the House Committee on Energy and Commerce, 97th Cong., 1st Sess. 2 (Comm. Print, Nov. 1981) (hereafter "Executive Privilege: Watt").

74. Martha M. Hamilton, "Executive Privilege Invoked to Back Watt," Washington Post, October 15, 1981, at D12.

75. 43 Op. Att'y Gen. at 331.

76. Id.

77. Watkins v. United States, 353 U.S. 178, 187 (1957).

78. Eastland v. United States Servicemen's Fund, 421 U.S. 491, 509 (1975).

liberative memoranda." Even after decisions have been made, disclosure of documents to Congress "could still deter the candor of future Executive Branch deliberations."[79] While Exemption 5 of FOIA exempts from public disclosure "inter-agency or intra-agency memorandums or letters which would not be available by law to a party other than an agency in litigation with the agency,"[80] Congress specifically provided in FOIA that the listed exemptions are "not authority to withhold documents from Congress."[81] Congress has often gained access to predecisional, deliberative memoranda in the executive branch.[82]

As a third point, Smith argued that the documents "relate to sensitive foreign policy considerations."[83] However, foreign policy is not an exclusive power of the President or the executive branch. In seeking the documents from Watt, Congress had a constitutionally-based need for the information: its power to "regulate Commerce with foreign Nations."[84] Throughout its history, Congress has legislated on international trade, foreign assistance, arms sales, and other matters of foreign policy.

In response to Smith's legal position, the subcommittee prepared a contempt citation against Watt.[85] Some of the documents, during this period, were shared with the subcommittee. On February 9, 1982, the subcommittee voted 11 to 6 to hold Watt in contempt.[86] By that time, all but seven of the 31 subpoenaed documents had been given to the subcommittee.[87] On February 25, the full committee voted 23 to 19 for contempt.[88] White House Counsel Fred Fielding offered to brief committee members on the seven documents, but lawmakers rejected his offer.[89]

---

79. 43 Op. Att'y Gen. at 330.
80. 5 U.S.C. §552(b)(5) (2000).
81. Id. at §552(d).
82. Memorandum from House General Counsel Stanley M. Brand, November 10, 1981, to Rep. John Dingell, in "Executive Privilege: Watt," at 7–8.
83. 43 Op. Att'y Gen. at 328.
84. U.S. Const., art. I, §8, cl. 3.
85. "House Subcommittee Moving to Cite Interior Secretary Watt for Contempt," Washington Post, November 27, 1981, at A9.
86. William Chapman, "House Subcommittee Votes to Cite Watt for Contempt," Washington Post, February 10, 1982, at A1.
87. "Watt Says Congress Likely to Hold Him in Contempt," Washington Post, February 11, 1982, at A9.
88. Philip Shabecoff, "House Panel Finds Watt in Contempt," New York Times, February 26, 1982, at D16.
89. William Chapman, "Hill Panel Votes to Cite Watt for Contempt," Washington Post, February 26, 1982, at A5.

Although Watt said he would rather go to jail than surrender the remaining materials,[90] those documents were reviewed by subcommittee members. The administration established several conditions. The documents would be delivered to a room in the Rayburn House Office Building, where committee members would have four hours to examine the documents and take notes. Lawmakers could not photocopy the documents or show them to committee staff. Also, the committee agreed not to release any information that might harm the national interest in dealing with Canada.[91]

A newspaper account reports that the ranking Republican on the subcommittee, Marc L. Marks, concluded there was "nothing sensitive in these documents. Watt would have given over the papers had the White House not intervened."[92] During a committee meeting, Marks attributed the impasse with Watt to "an irrational decision made by the White House, put into effect by a President who I cannot believe understood the ramifications of what he was doing."[93] Marks regretted the decision to exclude staff, calling it "illegal because...the first person that we are going to turn to that everybody expects us to turn to to discuss what the papers show, will naturally be our staff person."[94] Rep. Mike Synar pointed out that "23 members of the Interior Department and other departments saw these documents. We found in one case it was a law student, an intern at the time, who later became an official."[95]

Gorsuch Contempt

The experience with James Watt should have given the executive branch a better appreciation of legislative prerogatives. It was not to be. Senior attorneys in the Justice Department decided that their theory of executive privi-

---

90. Eleanor Randolph, "Watt Says He'd Rather Go to Jail Than Give Papers to Subcommittee," Los Angeles Times, February 11, 1982, at 10.
91. "Contempt of Congress," hearings before the House Committee on Energy and Commerce, 97th Cong. 385–94 (1982); H. Rept. No. 898, 97th Cong., 2d Sess. (1982); Margot Hornblower, "White House Avoids Hill Showdown Over Documents," Washington Post, March 17, 1982, at A5; Philip Shabecoff, "Data That Caused Citing of Watt Will Be Provided to House Group," New York Times, March 17, 1982, at A21.
92. Margot Hornblower, "White House Avoids Hill Showdown Over Documents," Washington Post, March 17, 1982, at A5.
93. "Contempt of Congress," hearings, at 386.
94. Id. at 389.
95. Id.

lege, having failed spectacularly with the Watt documents, had been correct all along. They waited for an opportunity to try it again, this time with perhaps greater success. Their second attempt came at great cost to many officials in the executive branch.

When the oversight subcommittee of the House Public Works Committee sought documents on the EPA's enforcement of the "Superfund" program, it was advised by the agency that there would be no objection "so long as the confidentiality of the information in those files was maintained."[96] The subcommittee had been investigating the $1.6 billion program established by Congress to clean up hazardous-waste sites and to prosecute companies responsible for illegal dumping.

Shortly thereafter the Reagan administration decided that Congress could not see documents in active litigation files. The administration's reversal may have been triggered by subpoenas from other committees for comparable documents. Another oversight panel from the House Energy and Commerce Committee wanted access to the same type of information. The administration expressed concern that executive branch control would be undermined by these multiple requests.[97] Both oversight subcommittees had reason to suspect that the major chemical companies were not paying their full share of the costs, requiring taxpayers to pick up the balance.[98]

EPA Administrator Anne Gorsuch, acting under instructions from President Reagan (meaning the Justice Department), refused to turn over "sensitive documents found in open law enforcement files." Reagan's memorandum to her, dated November 30, 1982, claimed that those documents represented "internal deliberative materials containing enforcement strategy and statements of the government's positions on various legal issues which may be raised in enforcement actions relative to the various hazardous waste sites" by the EPA or the Department of Justice.[99] On December 2, the administration withheld 64 documents from the subcommittee.[100] The administration's initial, discredited position in the Watt dispute had not changed. It still assumed that since documents shared with Congress might find their way into the public realm, they should not be shared at all. Following that logic, congressional oversight would have to be put on hold for years until the government completed its enforcement and litigation actions.

---

96. H. Rept. No. 968, 97th Cong., 2d Sess. 11 (1982).
97. Id. at 15, 21.
98. Id. at 7–9.
99. Id. at 42, 76.
100. 8 Op. O.L.C. 101, 107 (1984).

By a vote of 9 to 2, a subcommittee of the House Public Works Committee decided to cite Gorsuch for contempt.[101] The full committee did likewise, after rejecting a Justice Department proposal to give briefings on the contents of the documents.[102] The House of Representatives voted 259 to 105 to support the contempt citation. Although partisan overtones were present, 55 Republicans joined 204 Democrats to build the top-heavy majority.[103] Pursuant to the statutory procedures for contempt citations, the Speaker certified the facts and referred them to the U.S. Attorney for presentation to a grand jury.

The Justice Department, anticipating the House vote, moved quickly: "Immediately after the House vote and prior to the delivery of the contempt citation,"[104] the department chose not to prosecute the case. Instead, it asked a district court to declare the House action an unconstitutional intrusion into the President's authority to withhold information from Congress.[105] U.S. Attorney Stanley S. Harris, responsible for bringing the case to the grand jury, listed his name on the Justice Department complaint and advised Congress that "it would not be appropriate for me to consider bringing this matter before a grand jury until the civil action has been resolved."[106]

The Justice Department faced a conflict of interest. First it had advised Gorsuch to withhold the documents, and now it decided not to prosecute her for adhering to the department's legal analysis. In court, the department argued that the contempt action marked an "unwarranted burden on executive privilege" and an "interference with the executive's ability to carry out the laws." Counsel for the House of Representatives urged the court not to intervene, requesting it to dismiss the case.[107]

The court dismissed the government's suit on the ground that judicial intervention in executive-legislative disputes "should be delayed until all possibilities for settlement have been exhausted."[108] The court urged both parties

---

101. Mary Thornton, "House Subcommittee Votes to Cite EPA Administrator for Contempt," Washington Post, December 3, 1982, at A6.
102. 8 Op. O.L.C. at 107.
103. 128 Cong. Rec. 31746–76 (1982).
104. Stanley M. Brand and Sean Connelly, "Constitutional Confrontations: Preserving Prompt and Orderly Means By Which Congress May Enforce Investigative Demands Against Executive Branch Officials," 36 Cath. U. L. Rev. 71, 79 (1986).
105. Dale Russakoff, "Prosecution of Gorsuch Ruled Out," Washington Post, December 12, 1982, at A1.
106. H. Rept. No. 98-323, 98th Cong., 1st Sess. 49 (1983).
107. Al Kamen, "Attacked by Lawmakers, Executive Branch Defends Privilege," Washington Post, February 2, 1983, at A3.
108. United States v. U.S. House of Representatives, 556 F.Supp. 150, 152 (D.D.C. 1983).

to devote their energies to compromise and cooperation, not confrontation.[109] After the court's decision, which the Justice Department chose not to appeal, the administration agreed to release "enforcement sensitive" documents to the House Public Works Committee, beginning with briefings and redacted copies and eventually ending with the unredacted documents, which could be examined by committee members and up to two committee staff persons.[110]

The House Energy and Commerce Subcommittee on Oversight and Investigation, chaired by Rep. John Dingell, refused to accept an agreement with all these hoops. The documents covered by the subpoena were to be delivered to the subcommittee. There were to be no briefings and no multi-stage process of redacted documents leading to unredacted documents. The subcommittee agreed to handle any "enforcement sensitive" document in executive session, giving it confidential treatment. Even so, the subcommittee reserved for itself the right to release such documents or use them in public session, after providing "reasonable advance notice" to the EPA. If the agency did not agree, the documents would not be released or used in public session unless the chairman and ranking minority member concurred. If they did not concur, the subcommittee could vote on the release and use in public session. With regard to staff access, that would be decided by the chairman and ranking minority member.[111]

One of the casualties of the House investigation into the Superfund program was former EPA official Rita M. Lavelle. The House Energy and Commerce Committee voted unanimously to find her in contempt for defying a committee subpoena to testify.[112] The House voted 413 to zero to hold her in contempt.[113] She was sentenced in 1984 to six months in prison, five years' probation, and a fine of $10,000 for lying to Congress about her management of the Superfund program. She was the only EPA official indicted in the scandal, but more than 20 other top officials, including Anne Gorsuch, left the

---

109. Id. at 153.
110. "Memorandum of Understanding Between the Committee on Public Works and Transportation and the Department of Justice Concerning Documents Subpoenaed from Environmental Protection Agency," February 18, 1983; H. Rept. No. 323, at 18–20. For further details on the Gorsuch affair, see Ronald L. Claveloux, "The Conflict Between Executive Privilege and Congressional Oversight: The Gorsuch Controversy," 1983 Duke L. J. 1333 (1983).
111. "EPA Document Agreement,"CQ Weekly Report, March 26, 1983, at 635.
112. Cass Peterson, "House Panel Votes to Cite Rita Lavelle," Washington Post, April 27, 1983, at A3; Joseph A. Davis, "House Panel Votes to Cite Rita Lavelle for Contempt," CQ Weekly Report, April 30, 1983, at 839.
113. 129 Cong. Rec. 12717–25 (1983).

EPA amid allegations of perjury, conflict of interest, and political manipulation of the agency.[114]

Following the Gorsuch contempt, the Office of Legal Counsel wrote an opinion on May 30, 1984, concluding that as a matter of statutory interpretation and separation of powers analysis, a U.S. Attorney is not required to bring a congressional contempt citation to a grand jury when the citation is directed against an executive official who is carrying out the President's decision to invoke executive privilege.[115] The memo regarded the threat of criminal prosecution from a congressional contempt citation as an "unreasonable, unwarranted, and therefore intolerable burden" on the President's exercise of constitutional authority, pointing out that Congress "has other methods available to test the validity of a privilege claim and to obtain the documents that it seeks."[116] If an administration defies a committee subpoena, what effective methods exist other than contempt? The memo cautioned that its analysis was "limited to the unique circumstances that gave rise to these questions late in 1982 and early 1983,"[117] and suggested that "prudence" should limit the conclusions in the memo "to controversies similar to the one to which this memorandum expressly relates, and the general statements of legal principles should be applied in other contexts only after careful analysis."[118]

Travelgate and Jack Quinn

The House Committee on Government Reform and Oversight conducted an investigation into the 1993 firings of seven Travel Office employees in the Clinton White House. Although President Clinton had full authority to fire the employees, the manner of their discharge led to investigations by Congress, the General Accounting Office, the press, and the independent counsel. On May 19, 1993, they were dismissed with the charge that they followed poor management practices. Dee Dee Myers, Clinton's press secretary, also stated that the FBI had been asked to examine the records in the Travel Office, suggesting that the employees might have been guilty of criminal action as well.

---

114. "Burford Resigns From EPA Post Under Fire," 1983 CQ Almanac 332–35; Al Kamen, "Lavelle Gets Prison Term, $10,000 Fine," Washington Post, January 10, 1984, at A2.
115. 8 Op. O.L.C. 101 (1984).
116. Id. at 102.
117. Id.
118. Id. at 103.

The way the White House replaced the seven employees soon raised charges of nepotism and cronyism.[119]

The House Committee on Government Reform and Oversight received the documents it requested from the Justice Department and other federal agencies, but in September 1995 the White House informed the panel that President Clinton might claim executive privilege and refuse to turn over some or all of 907 documents.[120] In January 1996, the committee subpoenaed the records from the White House, and in May it announced that it would hold the White House in contempt unless it turned over the materials.[121] White House Counsel Jack Quinn drafted a remarkably insolent letter and sent it to Committee Chairman William F. Clinger, Jr.: "Let me be blunt: this threat can only be characterized as a desperate political act meant to resuscitate interest in a story that long ago died." Quinn objected to a legislative inquiry that had become, he said, "a tiresome fishing expedition" and a "wild good chase."[122] On May 9, the committee voted 27 to 19 to hold Quinn in contempt as well as two others: former White House Director of Administration David Watkins and his aide, Matthew Moore.[123]

Clinger offered to delay the next step—sending the contempt citation to the House for a vote—to leave open the possibility of an accommodation with the White House.[124] He offered to have Quinn come to the committee before floor action.[125] Thereafter, the administration released about 1,000 pages of documents to the committee just hours before the House was scheduled to take up the contempt vote.[126]

---

119. Louis Fisher, Constitutional Conflicts between Congress and the President 78–79 (1997 ed).

120. Ann Devroy, "Clinton May Assert Executive Privilege," Washington Post, September 8, 1995, at A11.

121. Susan Schmidt, "House Prober Presses Demand for Travel Office Documents," Washington Post, May 3, 1996, at A2.

122. "Correspondence Between the White House and Congress in the Proceedings Against John M. Quinn, David Watkins, and Matthew Moore," a report by the House Committee on Government Reform and Oversight, 104th Cong., 2d Sess. 409 (Comm. Print, May 1996).

123. Business Meeting in the Proceedings Against John M. Quinn, David Watkins, and Matthew Moore," House Committee on Government Reform and Oversight, 104th Cong., 2d Sess. 88 (Comm. Print, June 1996) (hereafter "Business Meeting: Quinn"); R. H. Melton, "House Panel Votes for Contempt Citation," Washington Post, May 10, 1996, at A4.

124. "Panel Moves to Gain Travel Office Files," New York Times, May 10, 1996, at A26.

125. "Business Meeting: Quinn," at 46.

126. Eric Schmitt, "White House Gives Committee More Papers in Dismissal Case," New York Times, May 31, 1996, at A20; Ann Devroy and John E. Yang, "White House Gives

Contempt Action against Reno

Late in 1997, Attorney General Janet Reno responded to a subpoena from the House Government Reform and Oversight Committee, chaired by Rep. Dan Burton. She declined to give the committee a memorandum sent to her by FBI Director Louis J. Freeh, who had urged the appointment of an independent counsel to investigate allegations of criminal conduct in campaign finance. Justice Department officials said that both Reno and Freeh advised the committee that it was inappropriate to provide a congressional committee with a departmental document that included analysis about an ongoing investigation. They agreed on the need to withhold the document because of "the need to protect the confidentiality and independence of an ongoing investigation and our prosecutorial decisionmaking."[127]

On July 27, 1998, the Justice Department refused to turn over two internal documents that recommended the appointment of an independent counsel in the campaign finance investigation. The House committee had subpoenaed a 27-page memo to Reno by Freeh and a 94-page report by Charles G. LaBella, former head of the department's campaign finance task force. Instead of turning over the two documents, the Justice Department offered to brief the committee members on the contents of the memos. Burton rejected the proposal.[128]

After the department's refusal to release the documents, the House committee voted 24 to 19 on August 6 to cite Reno for contempt. She warned that release of the documents would "provide criminals, targets and defense lawyers alike with a road map to our investigations."[129] Again, this response assumed that whatever the committee received, so would the public. Reno offered to brief the committee in public session "on the legal rationale" presented in the two memos, but only after she had made a decision on whether to seek an independent counsel.[130] At a news conference, she said that for a

---

Congress 1,000 Pages of Travel Office Papers," Washington Post, May 31, 1996, at A10. The contempt actions against Quinn, Watkins, and Moore are summarized in H. Rept. No. 104-598, 104th Cong., 2d Sess. (1996).

127. Roberto Suro, "Reno Declines To Hand Over Freeh Memo," Washington Post, December 9, 1997, at A6.

128. Roberto Suro, "Justice Dept. Defies House Subpoena for Campaign Finance Probe Memos," Washington Post, July 28, 1998, at A8.

129. George Lardner, Jr., "House Panel Votes to Hold Reno in Contempt," Washington Post, August 7, 1998, at A1.

130. Id. at A21.

committee to ask for an internal department document before she reached a decision "is a form of political tampering that no prosecutor in America can accept."[131]

The following month, Reno gave Chairman Burton access to heavily redacted versions of the memos, leaving him roughly thirty percent to read.[132] Burton asked Reno to allow three former prosecutors and a former White House deputy counsel to review the memos and give their opinions to him and to the House Republican leadership. She rejected that proposal.[133] She did agree, however, to allow six other Republican members of the committee to view the redacted copy, but insisted that Burton withdraw the subpoena and drop the contempt citation.[134] After these attempts to find common ground failed, Burton moved forward with the contempt citation. Although the committee recommended holding Reno in contempt, the matter was not taken to the floor for House action.

As part of the impeachment action against President Clinton, members of the House Judiciary Committee were allowed to read the Freeh and LaBella documents. On December 2, 1998, U.S. District Judge Norma Holloway Johnson granted the committee limited access to the two memos.[135] On June 6, 2000, the House Government Reform Committee released the Freeh and LaBella memos along with other Justice Department documents related to the refusal to appoint an independent counsel to investigate campaign finance issues of the 1996 presidential election.[136] WorldNetDaily made the two memos available to the general public on its website (www.worldnetdaily.com).

---

131. Sumana Chatterjee, "Panel Steps Up Confrontation Over Campaign Finance Memos, Voting to Cite Reno for Contempt," CQ Weekly Report, August 8, 1998, at 2175. For background documents on the contempt citation against Reno, see "Contempt of Congress," report by the House Committee on Government Reform and Oversight, H. Rept. No. 105-728, 105th Cong., 2d Sess. (September 17, 1998).

132. Sumana Chatterjee, "Reno Still Faces Citation for Contempt," CQ Weekly Report, September 5, 1998, at 2330.

133. Amy Keller, "Burton Pushes Contempt Against Reno," Roll Call, September 21, 1998, at 3.

134. "The Contempt Citation" (editorial), Washington Post, September 22, 1998, at A16.

135. Robert Suro and Ruth Marcus, "Justice Memos May Yield Very Little," Washington Post, December 3, 1998, at A18.

136. George Lardner, Jr., "Memos: Reno Was Warned," Washington Post, June 7, 2000, at A1.

Committee subpoenas and contempt citations have been effective instruments for gaining access to executive branch documents that are initially withheld. The pressure that builds from these two techniques generally results in the administration offering accommodations that satisfy legislative needs. Although both branches at times seek assistance from the courts, the general message from federal judges is that an agreement hammered out between the two branches is better that a directive handed down by a court. The contempt actions discussed in this chapter all resulted in access to disputed documents.

Executive-legislative conflicts offer several lessons about access to information. Congress has as much right to agency documents for oversight purposes as it does for legislation. Executive claims of "deliberative process," "enforcement sensitive," "ongoing investigation," or "foreign policy considerations" have not been, in themselves, adequate grounds for keeping documents from Congress. On the issue of withholding information from Congress, there are often sharp differences within an administration, especially between the Justice Department and the agencies.

Statutory language that authorizes withholding information from the public is not a legitimate reason for withholding information from Congress. Sharing sensitive information with congressional committees is not the same as sharing information with the public. Courts assume that congressional committees will exercise their powers responsibly. Legislative committees have demonstrated that they have reliable procedures for protecting confidentiality. Finally, congressional capacity to subpoena agency documents from private organizations is not an adequate substitute for receiving them directly from the agency.

7

House Resolutions of Inquiry

Another congressional procedure used to obtain information from the executive branch is the House resolution of inquiry. It is defined as "a simple resolution making a direct request or demand of the President or the head of an executive department to furnish the House of Representatives with specific factual information in the possession of the executive branch."[1] These resolutions gather only facts, not opinions. They may not be used to require new investigations by the executive branch.

Resolutions of inquiry are often much more effective than one would conclude from formal committee and floor action. There are many examples where a committee reports a resolution adversely and succeeds in tabling it on the floor, making it appear that the sponsor was defeated on all fronts. Yet these committee and floor actions are frequently justified because the administration has released the necessary documents and satisfied the resolution in full.

There is no counterpart in current Senate practice for resolutions of inquiry, although there are precedents dating to the end of the 19th century and an effort in 1926.[2] Nothing prevents the Senate from passing such resolutions, but apparently the Senate is satisfied with the leverage it has through other legislative means, including the nomination process and Senate "holds." Unlike the House, the Senate has no special practices for expediting consideration through committee discharge or non-debatable motions, and resolutions are not generally privileged for immediate consideration.[3]

---

1. Deschler's Precedents, H. Doc. No. 94-661, 94th Cong., 2d Sess., vol. 7, ch. 24, §8.
2. Riddick's Senate Procedure, S. Doc. No. 101-28, 101st Cong., 2d Sess. 799, 1205 (1992). The effort in 1926 was challenged on a point of order. When the sponsor of the resolution asked for unanimous consent to proceed, there was objection. 67 Cong. Rec. 2658–59, 2661–62, 2663.
3. Riddick's Senate Procedure, at 1204.

Origins of the Procedure

From its very first years, Congress requested information from the executive branch to further legislative inquiries. Examples already covered include the 1790 investigations into Robert Morris's term as Superintendent of Finance and the annuity given to Baron von Steuben. Those investigations, however, were conducted under the implied authority of Congress to function as the "Grand Inquest." A resolution of inquiry is different. Under it, the House operates by a special *rule* that grants privileged status to a lawmaker's motion to obtain documents from the executive branch. Early House rules contained no procedure for requesting information from the President or Cabinet officials.[4]

In 1820, the House clarified its rules for requesting information from the executive branch. There was concern that the House had not been acting with sufficient consideration before making such requests. In offering an amendment to House rules on December 12, 1820, Rep. Charles Rich noted that "six clerks had been constantly employed, from the close of the last session to the present time, in collecting the materials to enable one of the departments to answer a call at the last session."[5] Rich wanted requests for information from the President or departmental heads to "lie upon the table one day for consideration, unless otherwise ordered, with the unanimous consent of the House."[6] On the following day, the House agreed to his language.[7]

Two years later, the House made another change to its rules governing resolutions of inquiry, requiring not merely a day's delay but also committee consideration: "And shall be taken up for consideration on the next day, in the order in which they were presented, immediately after reports are called for from select committees, and, when adopted, the Clerk shall cause the same to be delivered."[8] The House rule now read:

> A proposition, requesting information from the President of the United States, or directing it to be furnished by the head of either of the Executive Departments, or by the Postmaster General, shall lie on the table one day for consideration, unless otherwise ordered by the

---

4. House rules adopted in 1789 made no mention of legislative procedures for obtaining executive documents; 1 Journal of the House of Representatives 8–14 (1826). Nor were such procedures in place in 1794; 4 Annals of Cong. 875–82.
5. Annals of Cong., 16th Cong., 2d Sess. 608 (1820).
6. Id. at 607.
7. Id. at 641.
8. Annals of Cong., 17th Cong., 1st Sess. 748 (1822).

unanimous consent of the House; and all such propositions shall be taken up for consideration in the order they were presented, immediately after reports are called for from select committees; and, when adopted, the Clerk shall cause the same to be delivered.[9]

That language survived until 1879, when the House Rules Committee reported language to eliminate the need for lawmakers to seek unanimous consent from the chamber in order to seek executive documents. Speaker Samuel J. Randall explained that it was "very seldom that it is in order for a member to offer a resolution calling for information; that is the difficulty. Any one member at any time may prevent a call for information."[10] Agreeing with Randall that procedures had to be changed to permit easier access to executive documents, Rep. Roger Q. Mills nevertheless objected to the requirement for committee referral: "What is the necessity for having a resolution calling for information from one of the Executive Departments referred to a committee? What is the use of my offering a resolution of that kind and having it referred to a committee and there buried?"[11]

Rep. James Garfield explained that the purpose of committee referral was to avoid the "constant danger of gentlemen upon this floor duplicating calls for information. Some one may want some information and offer a resolution calling for it and it passes by unanimous consent, and the same thing may have been asked already by somebody else and nobody has paid any attention to the fact that the same thing has already been called for...." Garfield thought it better that legislative requests for information "be referred to the committees, in order that they may not be duplicated so as to put the Departments to the necessity of employing a large number of clerks for a useless purpose."[12]

The House Committee on Rules recommended language that gave committees of jurisdiction full discretion over resolutions referred to them: "Under this call resolutions for information from the Executive Departments of the Government may be offered for reference to the appropriate committees, such committees to have the right to report at any time."[13] The language "under this call" referred to a procedure that required resolutions calling for executive information to be offered only during the morning hour of every Monday.[14]

---

9. Id. at 756 (the language on this page has "when appointed" rather than "when adopted," as originally proposed. "Appointed" appears to be a typographical error).
10. 9 Cong. Rec. 1018 (1879).
11. Id.
12. Id.
13. Id.
14. Id.

Mills objected to that procedure, pointing out that a resolution calling for information might be "of a partisan character," because a member of the minority wanted information in the possession of an executive officer of the majority party in the House. Did anyone believe, he asked, "that such a resolution would get out of any committee against the vote of a majority of its members, when the design of the resolution was, perhaps, to expose the malfeasance of some officer belonging to the party of the majority?"[15] Rep. William H. Calkins found Garfield's argument about duplication unpersuasive. If a lawmaker asked for information that an executive department had already made available to another lawmaker, "it would be a full answer to the resolution for such Department to reply that the information had already been given, and the Department would not be required to go over it again."[16]

As to Mills's argument that a committee could use its majority party power to block any action on a resolution, Randall pointed out that the majority party could also block floor action on the resolution, because "a single member of that majority could object to it." Mills conceded that point, but said "there would be a record."[17] Rep. John H. Baker thought that too much power had been centered in the committees of jurisdiction. Upon receiving a resolution requesting information, it should be "imperative for the committee to report either for or against the resolution, so as to allow the question to come before the House for its determination." Randall regarded that as "a very good suggestion" that did not occur to the Rules Committee.[18] Rep. Harry White sharpened Baker's proposal by requiring the committee to report "within one week."[19] Baker's amendment, as modified, was agreed to, resulting in this language: "And such committees shall report thereon within one week thereafter."[20]

Committee and Floor Procedures

Under House Rule XIII, clause 7, a Member may address a resolution of inquiry "to the head of an executive department." The resolution is privileged and may be considered at any time after it is properly reported or discharged

---

15. Id.
16. Id.
17. Id.
18. Id.
19. Id.
20. Id. at 1019.

from committee. If the resolution is not reported to the House by the deadline, a motion to discharge the committee from its consideration is privileged. The time allowed for committee review and consideration was extended from one week to 14 legislative days in 1983.[21] In calculating the days available for committee consideration, the first day and the last day are not counted.[22]

A resolution of inquiry is usually referred to the committee that has jurisdiction over the subject matter, but on a number of occasions two or more committees have been involved in responding to a resolution of inquiry. After a resolution of inquiry is introduced and referred to committee, the committee sends the resolution to the administration for action, requesting a timely response to allow the committee to act within the deadline for a committee report. While waiting for information from the executive branch, the committee may either act on the resolution in the form in which it was referred or consider amendments to it. The committee may vote to report the resolution favorably or adversely. It may also decide not to report at all, forcing the member who introduced the resolution to make a motion to discharge the committee.

When a resolution of inquiry is reported from committee, the chairman of the committee calls up the resolution and becomes floor manager, either to pass the resolution or table it. If the committee decides not to report, the sponsor of the resolution can call up the resolution as privileged business. The privileged status of the resolution applies only to requests for facts within the administration's control and not for opinions or investigations.[23] If part of the resolution is privileged but another is not, because it asks for opinions, the resolution as a whole may lose its privileged character.[24]

Resolutions of inquiry are directed "to the head of an executive department." There have been parliamentary challenges to resolutions that are directed to executive officials who are not considered the head of an executive department.[25] Although the President is not "the head of an executive department," resolutions of inquiry are routinely directed to the President. No one makes a parliamentary challenge that the President is not a departmental head.

---

21. 129 Cong. Rec. 34 (1983) (paragraph 7).
22. 3 Hinds' Precedents § 1858.
23. See House Rule XIII, Cl. 7 (Rules of the House of Representatives, H. Doc. No. 106-320, 106th Cong., 2d Sess. 619 (2001)).
24. 40 Cong. Rec. 593 (1905) (statement by Speaker Cannon).
25. 22 Cong. Rec. 1874–75 (1891); 38 Cong. Rec. 3181 (1904).

Administrative Discretion

Some House resolutions of inquiry give the administration discretion in providing factual information to Congress, particularly when they are directed to the President. In 1811, a resolution requested from the President, "as far as practicable," a list of Americans impressed by other countries, "with such other information on this subject as he in his judgment may think proper to communicate."[26] In the same year, a resolution requested from the President information relative to the situation in the Indiana Territory, "which may not be improper to be communicated."[27] Early in 1812, a resolution requested the President to furnish the House with copies of instructions given to the U.S. Minister at London, regarding the impressment of American seamen into the naval service of Great Britain, "excepting so much as it may be improper to disclose, on account of any pending negotiation."[28]

In 1876, the House passed a resolution requesting President Ulysses S. Grant to inform the House "if, in his opinion, it is not incompatible with the public interest," whether since March 4, 1869 (the date his term began) any executive offices, acts, or duties had been performed at a distance from "the seat of Government established by law, and for how long a period at any one time, and in what part of the United States; also, whether any public necessity existed for such performance, and, if so, of what character, and how far the performance of such executive offices, acts, or duties, at such distance from the seat of Government established by law was in compliance with the act of Congress of the 16th day of July, 1790."

President Grant could have withheld information on the ground stated in the resolution: That disclosure was not compatible with the public interest. Instead, he decided to use constitutional reasons to refuse the information. First, he said he could find nothing in the Constitution to justify congressional interest as to where the President discharged official acts and duties. What the House could require in terms of information from the executive branch was limited "to what is necessary for the proper discharge of its powers of legislation or of impeachment," neither of which, he said, applied. Asking where executive acts are performed and at what distance from the seat of Government

---

26. Annals of Cong., 12th Cong., 1st Sess. 370 (1811).
27. Id. at 582.
28. Id. at 779 (1812).

"does not necessarily belong to the province of legislation. It does not profess to be asked for that object."[29]

Second, if the House sought the information to assist in the impeachment process, "it is asked in derogation of an inherent natural right, recognized in this country by a constitutional guaranty which protects every citizen, the President as well as the humblest in the land, from being made a witness against himself."[30] This position was not well reasoned. Other Presidents, including George Washington and James Polk, had made it clear that if the House sought information as part of impeachment proceedings, the information would be supplied.

Third, Grant pointed out that previous Presidents found it necessary to discharge official business outside the nation's capital, and that "during such absences I did not neglect or forego the obligations of the duties of my office."[31] To his letter to the House he appended a study on the number of days other Presidents had conducted official business outside the nation's capital.

Finally, with regard to the statute of July 16, 1790, Grant said that no act of Congress could limit his constitutional duty to discharge governmental functions outside the nation's capital, and that the 1790 statute made no attempt to do so. He noted that on March 30, 1791, shortly after passage of the statute cited in the resolution, President Washington issued a proclamation "having reference to the subject of this very act from Georgetown, a place remote from Philadelphia, which then was the seat of Government...."[32]

In 1952, the House debated a resolution of inquiry to "direct" the Secretary of State to transmit to the House, "at the earliest practicable date, full and complete information with respect to any agreements, commitments, or understandings which may have been entered into" by President Harry Truman and Prime Minister Winston Churchill in the course of their conversations during January 1952, "and which might require the shipment of additional members of the Armed Forces of the United States beyond the continental limits of the United States or involve United States forces in armed conflict on foreign soil."[33] The resolution came to the floor accompanied by an adverse report from the Committee on Foreign Affairs.[34]

---

29. 9 Richardson 4316.
30. Id.
31. Id. at 4317.
32. Id. at 4318.
33. 98 Cong. Rec. 1205 (1952).
34. Id.

During debate on the resolution, which passed 189 to 143,[35] those who supported the resolution regarded it as non-binding. For example, Rep. John Martin Vorys advised his colleagues that "we cannot by this resolution make the Executive answer. We cannot make the President, we cannot make the Secretary of State, say anything. That has been passed on time and again under the precedents of this House. We can put a question up to them. All we can do, if we pass this resolution, is to say to the Secretary of State and the Department of State: 'Please try again. That answer you sent down was not very good.'"[36] Rep. James P. Richards, who voted against the resolution, said, regarding this resolution, "it is within the province of the President to refuse to divulge information that he considers would be dangerous or incompatible with the interests of our Nation."[37]

Discretion over the release of information to Congress has also been given expressly to departmental heads. In 1971 the House considered a resolution directing the Secretary of State to furnish certain information respecting U.S. military operations in Laos, but the language of the resolution included the phrase "to the extent not incompatible with the public interest."[38] The House tabled this resolution, 261 to 118.[39] In 1979, in the midst of an energy crisis, a resolution of inquiry requested certain facts from the President, "to the extent possible," regarding shortages of crude oil and refined petroleum products, refinery capacity utilization, and related matters. It was adopted 340 to 4.[40]

Committee Review

A committee has a number of choices after a resolution of inquiry is referred to it. It may vote the resolution up or down or amend it. It can report favorably or adversely, but an "adverse report" is often accompanied by a substantial amount of information prepared by the executive branch. The quality and quantity of this information can bring the administration into compliance with the resolution, making further congressional action unnecessary. Usually a

---

35. Id. at 1215.
36. Id. at 1208.
37. Id. at 1209.
38. 117 Cong. Rec. 23800 (1971).
39. Id. at 23807. See "Laos Secrets: House Defeat of Disclosure Move," CQ Weekly Report, July 9, 1971, at 1463–66.
40. 125 Cong. Rec. 15027, 15039 (1979).

committee issues a report on a resolution of inquiry; if it does not, it can be discharged.

Committee Amendments

Resolutions of inquiry may be amended at the committee level before action on the House floor. In 1980, the House acted on H. Res. 745, a resolution directing President Jimmy Carter to furnish information on the role of Billy Carter, the President's brother, as an agent of the government of Libya.[41] The House Judiciary Committee, after considering and adopting a number of amendments, reported the resolution favorably by a vote of 27 to 0.[42] The amendments included two that had been adopted by the Foreign Affairs Committee.[43] A third committee, the Permanent Select Committee on Intelligence, reported on the resolution with regard to classified material that touched on the relationship between Libya and Billy Carter. It concluded that the administration was in substantial compliance with H. Res. 745.[44]

During floor action, the chairman of House Judiciary, Peter Rodino, asked unanimous consent that the committee amendments be considered en bloc. There was no objection to his request and the committee amendments were agreed to.[45] He then noted that out of the previous 33 resolutions of inquiry, dating back to 1932, motions to table carried 25 times, largely because there had been substantial compliance to the committee of jurisdiction. It was Rodino's judgment that the administration had substantially complied with H. Res. 745 and that the issue was therefore "moot" and he would make a motion to table the resolution.[46]

Rep. Robert McClory, a member of the Judiciary Committee, disagreed with Rodino's position and his proposal to table the resolution. In McClory's view, "there has been something less than substantial compliance with the terms of the resolution," and that one omission from the materials assembled by the administration was President Carter's "conversation on June 17, 1980, with the Attorney General concerning the Billy Carter investigation."[47]

---

41. 126 Cong. Rec. 24948 (1980).
42. H. Rept. No. 96-1213 (Part 1), 96th Cong., 2d Sess. (1980).
43. 126 Cong. Rec. at 24950 (statement by Rep. Rodino); H. Rept. No. 96-1213 (Part 2), 96th Cong., 2d Sess. (1980).
44. H. Rept. No. 96-1269, 96th Cong., 2d Sess. (1980).
45. 126 Cong. Rec. at 24949.
46. Id. at 24951.
47. Id. at 24953.

Rodino's motion to table the resolution was rejected on a vote of 124 to 260, after which the House voted to agree to the resolution.[48] In defeating the tabling motion, 116 Democrats joined 144 Republicans.[49]

Adverse Reports

The fact that a committee reports a resolution of inquiry adversely does not mean that the committee opposes the purpose of the resolution or that the administration refuses to supply information. The documents delivered by the executive branch may bring it in substantial compliance with the resolution, thus making it unnecessary for the committee to report the resolution favorably for floor action. It often happens that a committee reports a resolution adversely and tables it on the floor, after the sponsor of the resolution has received all the information requested.

A good example of this executive-legislative exchange comes from 1979, when 81 Members supported H. Res. 291, a resolution that directed President Carter to provide the House with information on the energy crisis: shortages of crude oil and refined petroleum products, methods used in allocating oil supplies, possible actions within the private industry to withhold or reduce oil supplies, and any reduction in the supply of crude oil from any foreign country.[50] Within a week, 21 additional Members joined as sponsors of the resolution.[51]

The House Committee on Interstate and Foreign Commerce reported the resolution unfavorably and recommended that it not pass.[52] However, the committee had been seeking the information in a number of hearings, and had asked the Department of Energy to provide the information requested in the resolution. The committee stated that much of the information could be found in departmental publications, and that some of the information had been obtained in the course of committee investigations. Yet it also faulted the administration: "it cannot be said that all information necessary to a full understanding of the supply problem is collected by the DOE, nor that the information which is collected is timely. To the contrary, the Committee has found the DOE lacking vital information on such matters as secondary stocks and actual sales of products." The information supplied by the department was "rarely timely, as a result of long lag times in sending out forms and retrieving them," and the department was "heav-

---

48. Id. at 24961.
49. CQ Weekly Report, September 13, 1980, at 2740.
50. 125 Cong. Rec. 12626 (1979).
51. Id. at 12979.
52. H. Rept. No. 96-261, 96th Cong., 1st Sess. (1979).

ily reliant on unverified industry data despite the clear directives from the Congress in a variety of statutes, such as the Energy Supply and Environmental Coordination Act of 1974, and the Department of Energy Organization Act."[53]

The committee offered several reasons for reporting the resolution adversely: (1) the department had provided "all of the requested documents which were available at the time [the] resolution was considered, and has promised to provide the Committee additional information when it becomes available;" (2) much of the information was of a confidential or proprietary nature, which was appropriate to share with the committee of jurisdiction but less appropriate to share with the entire Congress; (3) the cost of reproducing the documents was substantial and unnecessary; (4) whatever information was available to the department had been shared with the committee and Congress; and (5) the data requested would probably not "quell public skepticism relating to the Nation's gasoline problems."[54] The committee then added a sixth reason:

> The Committee wishes to make clear that it is extremely interested in reliable information concerning the nature of our petroleum supply problems. The information currently available is far from adequate, and the Committee in reporting this resolution adversely does not suggest that the Congress and the public have been fully informed concerning these matters. Nor does the Committee wish to indicate that the Congress does not have a right to such information. To the contrary, the Congress clearly has such a right. Rather, the use of a resolution of inquiry is not the appropriate mechanism for obtaining this readily available data: it simply will not result in any new data.[55]

When the resolution came to the floor on June 14, Rep. John Dingell pointed to a desk covered with information provided by the Energy Department, including "the tables, data, and other documents. The total is a stack of papers nearly a foot high." Yet he also conceded that all of the committee members "believe that the Department's gathering system is inadequate and that data concerning the energy supplies, demands, and prices is not timely provided."[56] Dingell said he was not critical of those who filed the resolution of inquiry: "I do believe that continued inquiry by the Congress is highly desirable. I believe that the information must be made plain."[57]

---

53. Id. at 4.
54. Id. at 7.
55. Id. at 8.
56. 125 Cong. Rec. 14952 (1979).
57. Id. at 14953.

Instead of the mass of material sitting on the desk, several members wanted a summary of what the documents contained. Dingell said the department had prepared a summary but it was not yet available from the printer. After several members objected to voting on the resolution without a summary, Dingell agreed to withdraw his initial motion for the immediate consideration of the resolution.[58]

Debate continued the next day, with a number of members expressing dissatisfaction with the quality of departmental data. Minority Leader John J. Rhodes, who had introduced the resolution, said that "as far as the technicalities of the situation are concerned, those questions were answered, but they were answered in such a way as to be almost incomprehensible, and certainly not to inform either the House or the American people as to the reasons for the existence of these shortages."[59] When Dingell moved to table the resolution of inquiry he lost heavily, 4 to 338.[60]

As the debate moved along and members of both parties expressed support for the resolution, Dingell got the message: "I understand the temper of the House very clearly. I want to have my colleagues know that we have had the resolution of inquiry fully and fairly and properly complied with by the DOE, and it will be further fully, fairly, and properly complied with according to the letter of the rules of the House if this resolution is adopted." He wanted his colleagues to know he had "no objection to the vote which will take place, and I want them to know that the vote will, I regret to advise them, procure no new information other than that which was available at the committee table and which was made available to my Republican colleagues yesterday in response to the resolution." He pledged to "persist in my efforts to procure the information which I and my colleagues desire to have on this particular matter, and that the motion to table made earlier by me was simply to save the time of the House and to see to it that the information requested by the sponsors of the resolution of inquiry was presented to the House in a proper and appropriate fashion."[61] The resolution of inquiry passed on a vote of 340 to 4, with Dingell adding his support.[62]

Another example comes from 1986, after Rep. Leon Panetta introduced H. Res. 395 to receive documents regarding the administration's use of $27 million in appropriated funds for humanitarian assistance for the Nicara-

---

58. Id. at 14955.
59. Id. at 15028.
60. Id. at 15029.
61. Id. at 15035.
62. Id. at 15039.

guan democratic resistance. A subcommittee of the House Foreign Affairs Committee held a hearing on the resolution and made a tentative recommendation that the resolution be reported favorably to the full committee.[63] The subcommittee, after reviewing documents provided by the administration, agreed to recommend that the full committee report adversely if the subcommittee received information covering six categories.[64] A second effort by the administration convinced both the subcommittee and Panetta that the executive branch was in essential compliance with the resolution, but the subcommittee and Panetta also agreed that the documents demonstrated that the administration "has not complied with the law requiring it to set up appropriate monitoring procedures with respect to the so-called humanitarian assistance for the Contras authorized by the Congress."[65] Panetta, having met with representatives from the Central Intelligence Agency to review classified documents, wrote to the chairman of the full committee that the administration had complied with his resolution of inquiry.[66]

Competing Investigations

A committee may decide to report a resolution of inquiry adversely because it competes with other investigations that are regarded as more appropriate. In 1980, for example, H. Res. 571 directed the Attorney General to furnish the House with "all evidence compiled by the Department of Justice and the Federal Bureau of Investigation against Members of Congress in connection with the Abscam investigation," which was a Justice Department undercover operation that led to charges of criminal conduct against several members of Congress. The resolution also asked for "the total amount of Federal moneys expended in connection with the Abscam probe."[67]

The House Judiciary Committee reported the resolution adversely.[68] Committee opposition to the resolution was unanimous.[69] The Justice Department "vigorously oppose[d]" the resolution.[70] The objections raised by the depart-

---

63. H. Rept. No. 99-585, 99th Cong., 2d Sess. 1 (1986).
64. Id. at 4–5.
65. Id. at 5.
66. Id. at 6.
67. 126 Cong. Rec. 4071 (1980).
68. H. Rept. No. 96-778, 96th Cong., 2d Sess. (1980).
69. 126 Cong. Rec. 4073 (statement by Rep. McClory).
70. H. Rept. No. 96-778, at 2 (letter of Assistant Attorney General Philip B. Heymann).

ment, with which the committee agreed, centered on the concern that disclosure of evidence to the House would jeopardize the ability of the department to successfully conduct grand jury investigations and to prosecute any indictments, and that the release of unsifted and unevaluated evidence "would injure the reputations of innocent people who may be involved in no ethical or legal impropriety."[71]

Other considerations were present. The House Standards of Official Conduct Committee, conducting its own inquiry into Abscam, unanimously opposed the resolution of inquiry.[72] The committee had begun the process of negotiating with the Justice Department to obtain access to evidence needed for investigation by the House.[73] Moreover, two subcommittees of the House Judiciary Committee were planning hearings into the proper standards for the Justice Department to conduct undercover operations, particularly against members of Congress.[74] During House debate, Rep. John J. Cavanaugh expressed concern that Abscam "raises serious questions of the separation of powers and the ability of one branch of our Government—the executive—to employ investigative methods that are capable of subverting and intimidating and compromising the independence, the constitutional independence, of another and separate branch of our Government."[75]

In this case, Congress chose not to interrupt or interfere with Justice Department prosecutions because it might appear to be self-serving. Rep. William J. Hughes noted: "I can think of nothing that would be more damaging to the Congress than to be perceived as having obstructed an active criminal investigation."[76] Forcing the Justice Department to release evidence that might help some members who faced criminal prosecution would look as though lawmakers had greater protection than the average citizen.[77] By a vote of 404 to 4, the House decided to table the resolution of inquiry.[78]

In other situations, where members of Congress are not implicated in a criminal investigation, Congress may choose to investigate a scandal even if it jeopardizes successful prosecutions. In terms of public policy, it may be more important to investigate a matter promptly rather than wait years for the Jus-

---

71. Id.
72. 126 Cong. Rec. 4075 (statement by Rep. Bennett).
73. Id.
74. Id. (statement by Rep. Rodino).
75. Id. at 4077.
76. Id. at 4076.
77. Id. (statement by Rep. Lungren).
78. Id. at 4078–79.

tice Department or an independent counsel to investigate, prosecute, and pursue appeals. Such was the case with Iran-Contra, where both Houses of Congress concluded that the value of timely legislative investigation outweighed the needs of prosecutors. Lawrence Walsh, the independent counsel for Iran-Contra, recognized that if Congress "decides to grant immunity, there is no way that it can be avoided. They have the last word and that is a proper distribution of power.... The legislative branch has the power to decide whether it is more important perhaps even to destroy a prosecution than to hold back testimony they need."[79]

Discharging a Committee

If a committee receives a resolution of inquiry and fails to report it within the requisite number of days, a motion to discharge the committee is privileged. That procedure was used in 1971 after Rep. James M. Collins introduced H. Res. 539 directing the Secretary of Health, Education, and Welfare (HEW) to furnish certain documents.[80] The resolution directed the release, "to the extent not incompatible with the public interest," of any documents containing a list of the public school systems, from August 1, 1971 to June 30, 1972, that would be receiving federal funds and would be engaging in busing schoolchildren to achieve racial balance. Also requested were any documents regarding HEW rules and regulations with respect to the use of any federal funds administered by the department for busing to achieve racial balance.[81] The resolution was referred to the Committee on Education and Labor.

When the committee failed to report the resolution by the deadline, which was seven days in 1971, Collins moved to discharge the committee. His motion was agreed to, 252 to 129.[82] Rep. Thomas P. (Tip) O'Neill, Jr., who at that time was the House Majority Whip, voted against the discharge motion but admitted that he was uncertain about the meaning of the resolution: "What does the resolution do? Is there anything wrong? Is it a serious resolution? Is it something we should have had up today? Is it of that import?"[83]

---

79. Lawrence E. Walsh, "The Independent Counsel and the Separation of Powers," 25 Houston L. Rev. 1, 9 (1988).
80. 117 Cong. Rec. 24936 (1971).
81. Id. at 28863.
82. Id.
83. Id. at 28864.

He said that when Members came to the floor they were told: "Well, if you are for busing, you vote 'nay.' If you are against busing, you vote 'yea.' "[84] He now realized that the guidance given to Members was "inaccurate."[85] The vote was not for or against busing, but for or against receiving information from HEW. With this new understanding, O'Neill announced that he had no objection to the resolution and that "I will, and I hope all other Members will vote for the resolution."[86]

O'Neill asked the chairman of Education and Labor, Carl Perkins, why the committee had not acted on the resolution. Perkins explained that he and the committee's ranking member, Albert Quie, had difficulty in obtaining a quorum to discuss the resolution because they were marking up the Economic Opportunity Act. Perkins added: "To be perfectly truthful and frank, both he and I forgot about it. Neither of us, I believe, took the resolution too seriously because it was of the nature that the sponsor of the resolution could have picked up the telephone and gotten the information from HEW."[87]

Rep. Edith Green emphasized that the resolution "is simply a request for information," not "a bill to legislate." She could not understand what was wrong in asking the HEW Secretary "in a perfectly orderly fashion to supply within 60 days the amount of money that is now being spent and in which districts for busing and the guidelines, rules and regulations which HEW has drawn up to enforce this busing to achieve some magical racial balance."[88] With the purpose of the resolution clarified, it passed 351 to 36.[89]

Military Operations in Vietnam

Members of the House frequently use resolutions of inquiry to obtain information on matters of military policy. An especially heavy reliance came during the Vietnam War. In 1971, the House voted on two resolutions to give Members access to the "Pentagon Papers," the Defense Department study entitled "United States-Vietnam Relationships, 1945–1967." One of the cosponsors of the resolution, Rep. Bella Abzug, stated that the procedures adopted by the House Armed Services Committee, which had a single copy of the study, did not pro-

---

84. Id. at 28866.
85. Id.
86. Id. at 28867.
87. Id. at 28864.
88. Id. at 28866.
89. Id. at 28869.

vide Members adequate access to the 47-volume study: "they cannot take notes, cannot have staff people review and comment, cannot report on what they have read. Under such limitations, a Congressman must have an elephantine memory to retain the facts that would enable him to exercise his constitutional duty."[90]

H. Res. 489 directed the President "to furnish the House of Representatives within fifteen days after the adoption of this resolution with the full and complete text" of the Pentagon Papers. The House Armed Services Committee reported the resolution adversely, 25 to 2, and it was tabled on the floor, 272 to 113.[91] H. Res. 490, containing the identical language, was also reported adversely and tabled.[92]

Abzug and other legislators continued to press for facts about the war. In 1971, the House considered several resolutions of inquiry to obtain information about U.S. covert operations in Laos. H. Res. 492 directed the Secretary of State, "to the extent not incompatible with the public interest," to provide the House with any documents containing policy instructions or guidelines given to the U.S. Ambassador in Laos regarding covert CIA operations in Laos, Thai and other foreign armed forces operations in Laos, U.S. bombing operations other than those along the Ho Chi Minh Trail, U.S. armed forces operations in Laos, and U.S. Agency for International Development operations in Laos that assisted, directly or indirectly, military or CIA operations in Laos.[93] Rep. Benjamin Rosenthal, a cosponsor of the resolution, explained its purpose:

> This administration has steadfastly refused to report to the people and to the Congress the nature of the CIA covertly declared war in Laos where the CIA agents are advising the Meo tribesmen. The administration has steadfastly refused to admit that we are hiring Thai mercenaries and ferrying them to Laos in American aircraft to conduct a war in defense of the Laotian Government—a war which this administration has not declared.... Yet it is widely reported in the papers—the New York Times and the Washington Post and other newspapers, Life magazine and the Christian Science Monitor—that all of these events are taking place. We in Congress are forced to depend on what we are advised of in the public newspapers as to our involvement in Laos.[94]

---

90. 117 Cong. Rec. 23026 (1971).
91. H. Rept. No. 92-318, 92d Cong., 1st Sess. (1971); 117 Cong. Rec. at 23030–31.
92. H. Rept. No. 92-319, 92d Cong., 1st Sess. (1971); 117 Cong. Rec. at 23031.
93. 117 Cong. Rec. at 23800.
94. Id. at 23801.

After the House Foreign Affairs Committee reported the resolution adversely, it was tabled, 261 to 118.[95] Another resolution of inquiry, directing the Secretary of State—"to the extent not incompatible with the public interest"—to furnish the House with additional information regarding U.S. policy involving Laos,[96] was also tabled.[97]

House resolutions of inquiry are typically reported from committee without holding hearings. However, in 1972 the House Armed Services Committee held hearings on H. Res. 918, a resolution of inquiry introduced by Abzug to obtain information on U.S. bombing in Vietnam. Most of the resolution requested specific facts on U.S. military personnel in South Vietnam, the number of sorties flown during specific periods, the tonnage of bombs and shells fired or dropped during specific periods, and other statistics.[98] Testifying at the hearings, she said that the level of bombing constituted "the most dramatic proof yet that the Nixon administration is entirely committed to a full-scale and long-term U.S. air war in Indochina instead of negotiating a full withdrawal in return for the release of our captured pilots."[99] At the hearings, Dennis J. Doolin, Deputy Assistant Secretary of Defense for East Asia and Pacific Affairs, provided information on some of the elements in H. Res. 918.[100]

The committee reported the resolution adversely, 32 to 4.[101] During floor debate, Chairman F. Edward Hébert explained that the information sought in the resolution was in committee files, "available to any Member of the House for his examination, subject, of course, to the rules established by the committee which preclude the release or public use of such information without the consent of the committee."[102] After describing the material available in the committee's sessions, both open and closed, he said that the resolution "is directed to giving the Congress the information which is here printed for them to see. Every question is answered."[103] Another committee member, William J. Randall, noted that when the committee went into executive session, the answers

---

95. Id. at 23807–08.
96. Id. at 23808.
97. Id. at 23810.
98. 118 Cong. Rec. 13497–98 (1972).
99. "Full Committee Hearing and Consideration of H. Res. 918, a Resolution of Inquiry Concerning the Bombing in Vietnam by the United States Government," hearing before the House Committee on Armed Services, April 18, 1972, at 9043.
100. Id. at 9057–150.
101. H. Rept. No. 92-1003, 92d Cong., 2d Sess. (1972).
102. 118 Cong. Rec. 14349 (1972).
103. Id.

to the questions put by Abzug "were spread upon the record. We were given the very latest facts and figures on all of the things asked for in the resolution."[104]

House floor debate on the Abzug resolution, occupying 87 pages in the *Congressional Record*, includes the transcript from the open hearings before the Armed Services Committee and a number of articles on military operations in Vietnam. Some of the members who voted to table the resolution objected only to the part asking the administration to give the target date for full independence for Saigon. Otherwise, said Rep. Paul Findley, "the resolution seems to deal entirely with facts of past actions that should be available to Congress."[105] The House voted 270 to 113 to table the resolution.[106] Although the resolution was not agreed to, it forced delivery of information from the administration to the Armed Services Committee, and from there to individual members.

A similar pattern emerged in 1973, when the House acted on H. Res. 379, which directed the Secretary of Defense to furnish the House information on military operations in Cambodia and Laos: the number of sorties flown by the U.S. during certain periods, the tonnage of bombs and shells fired or dropped during certain periods, the number and nomenclature of U.S. aircraft lost over Cambodia and Laos, and other statistics.[107] The House Armed Services Committee held a hearing to review the 19 specific questions addressed in the resolution. Chairman Hébert asked the Defense Department "to be as responsive as possible to each of the questions, and to the maximum extent possible provide this information in open session." If necessary, the committee would go into closed session to "receive such additional classified information as may be necessary to permit the Department to be fully responsive to this privileged resolution."[108]

In open session, Deputy Assistant Secretary Doolin provided answers to each of the questions, with two exceptions. He told the committee that he would not be able to provide the answer for Question 10 for another 24 hours, at which time the committee received the information and placed it in the hearing record.[109] He also noted that Question 18, regarding the legal authority for U.S. military activity in Cambodia and Laos since January 27, 1973,

---

104. Id. at 14433.
105. Id. at 14432.
106. Id. at 14434.
107. 119 Cong. Rec. 14990–91 (1973).
108. "Full Committee Consideration of Privileged Resolution H. Res. 379, Concerning Certain Military Actions in Cambodia and Laos," hearing before the House Committee on Armed Services, 93d Cong., 1st Sess. 1–2 (1973).
109. Id. at 5–6.

would be addressed by DOD General Counsel J. Fred Buzhardt, who proceeded to provide a legal analysis.[110] As noted in the following exchange with Rep. Charles Wilson, all of the information given by Doolin and Buzhardt was released in open session:

> MR. CHARLES WILSON. There was no difficulty in presenting this to us in open session, was there?
> MR. DOOLIN. No, sir. I have tried to be as forthcoming as possible.
> MR. CHARLES WILSON. This information could have been furnished by a resolution asked for by any Member of the Congress, I assume?
> MR. DOOLIN. Yes, sir.[111]

Toward the end of the hearing, Chairman Hébert noted that the resolution "asks for certain information to be brought to the attention of the Congress. That information is now before the attention of the Congress. Therefore, making, in effect, the resolution a moot question." The sponsor of the resolution, Rep. Robert L. Leggett, agreed that "we answered all of the questions I think really very well."[112] When Chairman Hébert said "the resolution becomes moot," Leggett responded: "I concur in that."[113] The committee then voted 36 to zero to report the resolution adversely.[114] The answers to the 19 questions were placed in the *Congressional Record*, at which point the resolution was tabled.[115]

Forcing Other Legislative Actions

Resolutions of inquiry have been successful in prompting Congress to take other legislative actions that address the lack of information from the administration. The two examples included here relate to the calling of supplemental hearings beyond the scope of a resolution of inquiry and the adoption of substitute legislation.

Supplemental Hearings

A resolution of inquiry, after being partially satisfied by answers from the administration, can trigger supplemental information obtained through con-

---

110. Id. at 11–12.
111. Id. at 17.
112. Id. at 32.
113. Id. at 33.
114. Id. See H. Rept. No. 93-170, 93d Cong., 1st Sess. (1973).
115. 119 Cong. Rec. 14991–94.

gressional hearings. This was the result of H. Res. 552, introduced by Rep. Benjamin Rosenthal on June 18, 1975, to seek information about the administration's proposed sale of Hawk and Redeye missiles to Jordan.[116] On the following day, the House Committee on International Relations forwarded the resolution to President Gerald Ford, requesting a prompt reply. The White House responded on June 25, providing responses to the 20 questions put by the resolution.[117]

However, committee chairman Thomas E. Morgan questioned whether the resolution was a bona fide "privileged resolution of inquiry" under House rules. On June 26, the committee voted to table the resolution on the ground that it was not restricted to factual answers, but instead required "investigation" on the part of the President to answer several of the questions.[118] Rosenthal, having announced his intention to call up H. Res. 552 for House action because the committee had not reported on his resolution, agreed to withhold that motion in exchange for committee hearings. Morgan advised Rosenthal that the committee "should get the facts regarding the proposed sale, and I will be glad to cooperate with him in making that happen."[119]

The hearings came at an important time. Congress was about to decide whether to block the sale of the missiles by passing a resolution of disapproval under Section 36(b) of the Foreign Military Sales Act. On July 9, Rosenthal said that information about the proposed sale "was leaked to the press, not formally announced," and that "[n]o attempt was made to inform the Congress about the sale in the past 2 months, and there would have been none were it not for the questions posed in House Resolution 552, the resolution of inquiry." When the administration acknowledged the sale, it indicated that formal notice would be reported to Congress in late July or early August. Rosenthal pointed out that "Congress probably will be in recess at that time and unable to act on this very important arms sale and policy decision."[120]

Formal notice of the sale reached Congress on July 10. Under Section 36(b), Congress had 20 calendar days to pass a concurrent resolution of disapproval. Legislative action on the disapproval resolution therefore had to be completed by July 30. On July 14, Rep. Jonathan Bingham and ten other members introduced H. Con. Res. 337 to disapprove the sale. On July 16 and 17, a subcommittee of the House International Relations Committee held two days of hear-

---

116. 121 Cong. Rec. 19616 (1975).
117. Id. at 21664–67.
118. Id. at 21664.
119. Id. at 21882.
120. Id. at 21884.

ings on the proposed sale.[121] Administration officials defended the sale on the first day; eight Members of Congress raised their objections the following day.

With the disapproval resolution moving toward a vote, President Ford withdrew the proposed sale on July 28 and entered into negotiations with Congress. The administration announced a compromise on September 16, limiting the missiles to "defensive and non-mobile antiaircraft weapons."[122]

Triggering Legislation

In 1991, just prior to U.S. military operations against Iraq, Rep. Barbara Boxer and six Democratic colleagues introduced H. Res. 19 to call for certain information regarding casualty estimates, biological and chemical weapons, financial assistance from other countries (burden sharing), and other information.[123] House Minority Leader Bob Michel objected to Majority Leader Dick Gephardt that the resolution of inquiry "constitutes nothing less than legislative harassment." Michel said that "[j]ust how the sponsors of this resolution believe that implying the commander in chief is deceiving Congress will help the morale of our troops is beyond me."[124]

Members of both parties recognized that the House was entitled to budgetary and other information from the executive branch, but decided on a different approach. After the war began, Charles Schumer and Leon Panetta introduced H.R. 586 on January 18, for the purpose of requiring regular reports from the administration on U.S. expenditures for military operations and the financial contributions from other countries.[125] Action on a bill would avoid the 14-day deadline imposed by a resolution of inquiry.[126]

On February 21, the House moved to suspend the rules to pass H.R. 586. During debate on the bill, several members pointed out that the General Accounting Office had not been given access to any of the costs incurred in connection with the war.[127] Schumer said that until the resolution of inquiry and his bill were introduced, "we just were not getting those answers when we

---

121. "Proposed Sales to Jordan of the Hawk and Vulcan Air Defense Systems," hearings before the Subcommittee on International Political and Military Affairs of the House Committee on International Relations, 94th Cong., 1st Sess. (1975).
122. 1975 CQ Almanac 358–59.
123. 137 Cong. Rec. 105 (1991).
124. Susan B. Glasser, "Liberals Seek to Revive Little-Used Device for Desert Storm Oversight," Roll Call, February 7, 1991, at 8.
125. 137 Cong. Rec. 1910 (1991).
126. Glasser, "Liberals Seek to Revive," at 8.
127. 137 Cong. Rec. 3900 (statements by Rep. Spratt and Rep. Panetta).

asked questions."[128] Lawmakers received information on what allies had pledged but not "about how much they had actually paid."[129] Boxer announced that she would support H.R. 586 and the tabling of her resolution.[130] In a letter dated February 20, Brent Scowcroft of the administration provided specific information in response to H. Res. 19.[131] After H.R. 586 passed 393 to 1,[132] the House engaged in a brief debate on H. Res. 19 before tabling it by a vote of 390 to 0.[133] In discussing the resolution of inquiry, Rep. Dante Fascell said that it "has proven to be a catalyst for the executive branch to be more forthcoming with the Congress in providing necessary and appropriate information in order to satisfy the oversight responsibilities of the Congress."[134]

Mexico Rescue Package

In 1995, the Clinton administration offered a multibillion dollar rescue package for the Mexican peso. Rep. Marcy Kaptur responded with a resolution of inquiry requesting President Clinton to submit information to the House "concerning actions taken through the exchange stabilization fund to strengthen the Mexican peso and stabilize the economy of Mexico."[135] The House Banking and Financial Services Committee voted 37 to 5 to report the resolution favorably, but with a substitute directing the President to submit the documents "if not inconsistent with the public interest."[136] On March 1, the House adopted the committee substitute and agreed to the resolution, 407 to 21.[137]

Although the resolution established a deadline of 14 days, White House Counsel Abner J. Mikva sent a letter to Speaker Newt Gingrich stating that the administration would not be able to provide the documentary material until May 15, or two months after the date set in the resolution.[138] By April 6, the

---

128. Id. at 3902.
129. Id.
130. Id. at 3903.
131. Id. at 3904.
132. Id. at 3906–07.
133. Id. at 3907–11.
134. Id. at 3909.
135. H. Res. 80, 104th Cong., 1st Sess. (February 10, 1995).
136. H. Rept. No. 104-53, 104th Cong., 1st Sess. (1995).
137. 141 Cong. Rec. 6422 (1995).
138. "House GOP Considers Stance on Bailout of Mexico," CQ Weekly Report, March 25, 1995, at 880.

Treasury Department had supplied Congress with 3,200 pages of unclassified documents and 475 pages of classified documents, with additional materials promised.[139] The White House said it was in "substantial compliance" with the resolution.[140]

Iraq's Declaration on WMD

On February 12, 2003, Rep. Dennis Kucinich introduced a resolution of inquiry to give the House access to the 12,000-page Iraqi declaration on its weapons of mass destruction. The declaration had been provided to the UN Security Council on December 7, 2002. In his floor statement on H. Res. 68, Kucinich said that if the administration was intent on going to war against Iraq, "I believe it is incumbent upon them to make the document which was portrayed as evidence of an Iraqi threat available for all to evaluate." He asked that "the primary documents be transmitted in their complete and unedited form."[141]

The administration gave a copy of the declaration to the House on March 7, after which the House International Relations Committee voted to report H. Res. 68 adversely.[142] Rep. Doug Bereuter, who chaired the committee markup, said that the administration's release of the document rendered the resolution moot: "I would say, in short, Mr. Kucinich has won his point."[143] When the declaration reached the House on March 7, the Speaker directed the Permanent Select Committee on Intelligence to retain custody because of its facilities for handling classified documents. The declaration was available for review by members and to House staff "with appropriate security clearances who have executed a nondisclosure oath or affirmation."[144]

House resolutions of inquiry have been an effective means of obtaining factual material from the executive branch. Even when committees report the resolutions adversely or succeed in tabling them on the House floor, a substantial amount of information is usually released to Congress. Agreement that

---

139. "Treasury Says Congress Given Papers on Mexico," Washington Post, April 7, 1995, at F1.
140. 1995 CQ Almanac 10–17.
141. 149 Cong. Rec. H396 (daily ed. February 12, 2003).
142. CQ Today, March 13, 2003, at 16.
143. Id.
144. H. Rept. No. 108-38, 108th Cong., 1st Sess. 2 (2003).

the administration has complied with a resolution is frequently the reason for reporting it adversely and tabling it on the floor. On occasion, a resolution of inquiry is reported adversely because it competes with other investigations (either in Congress or in the executive branch) that are considered the more appropriate avenue for inquiry. In some situations, resolutions of inquiry have been instrumental in triggering other congressional methods of obtaining information, such as through supplemental hearings or alternative legislation.

Members turn to resolutions of inquiry for different reasons. A member may not be politically well positioned within a committee of jurisdiction to seek the information through regular investigatory procedures, or the committee might have advised the lawmaker that it had no intention of investigating the matter. Also, a resolution of inquiry is often a useful way for a member to bring attention to an issue, receive basic information from the administration, and perhaps spark more extensive legislative investigations. There is broad support within Congress whenever a member seeks factual information from the administration. Only in exceptional cases could an administration withhold from Congress facts that are readily available within the executive branch.

8

THE "SEVEN MEMBER RULE"

In 2001, seventeen Democrats and one Independent in the House invoked a seldom used statute, first enacted in 1928, that requires executive agencies to furnish information if requested by seven members of the House Committee on Government Reform or five members of the Senate Committee on Governmental Affairs. They sought census data from the Commerce Department. After the administration challenged the constitutionality of this statutory provision, a federal district court ruled in favor of the lawmakers.

This case, eventually mooted by the Ninth Circuit, raised the central question of what Congress needs to do to gain access to executive branch documents. Must congressional requests come only from the majority party, or may the minority operate effectively under the 1928 statute? May Congress act by committee, by a subgroup within a committee, or even by an individual member? Or does congressional access require action at least by a full chamber and perhaps even action by both chambers and presentation of a bill or resolution to the President?

Origin of the Statute

In 1928, as part of a statute that discontinued certain reports required to be made to the legislative branch, Congress added a section requiring every executive department and independent establishment of the federal government, upon request of "any seven members" of the House Committee on Expenditures in the Executive Departments, or "any five members" of the Senate Committee on Expenditures in the Executive Departments, to furnish "any information requested of it relating to any matter within the jurisdiction of said committee."[1] As presently codified, the statutory language requires an

---

1. 45 Stat. 996, §2 (1928).

"Executive agency," on request of seven members of the House committee or five members of the Senate committee, to submit "any information requested of it relating to any matter within the jurisdiction of the committee."[2]

The statutory language clearly gives seven members in the House and five members in the Senate, from the designated committees, the right to ask for certain executive information within the jurisdiction of their committee. One issue is the *type* of information that must be given to Congress. Part of the House legislative history suggests that the authority to request information is limited to what had been previously sent to Congress in agency reports, but was now being discontinued: "To save any question as to the right of the House of Representatives to have furnished any of the information contained in the reports proposed to be abolished, a provision has been added to the bill requiring such information."[3] Yet language on the same page of this House report suggests a much larger universe of information:

> The reports come in; they are not valuable enough to be printed, they are referred to committees, and that is the end of the matter. The departmental labor in preparation is a waste of time and the files of Congress are cluttered up with a mass of useless reports. If *any information* is desired by any Member or committee upon a particular subject that information can be better secured by a request made by an individual Member of committee, so framed as to bring out the special information desired.[4]

The House bill authorized access to executive branch information only by seven members of the designated House committee. In reporting the bill, the Senate decided to grant access to five members of its expenditure committee.[5] The Senate report included the language of the House report, but added language that seems to limit the request for agency information to what had been reported in the past in obsolete or useless reports: "This section makes it possible to require any report discontinued by the language of this bill to be resubmitted to either House upon its necessity becoming evident to the mem-

---

2. 5 U.S.C. § 2954 (2000). The codified language refers to the House Committee on Government Operations (now the Committee on Government Reform) and the Senate Committee on Governmental Affairs.

3. H.Rept. No. 1757, 70th Cong., 1st Sess. 6 (1928).

4. Id. (emphasis added). Floor debate in the House merely quotes the language of the section giving seven members of the House committee the right to request information from the executive branch. 69 Cong. Rec. 9417 (1928).

5. S. Rept. No. 1320, 70th Cong., 1st Sess. 1 (1928).

bership of either body."[6] Debate on the Senate floor reinforced that impression. The provision would enable either committee to "reinstate any report that was found to be needed."[7] The statutory language is broad, yet parts of the legislative history suggest a narrower field of information

In addition to disagreement about the type of information the two committees are entitled to receive, what legal remedies are available to Congress if an agency decides to ignore a request from seven members of the House committee or five members of the Senate committee? Would those legislators have to go to the full committee for support, or to the full chamber? Is their request enforceable in court?

Many of those issues were addressed during Senate hearings in 1975. Antonin Scalia, head of the OLC, testified on S. 2170, the Congressional Right to Information Act. Section 341(b) directed the head of a federal agency, "on request of a committee of the Congress or a subcommittee thereof or on request of two-fifths of the members thereof," to submit any information requested relating to matter within the jurisdiction of the committee or subcommittee. It was Scalia's position that committee action "normally presupposes majority support—and where this can not be achieved with respect to a proposed request for information from the Executive Branch, one suspects there would be good reason, based upon the unreasonableness of the request."[8]

Scalia compared S. 2170 to the "minority request" in the 1928 statute. He said the legislative history showed that "it did not represent a Congressional judgment that such a minority should have the power to demand all information, but rather only the information which was formerly contained in annual reports which the Congress abolished."[9] Congressional access, he said, applied only to "the information previously required." Any other interpretation, requiring presidential disclosure with respect to all material with a committee's jurisdiction, was of "questionable constitutionality."[10] Scalia regarded any provision that allowed a minority of a committee or subcommittee to obtain information from an executive agency as "surely extraordinary."[11]

---

6. Id. at 4.
7. 69 Cong. Rec. 10613 (1928) (statement by Senator Sackett).
8. "Executive Privilege—Secrecy in Government," hearings before the Subcommittee on Intergovernmental Relations of the Senate Committee on Government Operations, 94th Cong., 1st Sess. 105 (1975).
9. Id. at 107.
10. Id.
11. Id. at 106.

Subcommittee chairman Edmund S. Muskie moved Scalia from these general points to a specific: "Do you find it even more extraordinary for one Senator to ask for information? If it is extraordinary for two-fifths of the committee to ask for it, it is even more extraordinary for a single Senator to ask for information."[12] Scalia conceded that single Senators "are usually accommodated," but expressed concern that Section 341(b), if enacted, would "make it unlawful" for an executive official not to comply with a request that lacks support from a majority of the subcommittee.

Muskie took it to the next step: "That logic suggests that a single Senator ought not to ask for information, except as a matter of grace on the part of the executive, without getting the support of the majority of some committee."[13] Scalia said he had no objection to requests from individual members of Congress: "in the Justice Department and elsewhere we receive numerous requests from individual Senators and Congressmen which are complied with promptly." That response didn't satisfy Muskie, who charged that the "whole thrust" of Scalia's argument "is that we get information from the executive branch...only as a matter of grace," not as a matter "of constitutional right."[14]

Scalia held to his position that it was "extraordinary" to delegate to a minority of a subcommittee the authority to demand information that the majority of the subcommittee opposed.[15] As a matter of logic, he found it more reasonable "if the power were delegated to individual Senators."[16] However, Scalia assumed that a majority of a subcommittee might disagree with the minority's request. It might not. Also, the bill as a whole did not vest final authority in a minority. Under Section 342(a), an administration could decline to provide the information requested by two-fifths of a committee or subcommittee if the President, in writing, instructed an executive official to withhold the information and transmitted the instruction to the committee or subcommittee. At that point, the committee chairman, with the approval of the committee, was authorized under Section 343 to issue a subpoena requiring the executive officer to provide the information. Failure to comply with the subpoena would require the committee chairman to bring a civil action in the district court of the District of Columbia to enforce the subpoena.[17] Thus, the two-fifths minority marked only the first stage of a multi-step process that depended, in the end, on majority action.

---

12. Id. at 71.
13. Id.
14. Id. at 72.
15. Id.
16. Id. at 73.
17. Id. at 166.

Applying the Statute

Prior to the request in 2001, the 1928 statute had seen little action. Herman Wolkinson, an attorney in the Justice Department, discussed the statute in an article published in 1949. The statutory language might lead one to believe that "every executive department is obliged to furnish *any information*, when requested to do so, by the Committees on Expenditures of the House and Senate."[18] The legislative history convinced Wolkinson that the law "was not intended to enable the Committee on Expenditures to make blanket calls for information and papers upon the Executive Departments."[19] The purpose, he said, was to give the committees access only to "such information as they had theretofore been able to receive through the filing of the reports."[20] Notwithstanding the 1928 statute, the heads of departments could continue "to keep from public view matters which, in their judgment, should remain confidential."[21]

When Attorney General William Rogers appeared before the Senate Judiciary Committee in 1958, he identified a number of principles that guide the release of information to Congress. One principle indicated that there were limits on statutory efforts to obtain documents: "the legislative branch can make inquiry of the executive for its documents, but in response to congressional requests for documents, the executive should exercise a discretion as to whether their production would serve a public good or would be contrary to the public interest."[22] Rogers' testimony was guided by the Wolkinson study.[23]

Also in 1958, a subcommittee of the House Government Operations Committee held hearings on the withholding of information by the Agriculture Department. The subcommittee had twice asked for a copy of the original version of a pamphlet, "Farm Population Estimates for 1957," which was withheld from distribution. Each time the request was denied, with the explanation that the original version was a "working draft" that is "not available for

---

18. Herman Wolkinson, "Demands of Congressional Committees for Executive Papers" (Part III), 10 Fed'l Bar J. 319, 321 (1949) (emphasis in original).
19. Id. at 322.
20. Id.
21. Id. at 323.
22. "Freedom of Information and Secrecy in Government," hearing before the Subcommittee on Constitutional Rights of the Senate Committee on the Judiciary, 85th Cong., 2d Sess. 11 (1958).
23. Id. at 32–33. Wolkinson's analysis of the 1928 statute was included in the hearing record. Id. at 131–32.

release."[24] The second subcommittee request relied on the 1928 statute.[25] When the department again refused to comply, the subcommittee directed the assistant secretary to appear and to bring the original version of the document.[26] The department did so, and the original version was printed in the published hearings.[27] In withholding the document from the subcommittee, the department considered relying on executive privilege but soon dropped that as an argument.[28]

In 1970, seven members of the House Government Operations Committee asked the White House Office of Science and Technology for a report on a supersonic transport aircraft. William Rehnquist, as head of OLC, advised against releasing the report to the lawmakers. It was Rehnquist's position that the purpose of the 1928 statute "was to serve as a vehicle for obtaining information theretofore embodied in the annual routine reports to Congress submitted by the several agencies." To read the statute more broadly, he concluded, would bring it "into conflict with the constitutional prerogative of the President to withhold from Congress Executive branch documents the disclosure of which in his judgment does not comport with the national interest."[29] A broader reading, however, did not necessarily conflict with the constitutional authority of the President. If the report on the supersonic transport aircraft contained information that, if released, would be prejudicial to the national interest, the President could so state.

On September 20, 1994, twelve Republican members of the House Committee on Government Operations wrote to the Acting Director of the Office of Thrift Supervision, relying on the 1928 statute to request information regarding the failure of the Madison Guaranty Savings and Loan. The Acting Director complied with the request, while raising questions about whether the subject matter fell within the jurisdiction of the committee and whether release of the information might impair ongoing investigation of the company

---

24. "Withholding of Information by Department of Agriculture," hearing before a subcommittee of the House Government Operations Committee, 85th Cong., 2d Sess. 3 (1958) (letter from Assistant Secretary Don Paarlberg to Subcommittee Chairman L. H. Fountain, March 3, 1958).

25. Id. at 5.

26. Id. at 6.

27. Id. at 9, 63–74.

28. Id. at 32–33, 51–55

29. Letter from Rehnquist to Dr. Lee A. DuBridge, Director of the Office of Science and Technology, June 3, 1970, cited in "Memorandum of Law in Support of Plaintiff's Motion for Summary Judgment," Waxman v. Evans, Civil Action No. 01-04530 (LGB) (AJWx), August 3, 2001, at 15.

by an independent counsel.[30] Earlier that year, Republican members of the same committee invoked the 1928 statute to request documents from the Federal Deposit Insurance Corporation relating to a Texas savings and loan. Acting under the provisions of the 1928 statute, the corporation made the documents available to the lawmakers.[31] The previous year, on August 3, 1993, Chairman John Conyers and other members of the Government Operations Committee cited the 1928 statute as authority for requesting documents related to an equal employment opportunity complaint. The Merit Systems Protection Board released the documents with the understanding that the statute "compels [the agency] to disclose the information and material requested by the seven members of the Committee."[32]

The 1928 statute had not been adjudicated before the Waxman suit, although in two decisions federal courts made mention of it. A decision in 1971 footnotes a number of statutes, including the 1928 law, that require agencies to disclose information to Congress upon request.[33] A 1994 decision involved the effort of Rep. James Leach to obtain documents from the Resolution Trust Corporation and the Office of Thrift Supervision. He brought the action under the Freedom of Information Act (FOIA). A district court held that the lawsuit involved a dispute primarily between Leach and his fellow lawmakers, and for that reason it was inappropriate for the court to review the issues. The court noted that Leach had available to him a number of remedies, including an attempt to persuade the entire Congress, the House leadership, the chairman of the Banking Committee, or the committee as a whole to authorize his request for the documents. A footnote explained that if Leach was unable to gain the support of the majority party on the committee, he could avail himself of the 1928 statute, "through which small groups of individual congressmembers can request information without awaiting formal Committee action."[34]

The Waxman Request

Acting under the 1928 legislation, Rep. Henry A. Waxman, ranking member of the House Committee on Government Reform, wrote to Secretary of Commerce Donald L. Evans on April 6, 2001, requesting the adjusted census

---

30. Id. at 14.
31. Id.
32. Id. at 14–15.
33. Soucie v. David, 448 F.2d 106, 107, n. 9 (D.C. Cir. 1971).
34. Leach v. Resolution Trust Corp., 860 F.Supp. 868, 875 n. 7 (D.D.C. 1994).

data produced as part of the 2000 census.[35] Sixteen Democrats and one Independent from the committee signed the letter. The Census Bureau had compiled two sets of data. The population count determined by census forms returned by mail, supplemented by interviews conducted at addresses where no census form was returned, had been made public. A second set of data, using statistical techniques to correct for errors in the population count, was not released to the public. Relying on news reports, Waxman said that the unadjusted numbers released to the public "missed at least 6.4 million people and counted at least 3.1 million people twice."[36]

Waxman offered several reasons why his committee needed the information. The committee wanted the second set of data because it was "actively considering whether to amend the law regarding the timing and release of adjusted and unadjusted census data."[37] Second, the information "could have an enormous impact on the allocation by Congress of more than $185 billion in population-based federal grant funds."[38] Third, the information "could have a significant bearing on the appropriateness of congressional redistricting efforts currently being undertaken by state governments."[39] Waxman requested the adjusted data on or before April 20, 2001.

After receiving no response from the Commerce Department, Waxman wrote another letter to Evans, dated May 16, 2001.[40] Through phone calls from committee staff members, Waxman learned that the matter was under "active consideration" by the department's Office of General Counsel. He told Evans that if he did not receive a written response by the end of the week, he would conclude that the department had made a decision not to respond.[41]

District Court Decision

On May 18, Waxman and fifteen other members of the committee filed suit in federal district court, requesting declaratory and injunctive relief.[42] Three

---

35. Letter of April 6, 2001, from Rep. Waxman to Secretary Evans.
36. Id. at 1.
37. Id. at 2.
38. Id. at 2–3.
39. Id. at 3.
40. Letter of May 16, 2001, from Waxman to Evans.
41. Id.
42. Waxman v. Evans, Civil Action No. 01-04530, "Complaint for Declaratory and Injunctive Relief," May 18, 2001. Representatives Paul E. Kanjorski and Jim Turner, who had signed the April 6, 2001, letter to Evans, did not sign the Complaint.

months later, Waxman and the other plaintiffs filed a memorandum of law in support of a motion for summary judgment.[43] The brief argued that the Seven Member Rule compelled disclosure of the information, no exemption was claimed or applicable, and the use of "shall" in the statute mandated executive agencies to submit information requested by members of the committee.[44] Instead of identifying parts of the legislative history that suggested a limited reach to agency information, the brief cited the statutory adjective "any" (modifying "information") as evidence that the committee could request a broad range of information.[45] As to legislative history, the brief looked to language that encouraged lawmakers to make particularized, individual requests for information needed by the committee.[46]

Did Waxman and his colleagues have standing to sue in court? They referred to the Administrative Procedure Act as granting a cause of action, and empowering the district court to "compel agency action unlawfully withheld or unreasonably delayed."[47] It was a matter, they said, of enforcing a statutory right. Notwithstanding *Raines* v. *Byrd* (1997),[48] which denied standing to lawmakers who sued in their lawmaking capacity, the sixteen members said they were not suing in their lawmaking capacity, but rather to enforce a statutory right granted to them.[49]

The Justice Department filed its opposition to the plaintiff's motion on November 26.[50] The brief narrowed the issue to two disputes: the first between the executive and legislative branches over access to information possessed by executive officials, and the second between the minority and majority members of the House Committee on Government Reform. Justice advised the court to "decline to wade into this political thicket" and allow the controversy to be "sorted out in the political realm."[51] Moreover, even if the court decided the case, the plaintiffs's interpretation of the statute—singling out the words

---

43. Waxman v. Evans, Civil Action No. 01-04530 (LGB)(AJWx), "Memorandum of Law in Support of Plaintiff's Motion for Summary Judgment," August 8, 2001.
44. Id. at 1.
45. Id.
46. Id. at 1–2.
47. Id. at 18, citing 5 U.S.C. §§ 551(13), 706(1).
48. 521 U.S. 811 (1997).
49. "Memorandum of Law in Support of Plaintiff's Motion for Summary Judgment," at 20.
50. Waxman v. Evans, No. 01-04530-LGB (AJWx)," Secretary's Opposition to Plaintiffs' Motion for Summary Judgment and Memorandum in Support of Motion to Dismiss or, in the Alternative, Cross-Motion for Summary Judgment," November 26, 2001.
51. Id. at 1.

"shall" and "any"—ignored "entirely Congress's readily ascertainable purpose."[52] The government interpreted the statute as preserving access "to a limited universe of agency reports for members of two of Congress' numerous committees."[53] The legislative history "makes abundantly clear" that the statute "was merely intended to preserve access to the reports abolished by Section 1 of the Act."[54]

The Justice brief argued that the broader interpretation pressed by plaintiffs "would raise serious doubts about the constitutionality of the statute."[55] Justice warned that "[g]ranting unlimited access to agency files may cause unwarranted interference with the Executive branch function to 'take care that the laws be faithfully executed.'"[56] The "sweeping authority" advanced by the plaintiffs implied that an agency in possession of sensitive, national security material, or documents protected by executive privilege, "would have no choice…but to make the requested disclosure."[57] That was not a strong point. If Justice argued, as it did, that executive privilege is constitutionally based, no statute may dilute it. Justice also charged that the plaintiffs' interpretation was "constitutionally suspect, because this absolute power is proposed to be lodged not in any committee, or subcommittee, but in a mere fraction of the membership of only two of Congress' more than 40 full committees."[58]

On January 18, 2002, the district court ruled in favor of the plaintiffs. District Judge Lourdes G. Baird rejected the government's recommendation that the dispute should be "sorted out in the political realm" because "there is no room for compromise and cooperation."[59] In effect, the government's conduct made it clear that an accommodation was out of the question. Two letters from Waxman had been "to no avail."[60] As a result, the circumstances of the case "indicate that judicial intervention has become necessary to solve this inter-branch dispute."[61] Unlike some of the other cases cited by the government, where courts advised members of Congress that they could get relief by persuading their colleagues to repeal an objectionable statute, Judge

---

52. Id.
53. Id.
54. Id. at 10.
55. Id. at 2.
56. Id. at 18.
57. Id.
58. Id. at 19.
59. Waxman v. Evans, CV 01-4530 LGB (AJWx) (D. Cal. 2002), at 9.
60. Id. at 10.
61. Id.

Baird concluded that "Plaintiffs' rights cannot be vindicated by congressional repeal of a statute; rather, their rights may actually be vindicated by the effectuation of a statute."[62] She therefore denied the government's motion to dismiss.

Moving to the merits, Judge Baird ruled that the plain language of the Seven Member Rule "mandates that the Secretary release the requested data to Plaintiffs."[63] She cited Supreme Court decisions that "if no ambiguity in the plain statutory language is discerned, as in the instant situation, legislative history need not be consulted."[64] Nevertheless, "out of an abundance of caution,"[65] she examined what lawmakers had said in committee reports and floor statements. While it was clear that Congress intended either House to obtain information contained in discontinued reports, "such a recognition does not necessarily mean that the provision was designed to merely accomplish that narrow aim."[66] Because of ambiguity in the legislative history, she chose to follow "the text rather than the legislative history."[67]

Regarding the constitutional doubts raised by the government, Judge Baird recognized "the settled rule that a valid constitutional claim of Executive Privilege can defeat a congressional demand for information."[68] However, only after the government made an express claim of executive privilege would it be necessary for a court to consider "whether the disclosure provisions of the act exceeded the constitutional power of Congress to control the actions of the executive branch."[69] Earlier in her decision she indicated that a claim of executive privilege over adjusted census records would probably not be "viable."[70] She examined the government's claim that a constitutional issue exists because the congressional power to request information is not lodged in a committee or subcommittee but rather in a fraction of one committee. Baird noted that many committees and subcommittees give a single member of Congress (the chairman) the power to issue a subpoena.[71] Based on the available facts, she ordered Secretary Evans to release the requested census data to the plaintiffs.[72]

---

62. Id. at 12.
63. Id. at 15.
64. Id. at 16.
65. Id.
66. Id. at 18.
67. Id.
68. Id. at 19.
69. Id. at 20.
70. Id. at 8–9.
71. Id. at 20–21.
72. Id. at 21.

Request for Reconsideration

Following Judge Baird's decision, the government filed a memorandum in support of a motion for reconsideration.[73] Such motions are rare and usually unsuccessful. The motion implied that the government had prepared an inadequate brief the first time around and wanted to strengthen its case with arguments it had neglected to make. What new points could be offered to override the judge's skepticism? What had happened to elevate the importance of this case in the eyes of the Justice Department?

Quite likely the Waxman dispute became entangled with another case: *Walker v. Cheney*, in which Comptroller General David Walker relied on another statutory provision to demand documents from Vice President Dick Cheney. The Justice Department wanted to dismiss in each instance the capacity of Congress, either through its members or a legislative agency like the General Accounting Office, to use a compulsory process in court to obtain documents from the executive branch. The GAO case is discussed in the next chapter.

In the reconsideration motion, the government for the first time charged that the plaintiffs lacked Article III standing to sue and had no right of action in court either under the Seven Member Rule or the Administrative Procedure Act.[74] Moreover, the government now contended that the Seven Member Rule is a "rule of proceeding" within the meaning of Article I, §5, cl. 2, of the Constitution, and "has been superceded by House rules and is therefore no longer judicially enforceable."[75] It reiterated its position that Congress may not constitutionally delegate its investigatory powers to a few lawmakers and allow them to sue the executive branch to compel compliance with a request for information.[76]

In a separate brief on the reconsideration motion, the Justice Department argued that the court lacked authority to resolve "the quintessentially political dispute before it."[77] The court was unlikely to accept that position, given what appeared to be no chance of a political accommodation between the House members and the Commerce Department. This brief makes specific mention of *Walker v. Cheney*.[78]

---

73. Waxman v. Evans, No. 01-04530-LGB (AJWx), "Secretary's Memorandum in Support of Motion for Reconsideration," March 4, 2002.
74. Id. at 1.
75. Id. at 2.
76. Id. at 19.
77. Waxman v. Evans, No. 01-04-530-LGB (AJWx), "Secretary's Reply in Support of Motion for Reconsideration," March 25, 2002, at 2.
78. Id. at 18, n.13.

The plaintiffs opposed the motion for reconsideration, pointing out that Ninth Circuit law "makes clear that reconsideration is an 'extraordinary remedy' that may not be used to 'raise arguments...for the first time when they could reasonably have been raised earlier in the litigation.'"[79] The plaintiffs also found the government at error when it argued that Congress could not delegate to sub-parties the authority to acquire information, pointing to powers delegated to the GAO to gather information from the executive branch and the subpoena powers available to committees, subcommittees, and even individual committee chairmen.[80] Similarly, the plaintiffs found no merit in the argument that the Seven Member Rule had been superseded by subsequent House rules. Section 2954 is not an internal rule; it is a statute.[81]

In a brief opinion on March 21, 2002, Judge Baird denied the motion for reconsideration. She pointed out that although the plaintiffs discussed the standing issue in their opening brief, the government had not addressed that issue.[82] The government, in its initial brief, had also failed to raise arguments as to whether the plaintiffs possessed a judicially enforceable right of action, and whether the Seven Member Rule had been superseded by House rules.[83] She cited Ninth Circuit case law that a motion for reconsideration should not be granted, absent highly unusual circumstances, the presentation of newly discovered evidence, commitment of clear error, or an intervening change in controlling law.[84]

Briefs for the Ninth Circuit

In its appeal to the Ninth Circuit, the Justice Department repeated some of the arguments that had failed in district court: (1) the Seven Member Rule "marks a sharp departure from the settled means by which Congress seeks information from the executive branch," (2) those precedents preclude "small minorities from compelling disclosure of information when the majority believes that disclosure would be inappropriate or even harmful," and (3) there

---

79. Waxman v. Evans, No. 01-04530 (LGB) (AJWx), "Plaintiffs' Response to Defendant's Motion for a Stay," March 25, 2002, at 1 (citing Kona Enterprises, Inc. v. Estate of Bishop, 229 F.3d 877, 890 (9th Cir. 2000).
80. Id. at 17, 18.
81. Id. at 19–20.
82. Waxman v. Evans, No. CV 01-4530 LGB (AJWx) (D. Cal. 2002), at 3.
83. Id.
84. Id.

is a "general presumption that disputes between the branches will be resolved by political rather than judicial means."[85] The brief states that Congress "intended to preclude review of requests made under Section 2954 and to commit such decisions to the discretion of the executive branch."[86] How could there be a political resolution if the decision to release information to Congress is left solely to the discretion of the executive branch? The government also argued that the lawmakers lacked standing to bring the suit, but that if the Ninth Circuit were to grant standing, the lawmakers should have access only to what would be permitted under a restrictive reading of the 1928 statute: information from discontinued reports.[87]

The government brief acknowledged that Congress has authorized committees, subcommittees, and even committee chairmen to issue subpoenas,[88] but that enforcement of a subpoena requires a vote by the full chamber and dependence on a U.S. Attorney to file an action in federal court.[89] Allowing Waxman and the other lawmakers to file an enforcement action in their own name would be contrary to "[t]hat longstanding approach."[90] The government wavered on what Congress needed to do to obtain information from the executive branch. At times the test seemed to be "a majority of the House."[91] Elsewhere it insisted that even action by a full House would fail. Relying on *INS v. Chadha* (1983), the government stated that requests by Congress for information from the executive branch, since they affect the legal rights and duties of executive officials outside the legislative branch, would require bicameral action and presentment of a bill to the President for his signature or veto.[92] Under this analysis, the administration could ignore requests made under a House resolution of inquiry, but the political costs of pursuing this legal strategy would destroy the credibility and reputation of any administration.

The brief for Waxman and the other lawmakers argued that "[u]nder settled Ninth Circuit precedent, adjusted census data is not privileged and must be made available to anyone under the Freedom of Information Act...."[93] The brief repeated the district court's position that the case did not involve a claim

---

85. Waxman v. Evans, "Brief for the Appellant" (9th Cir.), May 10, 2002, at 5–6.
86. Id. at 6.
87. Id. at 8.
88. Id. at 21.
89. Id. at 22–23.
90. Id. at 23.
91. Id. at 12.
92. Id. at 8, 38.
93. Waxman v. Evans, "Brief for the Appellees" (9th Cir.), June 17, 2002, at 2.

of executive privilege, and that it was unlikely for the President to assert such a claim because the Seven Member Rule "applies only to agency records, and does not reach records of the President, his personal advisors, or White House staff."[94] As to the government's position that the Seven Member Rule merely allows lawmakers to ask for information, but not receive it, the Waxman brief stated that the government "points to no evidence" to support the theory that when Congress enacted § 2954 "it intended to render the provision unenforceable."[95]

Whereas the government asserted that § 2954 allows members of the two committees to request only documents from discontinued reports, the Waxman memo relied on statutory language and legislative history to argue for a broader universe of information: "If any information is desired by any Member or committee upon a particular subject that information can be better secured by a request made by an individual Member or committee, so framed as to bring out the special information desired."[96]

With regard to the government's argument that Congress "intended to preclude [judicial] review of requests made under Section 2954 and to commit such decisions to the discretion of the executive branch," the Waxman brief held that this argument "defies logic" and "depends on the submission that, when Congress enacted § 2954, it intended to render the provision a toothless tiger that agencies were free to ignore with impunity.... That submission is [at] war with the plain text of § 2954."[97] The government urged the court to dismiss lawsuits brought by members of Congress when the issue is essentially an intra-branch conflict, but the Waxman brief stated that the dispute raised by Waxman "is not with congressional colleagues.... [P]laintiffs do not seek to enact, amend or repeal legislation. They seek to enforce an existing statutory command against a federal officer...."[98]

Finally, the Waxman brief addressed the government's claim that under *INS v. Chadha*, legislative demands for information from the executive branch must comply with bicameralism and presentment. The distinction here is that "[a]lthough the Supreme Court has held that Congress may not *legislate* without action by both Houses,...it has never suggested that the Constitution places comparable limits on Congress' oversight and investigatory powers."[99]

---

94. Id. at 4.
95. Id. at 13.
96. Id. at 20 (citing H. Rept. No. 1757, 70th Cong., 1st Sess. 6 (1928)).
97. Id. at 34.
98. Id. at 50.
99. Id. at 54–55 (emphasis in original).

The Supreme Court has recognized the power of individual congressional committees to investigate and issue subpoenas.[100]

The House of Representatives submitted two amici briefs: one by the Office of General Counsel, and the other by the House Democratic Leadership. The first argued that executive-legislative struggles over access to information should be left to the political process, not to the courts. The second supports the district court ruling that §2954 mandates disclosure of the census data to Waxman and the other plaintiffs. The Office of General Counsel submitted its brief to the leadership of both parties, but the two Democratic leaders decided not to join. Thus, the brief represents only the views of the three Republican members of the bipartisan group: Speaker Dennis Hastert, Majority Leader Dick Armey, and Majority Whip Tom DeLay.

The House General Counsel brief pointed out that congressional efforts to obtain executive documents take place "almost entirely outside the judicial arena,"[101] through political negotiation, accommodation, compromise, and resort to subpoenas and contempt citations.[102] The district court's decision "would radically change the manner in which executive/legislative information access disputes are resolved," and would conflict with House rules "designed to maintain institutional control over the House's investigatory authority."[103] The point here is that the House, not the judiciary, should "decide what information is needed for legislative purposes, and when executive agencies may withhold information on matters such as national security or law enforcement."[104]

After reaching those judgments, the House General Counsel brief stated that Congress should be able to obtain executive documents needed for legislative and oversight functions, that the Commerce Department construed §2954 too narrowly, and that executive agencies have an obligation to respond "in good faith" to legislative requests under the 1928 statute.[105] When disputes arise under the 1928 statute, regarding congressional access to executive branch documents, resolution should be "through negotiation and accommodation, not through the judicial system."[106]

---

100. Id. at 55, citing McGrain v. Daugherty, 273 U.S. 135, 158, 160–61 (1927).
101. Waxman v. Evans, "Brief of Amicus Curiae Bipartisan Legal Advisory Group of the U.S. House of Representatives in Support of Reversal" (9th Cir.), May 21, 2002, at 1.
102. Id. at 2.
103. Id. at 3.
104. Id.
105. Id.
106. Id. at 4.

The two Democratic members, Minority Leader Dick Gephardt and Minority Whip Nancy Pelosi, filed a separate amicus brief, prepared by Charles Tiefer. It argued that the procedure for holding someone in contempt of Congress (requiring action by the full House or Senate) is distinct from statutes that mandate release of executive branch information to Congress.[107] The brief placed § 2954 in the "tradition of statutes mandating the public release of unprivileged Executive information, without resort to contempt powers or processes."[108] During the period from 1920 to 1927, each House consolidated oversight of executive branch expenditures in a single committee devoted to expenditure oversight, "capable of fully looking over the Executive Branch's documents."[109] Dismissing claims in the House General Counsel brief that the district court's ruling would "radically," "profoundly," and "drastically" change executive-legislative relations over information access disputes,[110] the Democratic brief described § 2954, like the Freedom of Information Act, "as a sensible mandatory disclosure statute for documents not subject to executive privilege."[111]

The Ninth Circuit held oral argument on the Waxman case along with a FOIA case brought by two Oregon lawmakers, who also sought access to the census documents. After argument, the two cases were submitted to the court for decision. On September 16, 2002, the court withdrew the submission of the Waxman case,[112] and on October 8 it decided the FOIA case in favor of the two lawmakers.[113] It rejected the government's argument that the adjusted data could be covered by the "deliberative process" privilege under Exemption 5 to FOIA. To the court, the data "were neither predecisional nor deliberative."[114] The Bush administration decided not to appeal.[115]

Although there was no final ruling on the Waxman case, the lawsuit revealed the extent to which the Justice Department would erect barriers to block legislative access to documents through compulsory process in court. In

---

107. Waxman v. Evans, "Brief of Amicus Curiae" (9th Cir.), June 21, 2002, at 3.
108. Id. at 4.
109. Id. at 7.
110. Id. at 13.
111. Id. at 15–16.
112. Waxman v. Evans, No. 02-55825 (9th Cir. 2002).
113. Carter v. U.S. Dept. of Commerce, 307 F.3d 1084 (9th Cir. 2002).
114. Id. at 1088.
115. Steven A. Holmes, "U.S. Won't Appeal Ruling on Release of Census Estimates," New York Times, November 23, 2002, at A15.

the end, the Justice Department argued that only by satisfying the standards of *Chadha*—bicameralism and presentment—could Congress enforce its demand for executive documents. Of course this greatly exaggerates the executive position, for agencies regularly surrender information in response to much lesser congressional actions, such as requests from individual members or through the House resolution of inquiry. Ironically, although 16 members of Congress were denied the census documents, they were turned over to two state lawmakers in a FOIA case. Evidently there were no legitimate grounds for the Commerce Department to initially withhold the documents. Finally, the 1928 law benefits the minority party when the majority in the House decides not to investigate the administration.

9

GAO INVESTIGATIONS

Congress relies on the General Accounting Office (GAO) to investigate executive agencies for inefficient and possibly corrupt practices. Various statutory authorities direct GAO to examine agency documents and papers. If agencies withhold documents, GAO has a number of options to force compliance, including efforts to gain the support of key lawmakers and committees. This chapter reviews the statutory authorities, the difficulties that GAO may encounter in gaining access to agency records, and the collision between GAO and Vice President Dick Cheney with regard to documents requested about the operation of the energy task force.

Statutory Authorities

Congress created the General Accounting Office in 1921 to strengthen legislative control over executive agencies. The enabling statute directed the Comptroller General, as head of GAO, to investigate "all matters relating to the receipt, disbursement, and application of public funds."[1] To enable the Comptroller General to perform that function, departments and establishments "shall furnish" information regarding the powers, duties, activities, organization, financial transactions, and methods of business "as he may from time to time require of them."[2] The Comptroller General and his assistants were to "have access to and the right to examine any books, documents, papers, or records of any such department or establishment."[3]

Comparable language appears in current law. The Comptroller General shall investigate "all matters related to the receipt, disbursement, and use of public money."[4] However, the scope of that investigative power is qualified by

---

1. 42 Stat. 25, §312(a) (1921).
2. Id. at 26, §313.
3. Id.
4. 31 U.S.C. §712 (2000).

other statutory provisions. When an agency record is not made available to the Comptroller General "within a reasonable time," the Comptroller General may issue what is called a "demand letter," which is a written request to the agency head, who has 20 days to describe the record withheld and the reason for its withholding. If the Comptroller General is not given an opportunity to inspect the record within the 20-day period, the Comptroller General may file a report with the President, the OMB Director, the Attorney General, the agency head, and Congress. Moreover, the Comptroller General may bring a civil action in federal court to require the agency head to produce a record and may subpoena a record of a person "not in the United States Government."[5]

The Comptroller General may not bring a civil action or issue a subpoena if the record relates to activities the President designates as "foreign intelligence or counterintelligence activities;" or if the record is specifically exempted from disclosure to the Comptroller General by a statute that "without discretion requires that the record be withheld from the Comptroller General," establishes particular criteria for withholding the record from the Comptroller General, or refers to particular types of records to be withheld from the Comptroller General; or by the twentieth day after the Comptroller General files a report regarding the withholding of a record the President or the OMB Director certifies to the Comptroller General and Congress that the record could be withheld under Exemptions 5 or 7 of the Freedom of Information Act "and disclosure reasonably could be expected to impair substantially the operations of the Government."[6] Those procedures, however, do not "authorize information to be withheld from Congress."[7]

Problems of Access

A 1960 Senate document provided examples over the previous five years in which the Defense Department, the State Department, and the National Aeronautics and Space Administration (NASA) had withheld information from GAO. These conflicts were reported to the Senate Committee on Government Operations and to other committees, sometimes leading to a resolution of the

---

5. Id. at §§716(b), 716(c).
6. Id. at §716(d). Exemption 5 of the FOIA refers to "inter-agency or intra-agency memorandums or letters which would not be available by law to a party other than an agency in litigation with the agency," while Exemption 7 covers certain records or information compiled for law enforcement purposes. 5 U.S.C. §552(b).
7. Id. at §716(e)(3).

dispute and sometimes not.[8] In the case of the State Department, Congress subsequently passed legislation to assist GAO in obtaining documents, even to the point of providing for a cutoff of agency funds 35 days after a refusal has been made to GAO or pertinent congressional committees, unless the information is delivered or the President certifies that he has forbidden its release and given his reasons.[9]

In 1972, Deputy Comptroller General Robert F. Keller told a congressional committee that GAO had received good cooperation in obtaining access to executive records except for the State Department, the Defense Department, and certain activities of the Treasury Department, the Federal Deposit Insurance Corporation, and the Emergency Loan Guarantee Board. He said that GAO had been experiencing "increasing difficulties" in obtaining access to information for programs involving U.S. relations with foreign countries.[10] In 1975, Comptroller General Elmer B. Staats told a House committee that GAO did not know how much the United States spent on intelligence. GAO had stopped auditing CIA expenditures in 1962 after being unable to obtain information, and had difficulty in getting information from other intelligence agencies, including the National Security Agency and the Defense Intelligence Agency.[11]

A 1979 study by Joseph Pois, a lawyer and professor of public administration, includes a chapter on GAO's access to information in executive agency and contractors' files and records. Much of the chapter is devoted to continuing GAO difficulty in obtaining documents from the Defense Department. Even when GAO ultimately prevailed or negotiated an acceptable compromise, lengthy delays detracted from the timeliness and usefulness of the eventual report.[12]

More recent studies describe the problems that GAO encounters in seeking information from the executive branch. A 1996 GAO report on National Intelligence Estimates (NIEs) stated that the scope of the study "was significantly impaired" by a lack of cooperation from the CIA, the National Intelligence Council, and the Departments of Defense and State. Officials from Defense and State referred GAO to CIA, which declined to cooperate, explaining that

---

8. S. Doc. No. 108, 86th Cong., 2d Sess. (1960).

9. Id. at 11–12; 73 Stat. 254, §401(i) (1959); 73 Stat. 720, §111(d) (1959).

10. 118 Cong. 18121 (1972).

11. Lawrence Meyer, "GAO Is Unable To Give Costs Of Intelligence," Washington Post, August 1, 1975, at A2.

12. Joseph Pois, Watchdog on the Potomac: A Study of the Comptroller General of the United States 115–59 (1979).

GAO review of certain NIEs would be contrary to oversight arrangements that Congress had established.[13] GAO requested statutory authority to expand its oversight role of CIA but has not received it.[14]

At House hearings in 1997, a GAO official described the problems that he and his colleagues had encountered in conducting a review of counternarcotics activities in Colombia. A lengthy screening program within the State Department delayed by several months delivery of documents to GAO. Moreover, the department denied access to some documents and deleted or redacted information from others.[15] The experience contrasted with State Department cooperation the previous two years when GAO conducted counternarcotics reviews in Colombia, Mexico, Bolivia, and Peru.[16]

In 1997, a subcommittee of the House Appropriations Committee held hearings on GAO's investigation of allegations that there had been 938 overnight guests in the Executive Residence of the White House. The subcommittee wanted to know whether the $550,000 in overtime pay for 36 full-time White House employees (maids, butlers, chefs, housekeepers, doormen, etc.) was related to these overnight stays. Seven months after the subcommittee had ordered the investigation, GAO was unable to comply because information had been withheld by the White House. The information was denied to GAO to "preserve the privacy of the First Family."[17] GAO had audited the Executive Residence in previous years without difficulty.[18]

On March 6, 2001, the GAO reported to the House Committee on International Relations regarding its study about U.S. participation in UN peacekeeping operations. After the Departments of State and Defense and the National Security Council had failed to provide GAO access to the records it requested, the Comptroller General issued "demand letters" to the head of each agency. After almost nine months of effort, GAO obtained from State

---

13. U.S. General Accounting Office, "Foreign Missile Threats: Analytic Soundness of Certain National Intelligence Estimates," GAO/NSIAD-96-225, B-274120, August 1996, at 15.

14. See Frederick M. Kaiser, "GAO Versus the CIA: Uphill Battles Against an Overpowering Force," 15 Int'l J. of Intell. & Counterintell. 330 (2002).

15. "International Drug Control Policy: Colombia," Hearing before the Subcommittee on National Security, International Affairs, and Criminal Justice of the House Committee on Government Reform and Oversight, 105th Cong., 1st Sess. 70 (1997).

16. Id. at 73.

17. "Treasury, Postal Service, and General Government Appropriations for Fiscal Year 1998 (Part 6: GAO Investigation of the White House)," hearings before a Subcommittee of the House Committee on Appropriations, 105th Cong., 1st Sess. 7 (1997).

18. Id. at 11.

"reasonable access" to records. Following the demand letter, Defense provided some material but GAO had access to only about one-quarter of the Defense records it had requested and many of those were heavily redacted. The NSC responded by denying GAO "full and complete access to the records."[19]

Access to FBI records continues to be a problem for the GAO. A report of June 20, 2001, disclosed that of all the law enforcement-related agencies, access to FBI records has been the "most sustained and intractable."[20] GAO's experience with the FBI "is by far our most contentious among law enforcement agencies."[21]

The GAO-Cheney Face-Off

GAO's statutory procedure for issuing a demand letter and taking a dispute to civil court were both used in 2001–02 in an effort to obtain information from Vice President Dick Cheney about his energy task force. Starting with little fanfare, the dispute escalated in intensity and publicity after Enron's bankruptcy in December 2001. As Enron executives came under fire for unethical and possibly criminal conduct, newspaper headlines began to suggest that Cheney's refusal to release documents to GAO might somehow be an obstruction of justice. That was a misconception, but misconceptions carry weight and are very difficult to correct. The controversy did damage to both Cheney and GAO. Several leading Republicans in the House and the Senate ripped the accounting agency and threatened deep cuts in its budget. The costs were so high that both sides looked for a graceful exit through some type of face-saving compromise.

A complicating factor in the GAO-Cheney standoff was Cheney's claim that the agency wanted to interfere with the "deliberative process" required for the executive branch. GAO insisted that it only wanted "facts" about the "development" and "formulation" of energy policy. At what point does a GAO inquiry into the development and formulation of energy policy shade into an

---

19. U.S. General Accounting Office, March 6, 2001 letter to Rep. Henry J. Hyde, Chairman, Committee on International Relations, and Rep. Benjamin Gilman, Chairman, Subcommittee on the Middle East and South Asia, Subject: U.N. Peacekeeping: GAO's Access to Records on Executive Branch Decision-making, at 2.

20. U.S. General Accounting Office, Testimony before the Senate Committee of the Judiciary, "GAO's Work at the FBI: Access to Data, Documents, and Personnel" (June 20, 2001), at 1.

21. Id. at 6.

investigation of the deliberative process? One analyst thought that if GAO were to prevail in this contest, it "could strengthen the ability of Congress, or even a single lawmaker, to find out details not only about the policy deliberations of federal agencies, but also about discussions in the West Wing."[22] That seems to me an overstatement, but the filing of a lawsuit is fraught with uncertainties for both sides.

The Legislative Request

The dispute began on April 19, 2001, when Representatives John Dingell and Henry Waxman wrote to Comptroller General David Walker, asking him to determine who served on the energy policy task force chaired by Vice President Cheney. It was their understanding that the task force had met in private with "exclusive groups of non-governmental participants—including political contributors—to discuss specific policies, rules, regulations, and legislation."[23] Dingell and Waxman, serving as ranking members of two committees with jurisdiction over federal energy policy (the House Committee on Energy and Commerce, and the House Committee on Government Reform), told Walker that they questioned the "apparent efforts of the task force to shield its membership and deliberations from public scrutiny."[24] The word "deliberations" would trigger a major dispute between the two legislators and the Vice President's office.

The April 19 letter directed GAO to produce a list of all task force members and staff, including their name, title, office, or employer represented. Moreover, the lawmakers wanted a list of all task force meetings, including the date, location, and duration of each meeting; the attendees at each task force meeting; the criteria used by the task force to determine which non-federal entities were invited to the meetings; the direct and indirect costs incurred by the task force; and other matters.[25]

On the same day, Dingell and Waxman wrote to Andrew Lundquist, executive director of the task force. They said it was their understanding that private meetings had been held at federal facilities "with the participation of both

---

22. Jill Barshay, "Risk Enough for All in *Walker v. Cheney*," CQ Weekly Report, March 2, 2002, at 562.
23. Letter of April 19, 2001, from Reps. Dingell and Waxman to Comptroller General Walker, at 1.
24. Id.
25. Id. at 2.

federal employees and private citizens and groups, including political contributors."[26] It was their concern that the closed-door meetings "may violate the letter and spirit of the Federal Advisory Committee Act (FACA)."[27] Attached to the letter were questions relating to the task force meetings, including some of the information requested of GAO, but also much more specific data: the purpose and outcome of each meeting; whether transcripts or detailed minutes of the meeting were kept; and whether invitations had been extended to governors, state public utility commissioners, representatives of organized labor, representatives of consumer advocacy groups, and small business representatives.[28] This information, including "copies of all documents and records produced or received by the task force," was to be delivered to the two lawmakers by May 4, 2001.[29]

On the date of the deadline, Cheney's counsel, David S. Addington, wrote to the two House committees, identifying both the chairmen (W. J. "Billy" Tauzin and Dan Burton) and the two ranking minority members, Dingell and Waxman. It was Addington's position that FACA did not apply to the task force because it "does not apply to a group 'composed wholly of full-time, or permanent part-time, officers or employees of the Federal Government.'"[30] However, as a matter of "comity between the legislative and executive branches," he provided information on the composition of the task force and pointed out that task force members "have met with many individuals who are not Federal employees to gather information relevant to the Group's work, but such meetings do not involve deliberations or any effort to achieve consensus on advice or recommendations."[31] The task force had met with "a broad representation of people potentially affected by the Group's work," including individuals from companies or industries from various sectors (electricity, telecommunications, coal mining, petroleum, gas, refining, bioenergy, solar energy, nuclear energy, pipeline, railroad and automobile manufacturing); environmental, wildlife, and marine advocacy; state and local utility regulation and energy management; research and teaching at universities; research and analysis at policy organizations (think-tanks); energy

---

26. Letter of April 19, 2001, from Reps. Dingell and Waxman to Andrew Lundquist, at 1.
27. Id.
28. Id. (three pages of "Questions for Andrew Lundquist").
29. Id. at 1.
30. Letter of May 4, 2001, from David S. Addington, Counsel to the Vice President, to Reps. Tauzin, Dingell, Burton, and Waxman, at 1.
31. Id. at 1 and page 2 of "Responses of Andrew Lundquist."

consumers; a major labor union; and about three dozen members of Congress and their staff.[32]

Addington's letter provided the dates and locations of all task force meetings and the general purpose and outcome of the meetings.[33] With regard to questions about whether the meetings were noticed in advance, open to the public, and on the record, an attachment to the letter explained that Section 3(2) of FACA provides that the term "advisory committee" excludes "any committee that is composed wholly of full-time, or permanent full-time, officers or employees of the Federal Government."[34]

On May 15, 2001, Dingell and Waxman wrote to Lundquist and told him it was inappropriate to refuse the records they requested. Lundquist's actions, they said, "only serve to deepen public suspicion over the administration's apparent efforts to shield the membership and deliberations of the task force and its staff from public scrutiny."[35] In order to help Lundquist "better understand" their request for records, they attached a definition that included such items as minutes, drafts, notes, logs, diaries, video recordings, e-mails, voice mails, and computer tapes.[36] In subsequent months, GAO would back away from the breadth of that definition and scale down its request.

---

32. Responses of Andrew Lundquist, at 2–3.

33. Id. at 3.

34. Id. at 4. Actually, the exemption in FACA reads: "any committee which is composed of full-time officers or employees of the Federal Government." 86 Stat. 770, §3(2)(C) (1972); 5 U.S.C. App. §3(2)(c) (1994).

35. Letter of May 15, 2001, from Dingell and Waxman to Lundquist, at 1.

36. Id. at 3. The definition construed "records" in the "broadest sense and shall mean any written or graphic material, however produced or reproduced, of any kind or description, consisting of the original and any non-identical copy (whether different from the original because of notes made on or attached to such copy or otherwise) and drafts and both sides thereof, whether printed or recorded electronically or magnetically or stored in any type of data bank, including, but not limited to, the following: correspondence, memoranda, records, summaries of personal conversations or interviews, minutes or records of meetings or conferences, opinions or reports of consultants, projections, statistical statements, drafts, contracts, agreements, purchase orders, invoices, confirmations, telegraphs, telexes, agendas, books, notes, pamphlets, periodicals, reports, studies, evaluations, opinions, logs, diaries, desk calendars, appointment books, tape recordings, video recordings, e-mails, voice mails, computer tapes, or other computer stored matter, magnetic tapes, microfilm, microfiche, punch cards, all other records kept by electronic, photographic, or mechanical means, charts, photographs, notebooks, drawings, plans, interoffice communications, intra-office and intra-departmental communications, transcripts, checks and canceled checks, bank statements, ledgers, books, records or statements of accounts, and papers and things similar to any of the foregoing, however denominated."

Challenging GAO's Legal Authority

The dispute sharpened on May 16, 2001, when Addington wrote to Anthony Gamboa, GAO's General Counsel, raising questions about a GAO fax transmittal sheet that asked to interview officials of the energy task force and the group's support staff. The fax explained that it was GAO's intent "to review the composition and workings of the President's Energy Policy Development Group." To Addington, GAO was seeking to inquire "into the exercise of the authorities committed to the Executive by the Constitution, including the authority to 'require the Opinion, in writing, of the principal Officer in each of the executive Departments, upon any Subject relating to the Duties of their respective Offices,' to 'take Care that the Laws be faithfully executed,' and, with respect to Congress, to 'recommend to their Consideration such Measures as he shall judge necessary and expedient.'" After citing these constitutional duties, Addington said it appeared that GAO "may intend to intrude into the heart of Executive deliberations, including deliberations among the President, the Vice President, members of the President's Cabinet, and the President's immediate assistants, which the law protects to ensure the candor in Executive deliberations necessary to effective government."[37] He closed by urging Gamboa to ask the Comptroller General to examine whether "the proposed inquiry is appropriate, in compliance with the law, and, especially in light of the information already provided as a matter of comity, a productive use of resources." Addington recommended that Walker "not proceed with the proposed inquiry." If Walker decided to go forward, Addington asked Gamboa to send a statement of GAO's legal authority.[38]

It took GAO two weeks to prepare a memo on its legal authorities. In the meantime, Dingell and Waxman wrote to Addington that they were "dismayed" by his letter questioning GAO's authority to conduct an investigation. Congressional oversight of the executive branch, they said, "includes the ability to examine all deliberations."[39] They asked whether the administration was relying on executive privilege, which can be invoked only by the President. If that was the intent, they wanted to receive clarification directly from President George W. Bush.[40] Executive privilege was never invoked. Dingell and Waxman closed by stating it "is a shame" that the Cheney task force "has begun deliberations" with such a "determined attitude of secrecy and stonewalling."

---

37. Letter of May 16, 2001, from Addington to GAO General Counsel Anthony Gamboa, at 1.
38. Id. at 2.
39. Letter of May 22, 2001, from Dingell and Waxman to Addington, at 1.
40. Id.

They said that Congress and the public had a right to know how the energy policy "was developed, including what special interests were consulted, what influence they had, and how competing interests were reconciled."[41]

Over time, the emphasis on "deliberations" by Dingell, Waxman, and GAO would be replaced by asking how the policy was developed and formulated. GAO seemed to think that an inquiry into *policy formulation* is not as intrusive as one into *policy deliberation*. Distinctions in this area are difficult to understand. For example, when Gamboa wrote to Addington on June 1, 2001, explaining GAO's legal authority to conduct the investigation, the subject of the letter is entitled "GAO's Review of the Development of the Administration's National Energy Policy."[42] The key word was now *development*. As to Addington's concern that GAO was intruding "into the heart of Executive deliberations," Gamboa insisted that GAO's legal authority "extends to deliberative process information." However, in the particular investigation of the Cheney task force, Gamboa said "we are not inquiring into the deliberative process but are focused on gathering factual information regarding the process of developing President Bush's National Energy Policy."[43] Gamboa denied that GAO "at this time" was requesting an interview with Cheney "or cabinet officials." He did want GAO to interview Lundquist and "other officials" involved in the energy task force.[44]

The first mention of Enron Corporation appears in a June 5, 2001, letter from Waxman to Representative Dan Burton, chairman of the House Committee on Government Reform. Waxman cites a May 25, 2001, *New York Times* article that the head of Enron, Kenneth L. Lay, had met with Cheney for thirty minutes earlier in the spring and that the task force report "includes much of what Mr. Lay advocated during their meeting." The article points out that Enron was a major donor to Republican causes.[45] Waxman told Burton that Congress and the public "have the right to know how the Administration develops policy in important areas such as energy issues, and the extent to which large donors are influencing such policy."[46] He urged Burton to hold hearings on the Cheney task force to examine a number of matters, including "meetings attended by nonfederal participants," the purpose of each meeting, and "what was discussed."[47]

---

41. Id. at 2.
42. Letter of June 1, 2001, from Gamboa to Addington, at 1.
43. Id.
44. Id. at 2.
45. Letter of June 5, 2001, from Waxman to Rep. Dan Burton, Chairman, House Committee on Government Reform, at 1.
46. Id. at 2.
47. Id.

On June 7, 2001, Addington wrote to Gamboa and commented upon the three statutes identified by GAO as the legal basis for its inquiry. Addington concluded that two of the statutes provided no legal basis for the inquiry, and the third statute provided a legal basis for only a limited inquiry. The first statute requires the Comptroller General to "evaluate the results of a program or activity the Government carries out under existing law" when a committee of Congress with jurisdiction over the program or activity "requests the evaluation."[48] Addington said that this statutory provision did not justify the GAO inquiry because (1) the task force functioned under executive authorities granted by the Constitution and thus was not a program or activity carried out "under existing law," and (2) the Dingell-Waxman request did not constitute a "request" from a "committee of Congress with jurisdiction over the program or activity."[49]

The second statute provided that each agency shall give the Comptroller General information that the Comptroller General requires about the duties, powers, activities, organization, and financial transactions of the agency, allowing the Comptroller General to inspect an agency record to get the information.[50] Addington said that this provision of law provided only "the means for conducting an otherwise authorized investigation," but even those investigations are limited by other legal authorities and privileges, "such as the constitutionally-based Executive privilege."[51] Bush did not invoke executive privilege in this dispute.

The third provision of law authorizes the Comptroller General to investigate "all matters related to the receipt, disbursement, and use of public money."[52] Addington promised to provide Gamboa with the direct and indirect costs incurred by Cheney and the task force staff. Addington also attached a presidential memorandum of January 29, 2001, establishing the Cheney task force. The memo lists the officers of the task force, its mission, required reports, and funding by the Department of Energy.

The Demand Letter

Three weeks later, Gamboa sent Addington a ten-page letter defending GAO's legal authority to conduct the inquiry. Gamboa argued that the three

---

48. Letter of June 7, 2001, from Addington to Gamboa, at 1, citing 31 U.S.C. §717(b)(3).
49. Id. at 2.
50. Id., citing 31 U.S.C.§716(a).
51. Id.
52. Id. at 3, citing 31 U.S.C. §712.

statutes and their legislative histories provided adequate authority to justify the inquiry.[53] As to responding to a request from Dingell and Waxman instead of a committee, Gamboa maintained that GAO's "Congressional Protocols" (practice rather than law) placed requests from "committee leaders" among GAOs top priorities for response.[54] Gamboa told Addington that the Comptroller General was prepared to issue a "demand letter" if he did not receive timely access to the information outlined in the GAO letter of June 1, 2001.[55]

Comptroller General Walker sent the demand letter on July 18, 2001, requiring Cheney to respond within twenty days. Walker said that his study "focuses on factual information, not the deliberative process."[56] However, the factual information was requested to understand "the development" of the administration's energy policy.[57] At what point does factual information edge into the deliberative process? Walker asked for (1) the names, titles, and offices represented by the attendees at each of the nine meetings conducted by the task force, (2) the names, titles, and offices of the six professional staff assigned to Cheney's office to support the task force, (3) the dates and locations of meetings between task force staff and individuals from the private sector, (4) the names, titles, and offices of those individuals, (5) the purpose and agenda of those meetings, (6) minutes or notes, (7) how the task force determined who would be invited to these meetings, (8) the same information (dates, locations, names, titles, offices, purpose and agenda, minutes or notes, and criteria for invitations) for the meetings that Cheney had, and (9) direct and indirect costs of the task force.[58] Much of this requested information (such as minutes or notes) would be dropped from subsequent GAO requests.

Cheney, refusing to release the names, said that if he responded to GAO's request "any member of Congress can demand to know who I meet with and what I talk to them about on a daily basis."[59] He stated that after meeting with outside groups, those private interests "were not in the meetings where we put together the policy and made the recommendations to the president. That's the big difference."[60] In a letter of August 2, 2001, Cheney told the

---

53. Letter of June 22, 2001, from Gamboa to Addington.
54. Id. at 8.
55. Id. at 2.
56. Letter of July 18, 2001, from Walker to Cheney, at 1.
57. Id.
58. Id. at 1–2.
59. Joseph Curl, "Cheney Refuses Demand by GAO," Washington Times, July 27, 2001, at A1, A16.
60. Id. at A16.

House of Representatives that Walker had exceeded his lawful authority by trying to "unconstitutionally interfere with the functioning of the Executive Branch."[61]

An appendix to the letter gave reasons for Cheney's refusal. First, it said that GAO was not evaluating the "results" of the task force; it was "attempting to inquire into the process by which the results of the Group's work were reached." Second, the statutes giving GAO authority to obtain documents from executive agencies did not apply because the term "agency" as used in those statutes "does not include the Vice President of the United States, who is a constitutional officer of the Government." Third, GAO would unconstitutionally interfere with the functioning of the executive branch. Its proposed inquiry as to how the President, the Vice President, and other senior advisers "execute the function of developing recommendations for policy and legislation" involved "a core constitutional function of the Executive Branch."[62]

Here the administration uses the same word that GAO had highlighted in its earlier letters: the development of policy.[63] A statement by GAO on August 6, 2001, insisted that the information it requested from the administration "is purely factual in nature and relates solely to the process used by the group."[64] How does one distinguish between the "process used" and the "deliberative process"?

GAO issued its "last best offer" to Cheney on August 17, 2001. Walker explained that the records sought "would not reveal communications between the President and his advisers and would not unconstitutionally interfere with the functioning of the executive branch."[65] He said he was not asking for "any communications involving the President, the Vice President, or the President's senior advisers."[66] Walker now boiled down his request to four categories: (1) the names present at the task force meetings, (2) the names of the professional staff assigned to the task force, (3) who the task force met with, including the date, subject, and location of the meetings, and (4) the direct and indirect costs incurred in developing the energy policy.[67] Walker re-

---

61. Letter of Aug. 2, 2001, from Cheney to the House of Representatives.
62. Id. (Appendix Two: Reasons).
63. GAO Letters of June 1 and June 22, 2001, from Gamboa to Addington, the subject of the letters being "GAO's Review of the Development of the Administration's National Energy Policy."
64. GAO Statement, Auust. 6, 2001.
65. Letter of August 17, 2001, from Walker to Cheney, at 1.
66. Id. at 4.
67. Id. at 2.

minded Cheney that in a previous letter GAO had offered to eliminate the earlier request for minutes and notes and for the information presented by private individuals. As a "matter of comity," Walker now excluded those two items from his request.[68]

Walker's letter to Cheney triggered a provision in law that authorizes the President or the Director of the Office of Management and Budget to "certify" that the information requested by GAO could not be made available for various reasons, including that "disclosure reasonably could be expected to impair substantially the operations of the Government."[69] Certification would permanently block a GAO lawsuit, and yet the administration chose not to issue a certification. Bottom line: If you want to go to court, go ahead.

Going to Court

By September 7, 2001, after the requested materials were not delivered, Walker began to prepare for the lawsuit. He said he expected to file by the end of the month.[70] However, the terrorist attacks of September 11 caused GAO to delay filing out of deference to an administration hard-pressed by the crisis.[71] With the administration strained by the need to obtain emergency legislation and to prosecute the war in Afghanistan, Walker decided to wait.

Two developments early in 2002 rekindled the GAO-Cheney dispute. First, after Enron declared bankruptcy in December 2001, the press began to highlight the meetings it had with the energy task force. Second, the administration for some reason disclosed that Cheney and his aides had met with Enron six times in 2001.[72] If that type of information could be released by the administration, why not the rest? When exceptions are made to a principle, the principle can begin to look a little threadbare.

On January 24, 2002, Dingell and Waxman wrote to Walker, urging him to proceed with a lawsuit. The need for the information "has only increased over time, particularly with recent questions concerning the influence of officials

---

68. Id.
69. 31 U.S.C. §716(d)(1)(C).
70. Ellen Nakashima, "GAO Prepares to Sue Cheney Over Records," Washington Post, September 8, 2001, at A13; Joseph Kahn, "Federal Agency Likely to Sue White House," New York Times, September 8, 2001, at A10.
71. Michael Grunwald and Ellen Nakashima, "Amid War, GAO Puts Legal Fight With Cheney on Hold," Washington Post, November 9, 2001, at A35.
72. Mike Allen, "Cheney, Aides Met With Enron 6 Times in 2001", Washington Post, January 9, 2002, at A3.

of Enron in the development of the National Energy Policy."[73] Walker announced the following day that he would sue the White House if it did not comply with his demands.[74] Newspaper headlines and subheads kept the spotlight on Enron. A subhead in the *Washington Post* declared: "Hill Probes Enron Influence on Task Force."[75] Cheney, defending his position on "Fox News Sunday," argued that "what's really at stake here is the ability of the president and the vice president to solicit advice from anybody they want in confidence—get good, solid, unvarnished advice without having to make it available to a member of Congress."[76]

Some Republicans began to desert the administration. Walker said that Senator Fred Thompson (R-Tenn.) and Rep. Christopher Shays (R-Conn.) wanted the White House to release the information.[77] Thompson, after deciding that the law favored the administration, thought release of the records would be politically wise.[78] Similarly, Rep. Dan Burton (R-Ind.) concluded that Cheney's legal position was stronger than GAO's, but counseled the administration to release the records to secure public trust.[79] Senator Charles E. Grassley (R-Iowa) advised the White House to release the information.[80]

On January 30, 2002, Walker announced that he would file a case in district court in order to obtain the documents he requested from the energy task force.[81] It was necessary to take this action, he said, because Congress

> has a right to the information we are seeking in connection with its consideration of comprehensive energy legislation and its ongoing oversight activities. Energy policy is an important economic and environmental matter with significant domestic and international implications. It affects the lives of each and every American. How it is formulated has understandably been a longstanding interest of the

---

73. Letter of January 24, 2002, from Dingell and Waxman to Walker, at 2.
74. Dana Milbank and Dan Morgan, "GAO Vows to Sue for Cheney Files," Washington Post, January 26, 2002, at 1.
75. Id.
76. Dana Milbank, "Cheney Refused Records' Release," Washington Post, January 28, 2002, at A12.
77. Id.
78. Richard A. Oppel, Jr. and Robert Pear, "G.O.P. Senators Divide Over Disclosing Information on Enron-White House Contacts," New York Times, January 30, 2002, at C6.
79. Jill Barshay, "Risk Enough for All in *Walker* v. *Cheney*," CQ Weekly Report, March 2, 2002, at 563.
80. Id.
81. Letter of January 30, 2002, from Walker to Waxman, at 3.

Congress. In addition, the recent bankruptcy of Enron has served to increase congressional interest in energy policy....[82]

On the same day, Dingell and Waxman wrote to Cheney to clarify what they considered to be misconceptions about the GAO inquiry. They agreed that the President and the Vice President are "generally entitled to confidentiality when discussing federal policies with senior White House staff." However, "confidentiality for discussions among the President and the Vice President and their top aides does not extend to external communications to the White House from outside groups."[83] Included in the letter were twelve recent precedents where GAO sought and received records of communications between outside groups and the White House.[84] Dingell and Waxman noted that President Bush "did not make—and could not reasonably have made—the certification required under section 716 for withholding the information."[85]

With Cheney taking a pounding in the press, Walker was not coming off unscathed either. Part of the criticism directed at Walker was the use of language that was unusual, if not unprecedented, for a Comptroller General. Because GAO is a nonpartisan agency funded by Congress, it is usually extremely cautious and circumspect in making public statements. Yet when Cheney said the task force could not be scrutinized because he headed it in his capacity as Vice President, Walker replied: "If all you have to do is create a task force, put the vice president in charge, detail people from different agencies paid by taxpayers, outreach to whomever you want and then you can circumvent Congressional oversight, that's a loophole big enough to drive a truck through."[86] After hearing Cheney object that GAO was overstepping its bounds, Walker remarked: "Talk is cheap."[87]

These and other comments prompted charges that GAO was conducting an overzealous and partisan inquiry. To House Majority Leader Dick Armey (R-Tex.), GAO "is being pressured here on a partisan political basis, and they are wrong."[88] Senator Ted Stevens (R-Alas.), the ranking member of the Ap-

---

82. Id. at 2.
83. Letter of January 30, 2002, from Walker to Cheney, at 2.
84. Id. at 4–6.
85. Id. at 7.
86. Stephen Labaton and Richard A. Oppel, Jr., "Bush Says Privacy Is Needed On Data From Enron Talks," New York Times, January 29, 2002, at A1.
87. Elizabeth Bumiller, "Cheney Is Set to Battle Congress To Keep His Enron Talks Secret," New York Times, January 28, 2002, at A1.
88. Dave Boyer, "GOP terms GAO's request a partisan hunt," Washington Times, January 30, 2002, at A4.

propriations Committee, said he was "appalled" at GAO's pursuit of the White House documents. He argued that the principle of separation of powers prevented such investigations,[89] and warned that the lawsuit could mark the decline of GAO.[90]

GAO finally filed its long-delayed lawsuit on February 22.[91] Other suits, filed under the Freedom of Information Act, also sought documents on the administration's energy policy. In one of these cases, a federal judge on February 27 ordered the Energy Department to turn over 7,500 pages of documents related to the Cheney task force.[92] On March 6, another federal judge in a FOIA case ordered seven government agencies to release thousands of documents related to the Cheney task force.[93] Several other courts were involved in lawsuits seeking documents from the task force.[94] In addition to information made available from litigation, reporters were talking directly to private groups involved in the task force meetings. A lengthy article in the *New York Times* identified the energy companies that met with the task force and contributions they made to the Republican and Democratic Parties in the 2000 election.[95] Some of the industry officials who met with the task force expressed surprise at the effort to keep the names secret: "Within the industry, there's this feeling like, 'Don't we already know who was there?'"[96]

The Court Decides

On December 9, 2002, District Judge John D. Bates dismissed the GAO complaint by holding that Comptroller General Walker lacked standing to bring the suit.[97] Walker, said the court, had suffered no personal jury, and

---

89. Id.
90. Jill Barshay, "GAO's Walker Says He Hopes To Avoid Court Fight With Cheney Over Energy Task Force Documents," CQ Weekly Report, February 9, 2002, at 396.
91. Don Van Natta, Jr., "Agency Files Suit For Cheney Papers on Energy Policy," New York Times, February 23, 2002, at A1.
92. Dana Milbank and Ellen Nakashima, "Energy Dept. Ordered To Release Documents," Washington Post, February 28, 2002, at A1.
93. Don Van Natta, Jr., "Judge Orders More Papers on Task Force Released," New York Times, March 6, 2002, at A18.
94. "Judges Knock Cheney Panel Court Efforts," Washington Post, March 1, 2002, at A5.
95. Don Van Natta, Jr. and Neela Banerjee, "Top G.O.P. Donors in Energy Industry Met Cheney Panel," New York Times, March 1, 2002, at A1.
96. Id. at A15.
97. Walker v. Cheney, 230 F.Supp.2d 51 (D.D.C. 2002).

any institutional injury would exist only "in his capacity as an agent of Congress—an entity that itself has issued no subpoena to obtain the information and given no expression of support for the pursuit of this action."[98] Walker had identified only two Congressmen (Dingell and Waxman) "and four Senators who have expressed support for his investigation as a general matter, and has not identified any Member of Congress (other than *amicus* Senator Reid) who has explicitly endorsed his recourse to the Judicial Branch."[99] When the case was before the court, Cheney's counsel noted that Congress "has 'plenty of practical leverage' to get the requested information, including refusing to act on the President's energy proposal until the information is produced."[100]

To obtain documents from the executive branch, Congress must be willing to use its considerable leverage and press its advantage. In this dispute, Congress and its committees decided not to do that, and Judge Bates interpreted the congressional silence as a grave weakness to GAO's position. Comptroller General Walker found himself, politically and institutionally, isolated. After checking with lawmakers in both Houses, Walker found inadequate support to continue the fight and announced that he would not seek an appeal.[101] He announced his willingness, "should the facts and circumstances warrant, to file suit to press our access rights in connection with a different matter in the future." However, on such occasions he would not step out alone: "I believe it would be appropriate to have an affirmative statement of support from at least one full committee with jurisdiction over any records access matter prior to any future court action by GAO."[102]

Lieberman's Subpoenas

Throughout this period, none of the committees or subcommittees of Congress had issued a subpoena for documents concerning the energy task force. On March 22, 2002, the Senate Committee on Governmental Affairs, chaired by Senator Joseph Lieberman (D-Conn.), issued 29 subpoenas to Enron to

---

98. Id. at 74.
99. Id. at 68.
100. Id. at 68, n.12.
101. Dana Milbank, "GAO Ends Fight With Cheney Over Files," Washington Post, February 8, 2003, at A4; Adam Clymer, "Agency Ends Pursuit of Cheney Energy Panel Data," New York Times, February 8, 2003, at A32.
102. 149 Cong. Rec. H433 (daily ed. February 12, 2003).

document its relationship to the administration's energy task force.[103] At the same time, Lieberman said he would write letters to the White House seeking information about its contacts with Enron, instead of resorting to subpoenas.[104] In response to Lieberman's letter, White House Counsel Alberto Gonzales directed more than 100 staff members to complete a questionnaire that would detail communications between the administration and Enron in the months just before the company's collapse.[105] These White House efforts were made under the threat of a subpoena that Lieberman held in reserve.[106]

As the weeks rolled by, Lieberman expressed dissatisfaction with the lack of progress.[107] Although Gonzales asked that the subpoena not be issued,[108] Lieberman decided on May 22, 2002, to subpoena the documents—the first congressional subpoenas on the Bush administration.[109] Four hours after the subpoenas were delivered, the White House faxed Lieberman a six-page letter showing that Enron executives had a number of meetings and phone calls with White House officials that had been previously disclosed.[110] The subpoenas flushed out a number of documents and e-mails related to White House communications with Enron.[111] In some cases, the White House refused to make copies of Enron-related documents but allowed Lieberman's staff to come to the Eisenhower Executive Office Building, which is next to the White House, and look at some of them.[112]

---

103. Dana Milbank, "Senate Panel Says Enron Must Detail Policy Role," Washington Post, March 23, 2002, at A1.
104. Id.
105. "White House Staff to Answer Enron Questionnaire," Washington Post, April 30, 2002, at A2; .
106. Richard A. Oppel, Jr., "Senator Presses for Information on Enron," New York Times, May 4, 2002, at B3; "Lieberman Angered by Response on Enron," Washington Post, May 4, 2002, at A5.
107. Mike Allen, "Subpoena Urged on Enron Records," Washington Post, May 18, 2002, at A7; Richard A. Oppel, Jr., "Senate Democrats Escalate Efforts to Get White House To Disclose Enron Contacts," New York Times, May 18, 2002, at B1.
108. "White House Asks Subpoena Not Be Issued," Washington Post, May 22, 2002, at A19.
109. Mike Allen, "Panel Demands Enron Papers," Washington Post, May 23, 2002, at A1.
110. Id.
111. Mike Allen, "White House Gathers Enron Data," Washington Post, May 25, 2002, at A4.
112. Mike Allen, "White House Gives Lieberman Limited Access to Enron Data," Washington Post, June 4, 2002, at A2. See also "Senate Panel Gets Some Enron Data," Washington Post, June 5, 2002, at A4.

The Waxman-Dingell request can be described as a "gotcha" legislative tactic: An effort by lawmakers to put the administration immediately on the defensive and possibly unearth some damaging information useful in political campaigns. No doubt a relatively small legislative investment in time and energy can put a White House in a tail-spin as it begins the laborious search for documents. An alternative is to concoct strained legal arguments that deny the lawmakers the documents, but at risk of appearing to engage in a cover-up or obstruction of justice. In the end, regardless of the merits of the legal doctrines, the documents are likely to become public anyway.

In the face of what appears to be a win-win legislative strategy, is the administration without a remedy? Resourceful executive officials have a number of ways to discourage or blunt a legislative inquiry. In the case of the energy task force, the administration came to power with a conspicuous spotlight trained on the business/industry backgrounds of President Bush, Vice President Cheney, Defense Secretary Don Rumsfeld, and other top officials. It would have been prudent for the administration to go out of its way by meeting with a plethora of environmental, consumer, and labor unit groups. When the time came for a legislative investigation of the energy task force, the administration could have released a lengthy list of the groups it met with, without embarrassment. If an administration fails to protect itself in advance, it will take a political hit, and deservedly so.

At that point, an administration has to decide whether it is better to release the damaging information early and absorb the blows—probably doing short-term damage—or drag out the investigation as the outside world, day by day, knows the truth anyway, because other lawsuits are bringing documents to light. Administrations are supposed to have an instinct for minimizing political damage. They live in a political world and have to expect opponents to score political points when they have an opportunity to do, just as the administration will exploit a political advantage when it sees an opening. In the case of the Cheney energy task force, the administration prevailed in court but took a political beating that could have been avoided.

10

Testimony by White House Officials

Administrations will often claim that White House aides are exempt from appearing before congressional committees. White House Counsels advise lawmakers that "it is a longstanding principle, rooted in the Constitutional separation of powers and the authority vested in the President by Article II of the Constitution, that White House officials generally do not testify before Congress, except in extraordinary circumstances not present here."[1] Take note of the two qualifications: "generally" and "except in extraordinary circumstances." Caution here is well advised.

Although White House aides do not testify on a regular basis, under certain conditions they do, and in large numbers. Intense and escalating political pressures may convince the White House that the President is best served by having these aides testify to ventilate an issue fully, hoping to scotch suspicions of a cover-up or criminal conduct. Chapter 4 on the appointment power explained how presidential aide Peter Flanigan testified in 1972 as part of the Kleindienst nomination to be Attorney General. This chapter provides many other examples of Congress taking testimony from White House aides.

Watergate and Its Aftermath

On March 2, 1973, President Nixon objected to allowing White House Counsel John Dean testify at congressional hearings. Nixon offered more general grounds, under the doctrine of separation of powers, for refusing any White House aide to testify. Under heavy political pressures and with impeachment in the House of Representatives looming, Nixon gradually gave

---

1. Letter from White House Counsel Jack Quinn to Rep. William H. Zeliff, Jr., Chairman, Subcommittee on National Security, International Affairs, and Criminal Justice, May 8, 1996.

ground, eventually agreeing to allow White House aides to testify before the Senate Select Committee on Presidential Campaign Activities. To emphasize the exceptional nature of allowing these individuals to testify, he set forth certain conditions.

As time went on Nixon relaxed those conditions, such as waiving executive privilege if possible criminal conduct was involved. With these understandings, many White House aides testified before the committee, including John Dean, former special assistant Jeb Magruder, former deputy assistant Alexander Butterfield, former chief domestic adviser John Ehrlichman, former White House aide H.R. Haldeman, former consultant Patrick Buchanan, and former staff coordinator Gen. Alexander M. Haig, Jr.

Confidentiality is especially valued among those who provide legal counsel to the President. Nevertheless, Nixon permitted these White House aides to testify: personal attorney Herbert W. Kalmbach, special counsel Richard A. Moore, Leonard Garment, former special counsel Fred C. LaRue, special counsel J. Frederick Buzhardt, and counsel Thomas H. Wakefield. Other White House aides who testified include Bruce A. Kehrli, Hugh W. Sloan, Jr., Herbert L. Porter, Gordon Strachen, Clark McGregor, William H. Marumoto, L. J. Evans, Jr., and Rose Mary Woods, who was personal secretary to Nixon.[2] Details on Nixon's constitutional position on these committee appearances for Watergate figures are included in Chapter 3 on impeachment. Following the Watergate hearings conducted by Senator Ervin, the House Judiciary Committee held hearings on the impeachment of Nixon. Several White House aides testified at those hearings, including Butterfield, Dean, Kalmbach, and Charles W. Colson.[3]

A White House aide testified about the "Huston Plan" developed during the Nixon years. On June 5, 1970, President Nixon met with FBI Director J. Edgar Hoover, CIA Director Richard Helms, National Security Agency Director Admiral Gayler, and Defense Intelligence Agency Director General Bennett. The purpose was to direct those officials to obtain better information about domestic dissenters. In a memo, White House aide Tom Charles Huston recommended a number of options, including illegal opening of mail, burglary, surreptitious entry, and other methods. President Nixon approved the oper-

---

2. "Presidential Campaign Activities of !972: Senate Resolution 60," hearings before the Senate Select Committee on Presidential Campaign Activities, 93d Cong., 1st Sess. (1973). For the particular volumes in which these aides appeared before the Senate Select Committee on Presidential Campaign Activities, see Louis Fisher, "White House Aides Testifying Before Congress," 27 Pres. Stud. Q. 139, 141–42 (1997).

3. "Testimony of Witnesses," hearings before the House Committee on the Judiciary, 93d Cong., 2d Sess. (1974); see Fisher, "White House Aides," at 142–43.

ation and submitted the plan to the FBI, the CIA, and the military intelligence agencies for implementation. Five days later he revoked the plan at the insistence of Hoover and Attorney General John Mitchell, but the intelligence agencies ignored the revocation and continued to carry out some of the recommendations, including mail-opening and surveillance.[4] In 1975, Huston was called before a Senate select committee to testify.[5]

The Senate select committee also heard from a number of former White House aides. On December 5, 1975, the committee received testimony from Clark Clifford, former counsel to President Truman; Cyrus Vance, former special representative of the President; and Morton H. Halperin, former assistant for planning, National Security Council staff.[6] The committee's report on assassination plots indicates that other former White House aides appeared in executive session to give testimony: Robert H. Johnson, a member of the National Security Council staff from 1951 to January 1962; Gordon Gray and Andrew Goodpaster, two members of President Eisenhower's staff responsible for national security affairs; Theodore Sorensen of President Kennedy's staff; McGeorge Bundy and Walter Rostow of President Lyndon B. Johnson's staff; and Henry Kissinger and Alexander Haig of President Nixon's staff.[7]

Also in 1975, the House created a Select Committee on Intelligence to investigate the CIA and other parts of the U.S. Intelligence establishment. Several White House aides, former and current, appeared at the hearings: Secretary of State Kissinger (who also served, at that time, in a dual capacity as National Security Adviser); McGeorge Bundy, former assistant for national security affairs to Lyndon B. Johnson; Arthur Schlesinger, former special assistant to President John F. Kennedy, and William G. Hyland, deputy assistant to the President for national security affairs for President Ford.[8]

---

4. S. Rept. 94-755, 94th Cong., 2d Sess. 926–27 (1976).

5. "Intelligence Activities: Senate Resolution 21" (Vol. 2), hearings before the Senate Select Committee to Study Governmental Operations with Respect to Intelligence Activities, 94th Cong., 1st Sess. (1975).

6. "Intelligence Activities: Senate Resolution 21" (Vol. 7), hearings before the Senate Select Committee to Study Governmental Operations with Respect to Intelligence Activities, 94th Cong., 1st Sess. (1975).

7. "Alleged Assassination Plots Involving Foreign Leaders," an interim report of the Senate Select Committee to Study Governmental Operations with Respect to Intelligence Activities, S. Rept. No. 94-465, 94th Cong., 1st Sess. 55, 64, 111–13, 148, 156–57, 186–87, 246–54 (1975).

8. "U.S. Intelligence Agencies and Activities: The Performance of the Intelligence Community," hearings before the House Select Committee on Intelligence, 94th Cong., 1st Sess. (1975), Parts 2 and 5.

Cutting One's Losses

In 1980, a special subcommittee of the Senate Judiciary Committee investigated whether Billy Carter, the President's brother, had influenced U.S. policy or committed criminal activities in his relationships with Libya. White House Counsel Lloyd Cutler and National Security Adviser Zbigniew Brzezinski appeared at the hearings.[9] President Carter instructed all members of the White House staff to cooperate fully with the subcommittee, with the understanding that Carter did not expect to assert claims of executive privilege with respect to these matters. He directed White House staff to "respond fully to such inquiries from the subcommittee and to testify if the subcommittee determines that oral testimony is necessary."[10] Carter was not about to fall on his sword for misjudgments committed by his brother.

In 1986, President Ronald Reagan told executive officials, including those in the White House, to assist in the congressional investigation into the Iran-Contra affair in any way possible, including testifying before Congress. He said he had "already taken the unprecedented step of permitting two of my former national security advisers to testify before a committee of Congress."[11] The two former national security advisers were Robert McFarlane and John Poindexter. Other former White House aides who testified at the hearings included Bretton G. Sciaroni, National Security Council member Lt. Col. Oliver North, and North's secretary, Fawn Hall. The extent to which Reagan waived executive privilege for the Iran-Contra hearings is discussed in Chapter 3 on impeachment.

Even when the White House will not allow an aide to testify, other mechanisms may be offered to satisfy congressional interests. For example, the White House may suggest that the aide meet with a committee or subcommittee chair to respond to inquiries and later answer any written questions submitted by the chair. Such an arrangement occurred in 1981, when Martin Anderson, President Reagan's assistant for policy development, refused to appear before a House Appropriations subcommittee responsible for funding Anderson's budget request for the Office of Policy Development. The subcommittee retaliated by deleting all of the requested $2,959,000. In doing so,

---

9. "Inquiry Into the Matter of Billy Carter and Libya" (Vol. II), hearings before the Subcommittee to Investigate the Activities of Individuals Representing the Interests of Foreign Governments, Senate Committee on the Judiciary, 96th Cong., 2d Sess. (1980).
10. Public Papers of the Presidents, 1980–81 (II), at 1420.
11. Public Papers of the Presidents, 1986, II, at 1595.

it pointed out that the previous heads of the office (Stuart Eizenstat in the Carter years, James M. Cannon in the Ford years, and Kennedy R. Cole in the Nixon years) had appeared before the subcommittee.[12]

White House Counsel Fred F. Fielding offered legal grounds to support Anderson's position. As a senior adviser to President Reagan, Anderson participated in the deliberative process by providing "frank and candid advice." Such candor "is possible only in an atmosphere that insures that the advice will remain confidential."[13] That argument is not persuasive. Cabinet heads are also senior advisers to Presidents and are also part of the deliberative process requiring candor and confidentiality, yet they regularly appear before congressional committees. They are at liberty at any time to decline to respond to committee questions that jeopardize confidentiality. In many cases a committee is interested in specific facts and general policies, not in the deliberative process. Anderson could have agreed to appear with this understanding.

In his legal memo, Fielding said that Anderson "remains willing to meet informally with the Subcommittee to provide such information as he can consistent with his obligations of confidentiality to the President."[14] If he could meet informally, why not formally? Informal meetings also pose some risk to confidentiality and inquiries into the deliberative process. White House aides can fend off such inquiries in informal meetings and can do the same in formal hearings. After the committee mark-up in 1981, Anderson bowed to the needs of reality and prudence by meeting informally and off the record with the subcommittee.[15] After the Senate restored almost all of the funds, Congress appropriated $2,500,000 instead of the budget request of $2,959,000.[16]

The Clinton Years

A series of congressional investigations throughout the Clinton years required a large number of White House aides to appear before legislative committees to testify about procedures and actions involving contacts with the Treasury Department, the dismissals of employees in the Travel Office, Whitewater, and access to FBI files. President Clinton's handling of pardons and clemency, normally considered a presidential prerogative, also required White

---

12. H. Rept. No. 97-171, 97th Cong., 1st Sess. 30 (1981).
13. Id. at 62.
14. Id. at 63.
15. Id. at 30.
16. Budget of the U.S. Government: Appendix, Fiscal Year 1983, at I-C5.

House aides to testify at congressional hearings. In 2002, Tom Ridge declined to testify before a Senate committee, citing separation of powers concerns because of his direct assistance to President Bush. Those actions are discussed at the end of this chapter.

White House-Treasury Contacts

Congressional hearings in 1994 focused on whether White House aides had inappropriately learned details of a Resolution Trust Corporation (RTC) investigation of the failed Madison Guaranty Savings and Loan. In March 1993, Deputy Treasury Secretary Roger C. Altman became interim chief of the RTC. William Roelle, an RTC senior vice president, said he briefed Altman that RTC had forwarded a criminal referral to the FBI and the U.S. Attorney in Little Rock, naming the Clintons as potential beneficiaries of alleged wrongdoing at Madison. On September 29, 1993, Treasury General Counsel Jean E. Hanson told White House Counsel Bernard Nussbaum of the referrals. Other contacts took place between the Treasury Department and the White House concerning the referrals. Both Houses of Congress held hearings to investigate these contacts.

Among those appearing at the hearings were White House Counsel Lloyd Cutler, who testified that "No White House staff witness has declined to appear."[17] Also appearing from the White House: Lisa Caputo, press secretary to Hillary Clinton; associate counsel to the President Neil Eggleston; assistant to the President Mark D. Gearan; assistant to the President and deputy chief of staff Harold Ickes; deputy counsel to the President Joel I. Klein; assistant to the President Bruce Lindsey; former White House Chief of Staff Thomas McLarty; associate counsel to the President Beth Nolan; former White House Counsel Bernard Nussbaum; assistant to the President John Podesta; associate counsel to the President Clifford Sloan; senior policy adviser to the President George Stephanopoulos; and Margaret Williams, chief of staff to Hillary Clinton. Some of these White House aides, after testifying before the House oversight committee, were called to appear before the Senate oversight committee as well.[18]

---

17. "White House Contacts with Treasury/RTC Officials About 'Whitewater'-Related Matters" (Part 1), hearing before the House Committee on Banking, Finance and Urban Affairs, 103d Cong., 2d Sess. 12 (1994).

18. "Hearings Relating to Madison Guaranty S&L and the Whitewater Development Corporation—Washington DC Phase," hearings before the Senate Committee on Banking, Housing, and Urban Affairs, 103d Cong., 2d Sess. (1994). For citations to the specific hearing White House aides appeared, see Fisher, "White House Aides," at 145–46.

Travel Office Firings

On May 19, 1993, seven employees of the White House Travel Office were dismissed with the charge that they followed poor management practices. Dee Dee Myers, President Clinton's press secretary, also stated that the FBI had been asked to examine the records of the Travel Office, suggesting that the employees might have been guilty of criminal actions as well. An effort by House Republicans to demand documents from the administration and investigate what happened was defeated by the Democratically-controlled Judiciary Committee.[19]

After the Republican victories in the 1994 elections, the House Committee on Government Reform and Oversight initiated an investigation that included hearings with former White House aides. Three days were set aside to explore what had happened: October 24, 1995, and January 17 and 24, 1996. Appearing at those hearings were former assistant to the President and White House staff secretary John Podesta and former director of the White House Office of Administration David Watkins.[20]

On May 17, 1995, the Senate created a Special Committee to Investigate Whitewater Development Corporation and Related Matters. The purpose of the committee was to look into a number of White House activities. Did improper conduct occur in the way White House officials handled documents in the office of White House Deputy Counsel Vincent Foster following his death? Did the White House engage in improper contacts with any other agency or department regarding confidential information held by the Resolution Trust Corporation? Was either the report issued by the Office of Government Ethics on July 31, 1994, or related transcripts of deposition testimony, improperly released to White House officials prior to their testimony before the Senate Committee on Banking?

Those issues precipitated testimony from a vast number of White House officials, major and minor. Some were required to make a return appearance. Here are the names: assistant to the President Mark Gearan; former special assistant to the President Sylvia Mathews; deputy assistant to the President Patsy Thomasson; former assistant to the President for management and administration David Watkins; White House deputy press secretary Evelyn

---

19. H. Rept. No. 103-183, 103d Cong., 1st Sess. (1993).

20. "White House Travel Office—Day One," hearing before the House Committee on Government Reform and Oversight," 104th Cong., 2d Sess. (1995); "White House Travel Office—Day Two," hearing before the House Committee on Government Reform and Oversight, 104th Cong., 2d Sess. 12ff (1996).

Lieberman; chief of staff to Hillary Clinton, Margaret A. Williams; assistant to the associate counsel to the President Deborah Gorham; executive assistant to the counsel to the President Linda Tripp; former chief of staff Thomas McLarty; chief of staff to the Vice President, John M. Quinn; assistant to the President Bruce Lindsey; special counsel to the President Jane Sherburne; special assistant to the President Carolyn Huber; deputy chief of White House staff Harold Ickes, and many others.[21]

Security of FBI Files

In June 1996, the House Committee on Government Reform and Oversight learned that the Clinton White House had obtained from the FBI hundreds of confidential files of individuals who had worked in the Reagan and Bush administrations. President Clinton explained that the request for files of people who were no longer with the White House was merely a "bureaucratic snafu."[22] Critics charged that the White House intended to use the files for partisan, political purposes, hoping to discover and disseminate derogatory information about Republicans. Bernard Nussbaum, who was White House Counsel at the time, acknowledged that the handling of the files marked "a serious breach of privacy."[23] Both Houses called a number of former and current White House aides to testify.

On June 19, the House Committee on Government Reform and Oversight heard from Jane Dannenhauser, director of the White House Office of Personnel Security in the Nixon, Ford, Reagan, and Bush administrations, until her retirement in March 1993; Nancy Gemmell, who worked for twelve years in the White House Office of Personnel Security; A.B. Culverhouse, White House Counsel for President Reagan; C. Boyden Gray, White House Counsel for President George H. W. Bush; and Richard Hauser, former Deputy White House Counsel for President Reagan.[24]

On the following day, June 20, the Senate Judiciary Committee held hearings to look into both the Travel Office firings and the White House use of FBI files. The committee called these White House aides to testify: Billy Ray Dale, former director of the White House Travel Office; Anita McBride, former di-

---

21. For the full list, see Fisher, "White House Aides," at 147–49.
22. Public Papers of the Presidents, 1996, I, at 903.
23. "Security of FBI Background Files, June 26, 1996," hearing before the House Committee on Government Reform and Oversight, 104th Cong., 2d Sess. 220 (1996).
24. "Security of FBI Background Files, June 19, 1996," hearing before the House Committee on Government Reform and Oversight, 104th Cong., 2d Sess (1996).

rector of the White House Personnel Office; Mary Kate Downham Carroll, former personnel assistant of the White House Personnel Office; Graven W. Craig, former intern, White House Office of Public Liaison; and Ellen J. Gober, former staff assistant, White House Office of Legislative Affairs.[25]

House Government Reform and Oversight held a second hearing on June 26, focusing on FBI files. It received testimony from several White House Office aides: former White House Counsel Nussbaum; director of White House Office of Personnel Security Craig Livingstone; Anthony Marceca, former detailee to the White House Office of Personnel Security; and Lisa Wetzl, former staffer with the White House Office of Personnel Security.[26] The committee held hearings on two other days, taking testimony from officials outside the White House who were familiar with standard procedures for handling of FBI files.

Senate Judiciary held two more hearings, on June 28 and September 25, to further its investigation into what had become known as Filegate. Gemmell, Livingston, and Wetzl appeared, along with Charles Easley, director of the White House Office of Personnel Security, and Mary Beck, associate director for human resources management, Office of Administration, in the Executive Office of the President. Marceca, at the June 28 hearing, declined to testify, citing the Fifth Amendment privilege against self-incrimination. At a closed-door session on July 18, Marceca repeatedly invoked his Fifth Amendment privilege. Senate Judiciary chairman Orrin G. Hatch announced that he would consider granting Marceca immunity to compel him to testify, but Independent Counsel Kenneth W. Starr said that congressional immunity would interfere with his investigation in the FBI file affair.[27]

Initially, the White House withheld from congressional committees documents related to Filegate. By September, however, the White House agreed to produce 10,000 pages of phone logs and other documents that had been requested by the Senate Judiciary Committee.[28]

The hearings discussed in this chapter do not include the annual hearings on the White House budget conducted by the Appropriations Com-

---

25. "White House Access to FBI Background Summaries," hearings before the Senate Committee on the Judiciary, 104th Cong., 2d Sess. (1996).

26. "Security of FBI Background Files, June 26, 1996," hearings before the House Committee on Government Reform and Oversight, 104th Cong., 2d Sess. (1996).

27. "Lisa Clagett Weintraub, "Aide's Resignation Does Little to Douse FBI File Fires," CQ Weekly Report, June 29, 1996, at 1860.

28. George Archibald, "White House Agrees to Turn Over Papers: Avoids Faceoff in FBI-files Probe," Washington Times, September 5, 1996, at A4.

mittees. White House aides in charge of management and administration appear at those hearings on a regular basis to support budget justifications submitted by the White House. For example, these White House aides appeared at the House hearings in 1995: Patsy L. Thomasson, special assistant to the President for management and administration and director of the Office of Administration; John W. Cressman, deputy director, Office of Administration, and Jurg E. Hochuli, director Financial Management division, Office of Administration.[29]

Presidential Pardons

If any area of White House activity were to be considered off-limits to congressional probes, it would be the President's decision to exercise the power to grant pardons and clemencies. Under the Constitution, the decision is vested entirely in the President. Article II gives the President the power to grant "Reprieves and Pardons for Offenses against the United States, except in Cases of Impeachment." Still, political situations can place in the hands of Congress many documents on the pardon process. The greatest access was during the Clinton years, after his decision in 1999 to grant clemency to Puerto Rican terrorists, followed by the pardons and clemencies he issued on his last day in office, covering Marc Rich and others. To understand the controversial nature of those actions, I need to explain the regular pardon process and the vehement protests that were directed against Clinton's decisions.

Scope of the Power

There are only two express restrictions on the President's power. The pardon power applies to offenses against the federal government, not against the states and localities. The President may not use the power to countermand a legislative decision to impeach and remove. There is also an implied restriction on the pardon power. Presidents may not use it to compensate individuals for what has been done or suffered; nor can they draw money from the Treasury Department for general amnesties, except as expressly authorized by

---

29. "Treasury, Postal Service, and General Government Appropriations for Fiscal Year 1996" (Part 2), hearings before the Subcommittee on the Treasury, Postal Service, and General Government Appropriations of the House Committee on Appropriations, 104th Cong., 1st Sess. (1995).

Congress.[30] The power of the purse belongs to Congress. On the other hand, certain statutory restrictions have been struck down by the Supreme Court as an invalid interference with the pardon power.[31] When a proviso in an appropriations statute attempts to control the President's power to pardon, or to prescribe for the judiciary the effect of a pardon, the statutory provision is invalid.[32]

Finally, presidential abuse of the pardon power may constitute an impeachable offense or lead to restrictive rulings in the courts.[33] Pardons and clemencies offered in return for presidential gain might fall in the category of bribery, and some conditions attached to a pardon could be found by the courts to be unconstitutional, such as conditions that limit First Amendment rights or other core constitutional freedoms.

Otherwise, the President has great latitude in deciding when and how to issue pardons and clemencies. The power of pardon may take a variety of forms: full pardon, conditional pardon, clemency for a class of people (amnesty), commutation (reducing a sentence), and remission of fines and forfeitures.[34] Through its appropriations and taxing powers, Congress may also remit fines, penalties, and forfeitures. Congress, with the support of the Supreme Court and the Justice Department, has vested that discretion in the Secretary of the Treasury and other executive officials.[35] Congress may also legislate a general pardon or amnesty by repealing a law that had imposed criminal liability. Congress derives this power not by sharing the President's pardon power but through its power to legislate and repeal legislation.[36]

Notwithstanding this great range of presidential discretion, under certain conditions congressional committees have successfully sought access to White House documents, White House aides, and even the direct testimony of the President. The most dramatic example resulted from the decision of President Ford on September 8, 1974, to grant a full pardon "for all offenses against the

---

30. Knote v. United States, 95 U.S. 149, 153–54 (1877). On the primacy of the appropriations power when pitted against the pardon power, see Hart v. United States, 118 U.S. 62 (1886); 8 Op. Att'y Gen. 281, 282 (1857); 23 Op. Att'y Gen. 360, 363 (1901).
31. Ex parte Garland, 71 U.S. 333, 380 (1866). See 12 Stat. 502 (1862) and 13 Stat. 424 (1865).
32. United States v. Klein, 13 Wall. 128 (1872); Hart v. United States, 118 U.S. 62 (1886).
33. David Gray Adler, "The Presidents Pardon Power," in Inventing the American Presidency, edited by Thomas E. Cronin (1989).
34. Humbert, W. W., The Pardoning Power of the President 22 (1941).
35. The Laura, 114 U.S. 411 (1885); 8 Op. Att'y Gen. 281, 282 (1857).
36. Humbert, The Pardoning Power, at 43–44.

United States which he, Richard Nixon, has committed or may have committed or taken part in during the period from January 20, 1969 through August 9, 1974."[37] Some members of Congress thought that Nixon might have made a deal with Ford when nominating him to be Vice President. If Nixon had conditioned the nomination on the promise of a pardon, or conditioned his own resignation on a pardon, the House might have charged Ford with accepting a bribe and impeached him. To allay such concerns, Ford took the extraordinary step of appearing before the House Judiciary Committee to explain the basis for his decision.[38]

To some lawmakers, it seemed improper for Ford to grant a pardon before formal charges had been lodged and without a formal admission of guilt from Nixon. It is established, however, that a pardon may be granted prior to a conviction and even before indictment.[39] Nevertheless, it is risky for a President to invoke the power prior to trial and condemnation. Without the facts produced through the regular trial procedure, a President may inadvertently grant a pardon for offenses that have yet to come to light.[40]

Basic Procedures

Justice Department regulations spell out the procedures for clemency. A person seeking executive clemency "shall execute a formal petition."[41] The pardon attorney in the Justice Department "shall submit all recommendations in clemency cases through the Associate Attorney General, who "shall exercise such discretion and authority as is appropriate and necessary for the handling and transmittal of such recommendations to the President."[42] The Attorney General "shall review each petition and all pertinent information developed by the investigation and shall determine whether the request for clemency is of sufficient merit to warrant favorable action by the President." Moreover, the Attorney General "shall report in writing his or her recommendations to the President, stating whether in his or her judgment the President should grant or deny the petition."[43]

---

37. Public Papers of the Presidents, 1974, at 61–62.
38. "Pardon of Richard M. Nixon and Related Matters," hearings before the House Committee on the Judiciary, 93d Cong., 2d Sess. (1974).
39. Ex parte Garland, 71 U.S. 333, 380 (1866); 1 Op. Att'y Gen. 341, 343 (1820); Murphy v. Ford, 390 F.Supp. 1372 (W.D. Mich. 1975).
40. 2 Op. Att'y Gen. 275 (1825); 6 Op. Att'y Gen. 20 (1853).
41. 28 C.F.R. §1.1.
42. Id. at §0.36.
43. Id. at §1.6[b].

When the pardon attorney receives a petition for clemency, the office reviews the petition to ensure that the applicant is eligible to apply. Once eligibility is established, the office contacts the warden at the federal prison where the inmate is held, requesting copies of the judgment of conviction, the pre-sentence report, and the most recent prison progress report. The pre-sentence report provides an account of the crime and a description of the defendant's criminal history. The progress report describes the prisoner's adjustment to incarceration and disciplinary history while in prison. The pardon attorney can also contact the U.S. Attorney's office that prosecuted the case and the sentencing judge. A report of approximately five hundred words is prepared for the use of the Deputy Attorney General's office, the Attorney General, and the White House Counsel.[44]

These regulations are advisory on the President. They do not in any way bind his exercise of constitutional power. However, part of the purpose of the regulations is to protect the President from making legal or political blunders because he lacks adequate information. Without close review by professionals in the Justice Department, Presidents can be easily blindsided. In both the clemency decision in 1999 for Puerto Rican terrorists and in his final day in office on January 20, 2002, Clinton ignored the Justice Department guidelines at considerable cost to his reputation.

Margaret Love, pardon attorney from 1990 to 1997, testified before a House subcommittee in 2001 that many of the concerns raised about Clinton's final pardons "are directly attributable" to his decision not to seek the advice of the Attorney General. She noted that "the irregularity and infrequency" with which Clinton acted on pardon applications "was calculated to invite public suspicion about the bona fides of even his most unexceptionable grants." The Clinton administration's "short-sighted and ill-advised" decision to abandon Justice Department assistance "led directly to the reported free-for-all at the end of his term, and the resultant appearance of cronyism and influence peddling."[45]

FALN Clemency

Clinton's willingness to circumvent the Justice Department on his last day in office was foreshadowed by his offer of clemency on August 11, 1999, to

---

44. "Clemency for FALN Members," hearings before the Senate Committee on the Judiciary, 106th Cong., 1st Sess. 100–02 (1999).
45. "The Controversial Pardon of International Fugitive Marc Rich," hearings before the House Committee on Government Reform, 107th Cong., 1st Sess. 30 (2001).

sixteen members of a Puerto Rican terrorist group, the FALN (Armed Forces of Puerto Rican National Liberation). Fourteen accepted the conditions attached to the clemency (such as renouncing violence). They had been convicted and imprisoned for seditious conspiracy in planting more than 130 bombs in public places in the United States, including shopping malls and restaurants. At least six people were killed and approximately 70 injured. The FALN operation marked the biggest terrorist campaign within U.S. borders, yet Clinton's clemency released individuals from prison after serving less than twenty years of terms running from 55 to 90 years.

Clinton's clemency action for the FALN did not receive the formal review of the pardon attorney, the Deputy Attorney General, or the Attorney General. Justice Department officials met several times with advocates for FALN clemency, but did not solicit the views of victims or other law enforcement officials. Background checks by the FBI were not requested. The White House was aware that the FBI was on record as opposed to clemency for the FALN members. Contrary to Justice Department regulations, the FALN members did not "execute a formal petition" to the pardon attorney.

The Justice Department had been involved earlier with the FALN issue, such as when Pardon Attorney Love advised against clemency in 1996.[46] Three years later, Clinton decided to cut the pardon attorney out of the picture. He was not the first President to skirt Justice Department procedures. President Ford pardoned Nixon in 1974 without Justice Department input, and President Bush in 1992 pardoned six Iran-Contra figures without asking for Justice Department advice.[47]

Clemency for the FALN members triggered bipartisan condemnation from lawmakers. Although Democrats in Congress regularly came to Clinton's defense on other matters, most Democrats were either silent on the clemency decision or issued strong public rebukes. Senator Dianne Feinstein (D-Cal.) was blunt: "Some have described these prisoners as political prisoners. They were not. They were terrorists."[48] Similarly, Senator Robert Torricelli (D-N.J.) pulled no punches: "The people of the FALN are not heroes, they are cowards. They hid in the night, they planned bombings against innocent people for a cause that has no merits."[49] Those who defended the clemency did so by arguing in favor of the right of the Puerto Rican people to self-determination and to rid themselves of their status as a "colony." Rep. Nydia Velázques re-

---

46. "No Clemency, Clinton Told," New York Times, October 20, 1999, at A21.
47. "Clemency for FALN Members," hearings before Senate Judiciary, at 115.
48. 145 Cong. Rec. S10770 (daily ed. September 13, 1999).
49. "Clemency for FALN Members," hearings before Senate Judiciary, at 62.

marked: "This is not about terrorism,...We have had...over 100 years of keeping a colony. That is a violation. That is a violation of the civil rights of the people of Puerto Rico."[50] Torricelli made short work of that argument:

> I do not know of any political cause that has less merits than those of the FALN. This is not the African National Congress. It is not any legitimate effort at national liberation. The people of Puerto Rico are in voluntary political association with the United States. They have voted repeatedly and overwhelmingly to be in voluntary political association with the United States. The day, the hour, the moment the people of Puerto Rico decide they do not want political association with the United States, they will have their independence.[51]

Both chambers passed resolutions condemning Clinton's pardons. The House adopted language stating that Clinton's decision violated "longstanding tenets of United States counterterrorism policy" and was "an affront to the rule of law, the victims and their families, and every American who believes that violent acts must be punished to the fullest extent of the law." The House resolution further stated that "making concessions to terrorists is deplorable and that President Clinton should not have offered or granted clemencies to the FALN terrorists." The resolution passed 311 to 41.[52] The party split: 218 to 0 Republican, 93 to 41 Democrat.

A Senate resolution deploring the clemency to FALN terrorists passed five days later by a vote of 95 to 2.[53] The resolution pointed out that "no petitions for clemency were made by these terrorists, but other persons sought such clemency for them." Like the House resolution, the Senate condemned the making of concessions to terrorists and said that Clinton should not have granted clemency to the FALN members. Politically, Clinton took a terrific beating. Throughout his administration, he and his party moderates had successfully taken the law-and-order issue away from the Republicans. Clinton supported the death penalty, called for more police on the streets, and took initiatives against international terrorism. Yet nothing could have poisoned his relationship with the law enforcement community more than his clemency order for the FALN.

At Senate hearings, several members of the law enforcement community testified and submitted statements. One of those who appeared was Gilbert G. Gallegos, national president of the Fraternal Order of the Police, the largest

---

50. 145 Cong. Rec. H8008 (daily ed. September 9, 1999).
51. "Clemency for FALN Members," hearings before Senate Judiciary, at 61.
52. 145 Cong. Rec. H8019–20 (daily ed. September 9, 1999).
53. Id. at S10818 (daily ed. September 14, 1999).

police organization in the country with 283,000 members. He included the letter he wrote to President Clinton protesting the clemency decision.[54] The police officers who testified at the Senate hearings all reported the same fact: not one had been asked by the administration for his or her views on giving clemency to the FALN members. The only witness who gained entry to the administration was Dr. C. Nozomi Ikuta, an ordained minister of the United Church of Christ. She was able to talk to White House Counsel Jack Quinn, White House Counsel Charles Ruff, Deputy Attorney General Eric Holder, and Pardon Attorney Roger Adams about the clemencies.[55] That is extraordinary access to top administration officials.

When asked about the clemencies, Clinton told two reporters on January 18, 2000, that a President "should rarely commute sentences and should have good reasons for doing so if he does, knowing that they will always be somewhat controversial."[56] Yet he then said that his White House Counsel, Charles Ruff, "handled it entirely, and only he handled it." With such politically sensitive decisions, why place the matter in the hands of one person, no matter how gifted and trusted? Why not seek outside assistance from federal agencies to assure that Ruff (and Clinton) had full access to available information and considerations?

In the same meeting with reporters, Clinton insisted that "categorically there was no politics in it." If there were no politics, why keep the process so closely guarded in the hands of one White House official? Clinton acknowledged that the Justice Department has "its own independent bureaucracy for evaluating these things. And the tradition is that the President doesn't rule on them, one way or the other, until you get all these recommendations sent to you. And I think what I believe is that—although this operation had a life of its own... is that we should be granting more pardons."[57] His reference to "independent bureaucracy" was an exaggeration. The pardon attorney's office consists of six attorneys.[58] The phrase "a life of its own" suggested that there was something unique and highly special about the FALN clemency, implying that the decision was anything but routine and nonpolitical. In a letter to Rep. Henry Waxman (D-Cal.), Clinton insisted that "political considerations played no role in the process."[59] Clinton's statement lacks credibility. Political

---

54. "Clemency for FALN Members," hearings before Senate Judiciary, at 8–9.
55. Id. at 56–57.
56. Public Papers of the Presidents, 2000–2001, I, at 77.
57. Id. at 78.
58. "Clemency for FALN Members," hearings before Senate Judiciary, at 117.
59. "Clemency for the FALN: A Flawed Decision?," hearings before the House Committee on Government Reform, 106th Cong., 1st Sess. 10 (1999).

considerations on a clemency decision like the FALN always play a role, and they should.

Clinton justified the clemency on various grounds. He said it was requested "by hundreds of people, including President Carter, Bishop Tutu, and many other religious leaders and Members of Congress." He conceded that "obviously, there were those who disagreed."[60] This explanation makes the decision sound quite political, with supporters and detractors lining up on different sides. He cited Carter and Tutu to build political support for a decision that was politically unpopular. However, a presidential decision to pardon someone should stand on its merits. It is not better or worse because Carter or Tutu offered support. The decision is meant to be *presidential*, not part of a polling operation.

In that same statement, Clinton said he "did not believe they should be held in incarceration, in effect, by guilt by association." Here he seriously abuses a well-known expression. Someone becomes a victim of "guilt by association" when arrested and punished because of something a family member or associate did, or perhaps because the person belongs to the race or ethnic group of someone suspected of a crime. The FALN members were in prison because of what *they* did. They conspired to support violence and terrorism. They helped build bombs and transport explosives. Several were caught with weapons in their van on the way to a terrorist attempt. Their intent to commit violence failed because they were first apprehended. As a former law professor, Clinton should know the meaning of "guilt by association."

Clinton further justified the clemency because "none of them, even though they belong to an organization which has espoused violent means, none of them were convicted of doing any bodily harm to anyone."[61] The FALN members did not just belong to an organization that "espoused" violence. Their organization *practiced* it. As for not doing any bodily harm to anyone, they worked with an organization dedicated to violent action and they knew it. That knowledge alone was sufficient to justify conviction and incarceration. Several of them intended to commit violence but were arrested before they could complete their assigned task.

Legislative efforts to learn more about the FALN matter came to an end when Clinton invoked executive privilege after congressional subpoenas asked for the records of private deliberations that led to the clemency decision. Cheryl Mills, White House Deputy Counsel, told the House Committee on

---

60. Public Papers of the Presidents, 1999, II, at 1513.
61. Id.

Government Reform that the President's constitutional authority to grant clemency "is not subject to legislative oversight."[62] Actually, that is an overstatement. Congress conducted considerable oversight on the FALN clemency decision and received thousands of pages of documents related to the decision.[63] Several senior administration officials testified, including Deputy Attorney General Holder and Pardon Attorney Adams.[64]

Marc Rich et al.

Two years later, Congress and the White House again battled over access to documents concerning presidential pardons. The subject this time were the pardons issued by President Clinton during his last day in office, particularly the pardon of Marc Rich. Pulling an all-nighter, Clinton issued pardons to 140 people and commuted 36 prison sentences. The magnitude of the operation and the nature of the procedures (or lack of them) prompted Pardon Attorney Adams to remark: "I've never seen anything like this." He said that many of the people on the list had not applied for pardons and that there was often no time to conduct record checks with the FBI.[65]

The names included such prominent people as Susan McDougal, Henry Cisneros, Patricia Hearst Shaw, and Clinton's brother, Roger. Media attention also focused on names not well known. One was Susan L. Rosenberg, a one-time member of the Weather Underground terrorist group charged in the 1981 Brinks robbery that left a guard and two police officers dead. She admitted her role in a 1984 New Jersey case, where she was found with a companion loading 740 pounds of dynamite and weapons, including a submachine gun.[66]

The commutation of prison sentences for four Hasidic men from New York, convicted of defrauding the government of tens of millions of dollars, stayed in the spotlight for months. After their supporters met with Clinton and his wife in 2000, the religious community voted overwhelmingly for Mrs. Clin-

---

62. H. Rept. No. 106-488, 106th Cong., 1st Sess. 115 (1999).

63. See the documents reprinted in H. Rept. No. 106-488 and these hearings: "Clemency for the FALN: A Flawed Decision?," hearings before the House Committee on Government Reform, 106th Cong., 1st Sess. (1999); "Clemency for FALN Members," hearings before the Senate Committee on the Judiciary, 106th Cong., 1st Sess. (1999).

64. "Clemency for FALN Members," at 96–148.

65. Amy Goldstein and Susan Schmidt, "Clinton's Last-Day Clemency Benefits 176," Washington Post, January 21, 2001, at A1, A16.

66. Eric Lipton, "Pardon Given Ex-Terrorist is Criticized," New York Times, January 22, 2001, at A17.

ton that fall in her successful campaign for the U.S. Senate.[67] Federal prosecutors investigated whether President Clinton commuted the four prison sentences as payback for the community's support of her campaign.[68] Also criticized was the pardon of Almon Glenn Braswell, convicted in 1983 of mail fraud and perjury related to his vitamin and health supplement business. He was still under investigation by federal prosecutors on another matter when the pardon was announced.[69] Another focal point was the commutation of a fifteen-year prison sentence for Carlos Vignali, a convicted Los Angeles cocaine dealer. His father, a major donor to Democrats in California, made contributions in excess of $150,000.[70]

Clinton's family and in-laws were actively involved in these pardons. His brother-in-law, Hugh Rodham, received about $400,000 for helping two felons (Braswell and Vignali) receive clemency. After the matter became public, he returned the money.[71] Another brother-in-law, Tony Rodham, helped obtain a pardon for a Tennessee couple.[72] The next shoe to drop concerned Clinton's brother, Roger. Several friends described how he received money for promising pardons to two people convicted of drug offenses.[73]

As captivating as these stories were, the lion's share of attention fell on Clinton's pardon of Marc Rich and Pincus Green, charged in 1983 with conduct-

---

67. Clifford J. Levy, "Both Clintons Met With Backers of 4 Hasidim Who Got Leniency," New York Times, January 24, 2001, at A19; Randal C. Archibold and Elissa Gootman, "Behind 4 Pardons, a Hasidic Sect Desperate for Subsidies, and for Political Influence," New York Times, February 5, 2001, at A23; and Christine Haughney, "Orthodox Town Under Scrutiny," Washington Post, February 25, 2001, at A6.

68. Michael Grunwald and Christine Haughney, "4 Pardons Probed for Ties to N.Y. Senate Bid," Washington Post, February 24, 2001, at A1; and Benjamin Weiser, "Inquiry Focuses on Commuted Sentences for 4 New Yorkers," New York Times, February 24, 2001, at A8.

69. Kurt Eichenwald and Michael Moss, "Pardon for Subject of Inquiry Worries Prosecutors," New York Times, February 6, 2001, at A3; Michael Moss, "Officials Say Investigation Will Go On Despite Pardon," New York Times, February 8, 2001, at A20; and Peter Slevin, "Another Pardon Stirs Controversy," Washington Post, February 6, 2001, at A3.

70. Todd S. Purdum, "A Convict in the Storm's Eye Had Plenty of Help," New York Times, February 22, 2001, at A21; and Rene Sanchez, "Drug Felon's Powerful Supporters Retreat on Pardon," Washington Post, February 24, 2001, at A6.

71. James V. Grimaldi and Peter Slevin, "Hillary Clinton's Brother Was Paid for Role in 2 Pardons," Washington Post, February 22, 2001, at A2.

72. Marc Lacey and Don Van Natta, Jr., "Second Clinton In-Law Says He Helped to Obtain Pardon," New York Times, March 1, 2001, at A1.

73. Susan Schmidt, "Clinton's Brother Promised Pardons," Washington Post, February 24, 2001, at A7; Alison Leigh Cowan, "Allegations on Cash and Pardons Put Focus Back on Roger Clinton," New York Times, June 17, 2001, at 16.

ing the largest tax-evasion scheme in U.S. history. Rather than stand trial, they fled to Switzerland. Rich became naturalized as a citizen of Spain, purporting to renounce his U.S. citizenship. Both Rich and Green became citizens of Israel. In 1983, a grand jury issued a 51 count indictment against Rich, Green, and others for wire fraud, mail fraud, racketeering, racketeering conspiracy, tax evasion, and trading with the enemy. The latter charge reflects their purchase of oil from Iran during the 1979 hostage crisis. In 1984, the government filed an amended 65 count indictment. U.S. efforts to extradite Rich and Green from Switzerland and Spain were unsuccessful.

In early 2000, with Clinton in his last year in office, the attorneys for Rich and Green pressed hard for a presidential pardon. One strategy was to have Rich's ex-wife, Denise Rich, meet with President Clinton to discuss the pardon. An e-mail of March 18 from Avner Azulay, a friend of Marc Rich, spoke of sending "DR on a 'personal' mission to NO. 1, with a well prepared script."[74] She spoke with President Clinton at a White House social event. Over the years, she had contributed more than a million dollars to the Democratic Party and donated $450,000 to Clinton's presidential library in Little Rock. Beth Dozoretz, a close friend of Denise Rich, also played a substantial role as Democratic fund-raiser. She and her husband had visited the Clintons at Camp David and vacationed with them at Martha's Vineyard. Jack Quinn, a former White House Counsel and subsequently one of Rich's lawyers, asked her to contact President Clinton about the pardon request. She did so at least twice and pledged to raise $1 million for the Clinton library.[75]

In October 2000, Marc Rich and his advisers decided to move on the pardon request. On December 11, the pardon petition was delivered to the White House. Two letters from Denise Rich were attached to the petition. On the evening of January 19, the day before Clinton had to yield power, White House Counsel Beth Nolan called Deputy Attorney General Eric Holder to discuss the Rich pardon. He told her that his earlier position of "neutral" would change to "neutral, leaning towards favorable" if Clinton thought the pardon would yield foreign policy benefits in the Middle East.[76] Denise Rich, after invoking the Fifth Amendment rather than testify at congressional hearings, was given immunity as part of the pardon probe. Beth Dozoretz, when

---

74. In re Grand Jury Subpoenas Dated March 9, 2001, 179 F.Supp.2d 270, 277 (S.D. N.Y. 2001).

75. George Lardner, Jr., "House Panel Given List of Clinton Library Donors," Washington Post, March 3, 2001, at A14.

76. Peter Slevin and James V. Grimaldi, "Ex-Aides say They Fought Rich Pardon," Washington Post, March 2, 2001, at A12.

called before the House Government Reform Committee to testify about her role in the pardon of Rich and Green, also invoked the Fifth Amendment.[77]

The House Government Reform Committee held hearings on February 8 and March 1, 2001, taking testimony from former Deputy Attorney General Holder, former White House Counsel Jack Quinn, former counsel to the President Beth Nolan, former deputy counsel to the President Bruce Lindsey, and former White House Chief of Staff John Podesta.[78] A number of documents— including letters, notes, e-mails, and phone logs—that explain the process leading to the Rich pardon are reprinted in the hearings.[79] Additional documents on the Rich pardon appear in a subsequent committee report.[80]

Clinton's Defense

On February 18, 2001, Clinton defended the pardons of Rich and others in a lengthy op-ed piece for the *New York Times*. He explained that "the common denominator was that the cases, like that of Patricia Hearst, seemed to me deserving of executive clemency. Overwhelmingly, the pardon went to people who had been convicted and served their time."[81] Yet the most controversial figure, Marc Rich, had not been convicted and had not served time. Clinton conceded that "the process would have been better served had I sought [the] views directly" of Mary Jo White, the U.S. Attorney for the Southern District of New York, whose jurisdiction covered the Marc Rich case.

In the op-ed piece, Clinton claimed that the case for the pardons of Rich and Green "was reviewed and advocated not only by my former White House counsel Jack Quinn but also by three distinguished Republican attorneys: Leonard Garment, a former Nixon White House official; William Bradford Reynolds, a former high-ranking official in the Reagan Justice Department; and Lewis Libby, now Vice President Cheney's chief of staff." This would have been a powerful and politically adroit defense, but within hours all three men denied offering any assistance or encouragement to the pardons. Garment said it was "absolutely false that I knew about and endorsed the idea of a pardon."

---

77. Jerry Seper, "Dozoretz had Integral Role in Pardon," Washington Times, March 6, 2001, at A8.

78. "The Controversial Pardon of International Fugitive Marc Rich," hearings before the House Committee on Government Reform, 107th Cong., 1st Sess. 192, 309 (2001).

79. E.g., id. at 75, 80–87, 115, 185, 247, 250, 259, 265, 305, 330, 350–51, 368, 971–72.

80. H. Rept. No. 107-454, 107th Cong., 2d Sess. 463–708 (2002).

81. William Clinton, "My Reasons for the Pardons," New York Times, February 18, 2001, at 12.

Libby, although a former lawyer for Rich, was not involved in the pardon. Reynolds said he "never reviewed nor advocated the pardon."[82] At that point, Clinton's office acknowledged that none of the three lawyers had reviewed the pardon application or lobbied for it.[83]

On February 8 and March 1, 2001, the House Government Reform Committee held hearings on the Rich pardon. Several former Clinton White House aides testified that they strongly opposed the decision to pardon Rich. Chief of Staff John Podesta and White House Counsel Beth Nolan thought they had argued successfully against the pardon. Bruce Lindsey, a former counsel to Clinton, said he opposed the pardon because Rich was a fugitive. That factor alone, he said, "was the beginning and the end." The three Clinton aides testified about the intensity of lobbying efforts for various pardons.[84]

Clinton's library came under further scrutiny when it was learned that John Catsimatidis, a Clinton library advisory board member who pledged to raise $1 million for the library, had lobbied successfully for the pardon of convicted perjurer William Fugazy. After the Justice Department denied the request, Catsimatidis appealed directly to Clinton's chief of staff, John Podesta.[85] Also, former White House lawyer Cheryl Mills, a member of the library's board, participated in a White House meeting on the evening of January 19, 2001, to discuss the pardon of Rich. The House Committee on Government Reform, watching this story unfold, asked that the library release the names of major contributors. The library agreed to give the committee a list of more than one hundred people who had given or promised to raise at least $5,000 for the building.[86]

Clinton's efforts to justify the pardon of Rich and Green invariably backfired, but he tried again in an April 8, 2002 interview with Jonathan Alter of *Newsweek*. In discussing the pardons he issued on his last day in office, he spoke about being "mugged one more time on the way out the door." An interesting picture. Being "mugged" is the language of an innocent victim, someone attacked and robbed on a street. Clinton was hardly innocent. He seemed

---

82. Jill Abramson, "A Clinton Fund-Raiser is Said to be Behind Gifts in Rich Case," New York Times, February 18, 2001, at 17.

83. Joseph Kahn, "Clinton's Defense of Pardons Brings Even More Questions," New York Times, February 19, 2001, at A1, A15.

84. Peter Slevin and James V. Grimaldi, "Ex-aides Say They Fought Rich Pardon," March 22, 2001, at A1; "The Controversial Pardon of International Fugitive Marc Rich," hearings before the House Committee on Government Reform, 107th Cong., 1st Sess. (2001).

85. Greg B. Smith, "Clinton Library Fundraiser Helped Perjurer Get Pardon," Washington Post, March 4, 2001, at A2.

86. Don Van Natta, Jr. and David Johnston, "Clinton Library to Yield Details on Big Gifts," New York Times, March 3, 2001, at A10.

unable to reflect on how much his personal judgments and misjudgments had contributed to—and deserved—the criticism that came his way.

Alter asked: "If you had to do it all over again, would you pardon Marc Rich"? Clinton expressed regret about the personal cost to him, but did not acknowledge any error on his part: "Probably not, just for the politics. It was terrible politics. It wasn't worth the damage to my reputation. But that doesn't mean the attacks were true. The fact that his ex-wife—I didn't think they got along—was for it and had contributed to my library had nothing to do with it."[87]

Clinton gave Alter three justifications for the Rich pardon: "Number one, the Justice Department said they were no longer opposed and they were really for it. Had I not granted it, it would have been the only one they wanted publicly that they didn't grant." Here Clinton shifted the blame to the Justice Department. Did it want the pardon "publicly"? There is no such public record. Clinton's response assumed that the department and the pardon attorney had some formal role in investigating the pardon petition and in seeking outside comment, but Jack Quinn clearly bypassed that process and went directly to Clinton. As for the department withdrawing its opposition and being "really for it," that can only refer to the brief conversation between White House Counsel Nolan and Deputy Attorney General Holder on the evening of January 19. That telephone conversation does not represent a department position and it hardly reflects enthusiasm on Holder's part. He merely told Nolan that if the pardon of Marc Rich would somehow yield foreign policy benefits in the Middle East, he would shift from his former position of "neutral" to "neutral, leaning towards favorable." It takes a rich imagination to read that as "really for it."

The second reason offered by Clinton is that Marc Rich "waived his statute-of-limitations defenses so we can get lots of money from him [in a civil suit, if Rich returns to the United States]. Justice Ginsburg's husband—the tax expert—said he wasn't guilty. And the Justice Department under President Reagan said he was wrongly indicted in the first place." In brackets, *Newsweek* inserted this comment: "a claim former Reagan officials deny." Moreover, there is no evidence that Rich will ever return to the United States to pay any claims in a civil suit. As for Martin Ginsburg's work, as a tax attorney he only examined the issue of tax evasion. He did not analyze the dozens of other charges included in the grand jury indictment, much less venture opinions about Rich's guilt or innocence on those charges.

---

87. Jonathan Alter, "Life is Fleeting, Man," Newsweek, April 8, 2002, at 44.

The third and final reason is that Clinton received "a request from the government of Israel. They wanted him and [Jonathan] Pollard, and I considered Pollard an unrepentant spy and I didn't think I could pardon him. And I wanted to do something to support the peace process. Furthermore, [Rich's] main lawyer was Vice President Cheney's chief of staff [Lewis Libby] and they [conservative critics] tried to hide that." It's quite a stretch to find some relationship between the Rich pardon and the peace process. As for Libby's role, the credibility of the pardon depends on Clinton's judgment and the facts surrounding it, not on who provided legal advice to Rich.

Later in the interview, when asked about Rich's fugitive status, Clinton responded: "Look, I'm not justifying the fugitive status. But if we can get a couple of hundred million dollars, whatever it is he allegedly owes, it is in the interests of the United States to recover from him the way we recovered from other people who violated these oil-pricing schemes."[88] By implying that Rich was guilty with others in violating oil-pricing schemes, Clinton contradicts the claim that Martin Ginsburg had found Rich to be innocent.

Clinton felt the hurt and frustration that came with the pardons. On that part of the experience he articulated strongly. However, nothing in his public statements suggests that he understood how much his actions and decisions contributed to the damage. Earlier in the *Newsweek* story he offered a comment that opens the door to possible understanding: "The biggest wounds in life are all self-inflicted."[89]

Grand Jury Probe

Just as it is rare for Congress to supervise presidential decisions over the pardon process, so is that the case with the judiciary. Yet both Congress and the courts were quite involved in monitoring the Clinton pardons. In February 2001, the Justice Department in the Southern District in New York began to investigate the circumstances surrounding the pardons to Marc Rich and Pincus Green, the four Hasidic Jews, and the role of Roger Clinton. The probe soon widened to cover any of the controversial pardons handed down on Clinton's last day in office.[90] The following month, the grand jury issued subpoenas to five lawyers who had represented Rich and Green in connection with the pardon application.

---

88. Id.
89. Id. at 41.
90. Dan Eggen, "All of Clinton's Pardons Subject to Probe," Washington Post, March 13, 2001, at A22.

The lawyers provided some documents in response to the subpoenas, including conversations and communications with Denise Rich, Beth Dozoretz, Eric Holder, Avner Azulay, and others. But they cited the work-product doctrine and the attorney-client privilege as grounds for withholding other documents and testimony. The work-product doctrine protects a lawyer's work product prepared "in anticipation of" litigation. The doctrine keeps the materials out of the hands of adversaries. The attorney-client privilege protects confidential communications made for the purpose of obtaining legal advice.

On December 13, 2001, a federal district judge held that once Rich and Green decided to seek a pardon, their lawyers ceased providing legal services in an adversarial context. By remaining fugitives for seventeen years, Rich and Green avoided further litigation on the criminal charges. Moreover, by going directly to the White House instead of through the pardon attorney and the Justice Department, the attorneys faced no opposing parties or adversaries. The pardon petition went directly to the White House; no copies were filed with the pardon attorney. The efforts of Rich's attorneys were entirely ex parte.

The judge concluded that the attorneys functioned principally as lobbyists, not lawyers. They worked with public relations specialists, foreign government officials, prominent citizens, and personal friends of President Clinton. The pardon petition was couched in political, not legal, terms: "Under the circumstances, then, this case will not be resolved through trial, settlement or the withdrawal of the indictment."[91] The judge concluded that Jack Quinn was hired not "for his ability to formulate better legal arguments or write better briefs...[but] because he was 'Washington wise' and understood 'the entire political process.' He was hired because 'he could telephone the White House and engage in a 20-minute conversation with the President.'"[92]

On these grounds, the judge overruled the objections raised by the attorneys regarding the work-product doctrine and attorney-client privilege. As a result of the grand jury inquiry, additional documents would be forthcoming about the process used by Clinton to grant pardons to Rich and Green. The White House was able to withhold many documents from congressional committees by arguing that the President possesses exclusive control over the pardon power. It is much more difficult to make that argument persuasively in the context of a criminal investigation.

---

91. In re Grand Jury Subpoenas Dated March 9, 2001, 179 F.Supp.2d 270, 278 (S.D. N.Y. 2001).

92. Id. at 289.

One would think that presidential power is most secure when it involves powers that are given expressly and solely to the President. Yet probably the gravest injuries to Clinton resulted from the exercise of powers that unquestionably belonged to him: the removal and pardon powers. The range of his actions, from firing people in the White House Travel Office, to giving clemencies to FALN terrorists, to the last-minute pardons of Marc Rich and others, did lasting damage to the legacy of Clinton's years in office. Even if corruption is not proved, the slapdash nature of the process displayed a lack of professionalism, discipline, and judgment. Procedures and due process are important not just to protect individuals but to safeguard presidential power and constitutional government. Clinton's failure to respect procedure opened the door to unprecedented congressional access to documents, judicial review of the pardon process, and public scrutiny of a presidential power formerly considered highly privileged.

Tom Ridge

After the September 11, 2001, terrorist attacks, President Bush issued an executive order to establish the Office of Homeland Security, to be located within the Executive Office of the President.[93] Because of its location within the President's office and its creation by executive order instead of by statute, the White House argued that the head of the Office of Homeland Security would have protection against testifying before congressional committees. President Bush appointed Tom Ridge to head the office.

In a letter of March 4, 2002, Senators Robert C. Byrd (D-W.Va.) and Ted Stevens (R-Alas.), the chairman and ranking member of the Appropriations Committee, invited Ridge to testify before their committee on April 9, 10, and 11.[94] The White House announced that Ridge would not appear because he was an "adviser" to President Bush, not a Cabinet officer.[95] A letter of March 13 from White House liaison Nicholas Calio advised the two Senators that "members of the President's staff do not ordinarily testify before congressional committees."[96]

---

93. 66 Fed. Reg. 51812 (2001).
94. Letter from Byrd and Stevens to Ridge, March 4, 2002.
95. "Letter to Ridge Is Latest Jab in Fight Over Balance of Powers," New York Times, March 5, 2002, at A8.
96. Calio's language is cited in a letter from Byrd and Stevens to President Bush, March 15, 2002, at 1.

Not receiving a response from Ridge, Senators Byrd and Stevens wrote to President Bush, pointing out that the budget he submitted to Congress proposed $38 billion for over eighty federal departments and agencies for homeland defense. It was their position that Ridge "is the single Executive Branch official with the responsibility to integrate the many complex functions of the various Federal agencies in the formulation and execution of homeland defense programs."[97] They further argued that the duties and responsibilities that President Bush had assigned to Ridge are "much broader in scope than the staff role of advising the President," and that unless Ridge testified they would have "no recourse but to invite witnesses from more than eighty Federal departments and agencies that participate in homeland defense programs."[98] Byrd and Stevens renewed their request for Ridge to testify before the Appropriations Committee. They said they had "no interest in questioning Governor Ridge about his private advice to you." Also, they asked to meet with President Bush to explain their intentions.

The meeting with President Bush did not take place, but the letter from Byrd and Stevens prompted a letter from Ridge to Byrd, offering a compromise designed to "avoid the setting of a precedent that could undermine the Constitutional separation of powers and the long-standing traditions and practices of both Congress and the Executive Branch."[99] Ridge proposed that he provide a public briefing in April to Senators and members of Congress. Joining him would be executive officials with operational authority over the homeland security programs. Lawmakers would have the opportunity to ask questions of Ridge and the other executive officials, with the proceedings open to both the public and the press.[100] How that proposal protects the constitutional separation of powers and "long-standing traditions and practices" is difficult to fathom. Probably no credible explanation could be offered by the administration. Pressured by both parties, the White House offered an accommodation it hoped would settle the dispute.

While Senators Byrd and Stevens were considering this proposal, Ridge offered to "informally" brief two House committees.[101] He followed through by

---

97. Id.
98. Id.
99. Letter from Ridge to Byrd, March 25, 2002.
100. Id.
101. "Ridge to Brief 2 House Panels, but Rift With Senate Remains," New York Times, April 4, 2002, at A15; "Ridge Will Meet Informally With 2 House Committees," Washington Post, April 4, 2002, at A15.

meeting informally with a subcommittee of House Appropriations and the House Government Reform Committee.[102] Ridge also met with a group of Senators to discuss border security issues.[103] Ridge explained that he was willing to meet with lawmakers in "briefings" but not "hearings."[104]

These artificial distinctions created by the White House—allowing Ridge to meet informally and take questions but not appear formally to take questions, or to participate in briefings but not hearings—added fuel to congressional efforts to create a Department of Homeland Security and have the agency headed by someone who must be confirmed by the Senate and subject to being called to testify. Statutory action would override President Bush's executive order and neutralize White House arguments about Ridge functioning as a presidential adviser. Congress could have compromised by creating both a statutory agency and a small Office of Homeland Security located in the White House. However, the statute creating a Department of Homeland Security makes no mention of a White House office.[105] The Office of Homeland Security remains within the White House, as a presidential creation. Ridge became head of the Department of Homeland Security.

The White House is usually insulated from congressional inquiry because of a long-standing comity that exists between Congress and the presidency. By and large, each branch concedes a certain amount of autonomy to the other. However, in clear cases of abuse and bad faith, Congress may require White House aides to appear and give an account of their activities. The White House could minimize such requests by conducting its operations with integrity, good judgment, and respect for Congress. However, the growing reliance on White House aides who have little experience other than helping in a campaign, and little commitment to or understanding of constitutional processes, suggests that future White House mishaps—especially during first terms—will remain more the rule than the exception. As the

---

102. "From Bush Officials, A Hill Overture and a Snub: Ridge Meets House Panel in a Closed, Informal Session, but Criticism Persists," Washington Post, April 11, 2002, at A27; "Ridge Briefs House Panel, but Discord Is Not Resolved," New York Times, April 11, 2002, at A17.
103. "Ridge to Brief Senators About Border Security," Washington Post, May 2, 2002, at A2.
104. "On Homeland Security Front, a Rocky Day on the Hill," Washington Post, May 3, 2002, at A25.
105. 116 Stat. 2135 (2002).

White House continues to expand its operations to determine policy and power that used to reside in the executive departments, where legislative oversight is strong, Congress has less reason to grant the White House its customary independence.

11

NATIONAL SECURITY CLAIMS

Those who write about executive privilege sometimes imply that the mere claim by an administration of "national security" (or "foreign affairs" or "diplomacy") is sufficient to establish presidential primacy. In one article, Saikrishna Prakash writes that "national security considerations strongly bolster the case for an executive privilege.... Properly wielded, an executive privilege could lead to...enhanced [presidential] supervision of foreign affairs...."[1] Writing for the Court in the Watergate Tapes Case, Chief Justice Burger rejected an "absolute, unqualified" presidential privilege of immunity from judicial process.[2] However, in clumsy dicta, he seemed to cede ground if the President claimed a "need to protect military, diplomatic, or sensitive national security secrets."[3] If the Court wants to acquiesce to such presidential arguments, it is free to do so. But Congress has no reason to follow in its steps. The Watergate Tapes Case concerned *judicial*, not *congressional*, access to executive branch information.[4]

In 1973, President Nixon was asked to compare the congressional investigation of Watergate with his earlier inquiry—as a member of Congress—in the Alger Hiss case. A reporter noted that the Hiss investigation involved "foreign affairs" and "possibly security matters," whereas the pending questioning of John Dean concerned the Watergate break-in. Should lawmakers have reduced access to national security documents? Nixon argued that they needed *greater* access: "when a committee of Congress was investigating espionage against the Government of this country, that committee should have had com-

---

1. Saikrishna Bangalore Prakash, "A Critical Comment on the Constitutionality of Executive Privilege," 83 Minn. L. Rev. 1143, 1145 (1999).
2. United States v. Nixon, 418 U.S. 683, 706 (1974).
3. Id.
4. A footnote in the Court's decision makes this distinction clear: "We are not here concerned with...congressional demands for information." Id. at 712 n.19.

plete cooperation from at least the executive branch of the Government in the form that we asked." The Watergate investigation, he said, "does not involve espionage against the United States." Nixon insisted that Congress "would have a far greater right and would be on much stronger ground to ask the Government to cooperate in a matter involving espionage against the Government than in a matter like this involving politics."[5]

Unlike the judiciary, Congress has express constitutional powers and duties in the fields of military affairs and national security. When Congress passed the Freedom of Information Act (FOIA), requiring executive agencies to make documents available to the public, it set forth nine exemptions, including matters that are "(A) specifically authorized under criteria established by an Executive order to be kept secret in the interest of national defense or foreign policy and (B) are in fact properly classified pursuant to such Executive order."[6] Another exemption: "inter-agency or intra-agency memorandums or letters which would not be available by law to a party other than an agency in litigation with the agency."[7] Yet another exemption: "records or information compiled for law enforcement purposes...."[8] Those are some of the grounds for denying *members of the public* information from executive agencies. They do not apply to Congress. FOIA specifically provides that those exemptions do not constitute "authority to withhold information from Congress."[9]

Controlling National Security Information

A 1996 memorandum prepared by the Office of Legal Counsel argued that a congressional enactment "would be unconstitutional if it were interpreted 'to divest the President of his control over national security information in the Executive Branch' by vesting lower-ranking personnel in that Branch with a 'right' to furnish such information to a Member of Congress without receiving official authorization to do so.'"[10] OLC based this position on the following separation of powers rationale:

---

5. Public Papers of the Presidents, 1973, at 211–12.
6. 5 U.S.C. §552(b)(1) (2000).
7. Id. at §552(b)(5).
8. Id. at §552(b)(7).
9. Id. at §552(d).
10. Memorandum from Christopher H. Schroeder, Office of Legal Counsel, Department of Justice, to Michael J. O'Neil, General Counsel to the Central Intelligence Agency, November 26, 1996, at 3 (hereafter "OLC Memo").

[T]he President's roles as Commander in Chief, head of the Executive Branch, and sole organ of the Nation in its external relations require that he have ultimate and unimpeded authority over the collection, retention and dissemination of intelligence and other national security information in the Executive Branch. There is no exception to this principle for those disseminations that would be made to Congress or its Members. In that context, as in all others, the decision whether to grant access to the information must be made by someone who is acting in an official capacity on behalf of the President and who is ultimately responsible, perhaps through intermediaries, to the President. The Constitution does not permit Congress to circumvent these orderly procedures and chain of command—and to erect an obstacle to the President's exercise of all executive powers relating to the Nation's security—by vesting lower-level employees in the Executive Branch with a supposed "right" to disclose national security information to Members of Congress (or anyone else) without the authorization of Executive Branch personnel who derive their authority from the President.[11]

As explained later in this chapter, OLC's analysis led to the conclusion that two congressional statutes—one dating back to 1912, and pending language in a Senate bill—were unconstitutional. However, the department's position relies on faulty generalizations and misconceptions about the President's roles as Commander in Chief, head of the Executive Branch, and "sole organ" of the Nation in its external relations.

Commander in Chief

The Constitution empowers the President to be Commander in Chief, but that title must be understood in the context of military responsibilities that the Constitution grants to Congress. Article II reads: "The President shall be Commander in Chief of the Army and Navy of the United States, and of the Militia of the several States, when called into the actual Service of the United States."[12] For the militia, Congress—not the President—does the calling. The Constitution gives to Congress the power to provide "for calling forth the Militia to execute the Laws of the Union, suppress Insurrections and repel invasions."[13]

---

11. Id. at 4.
12. U.S. Const., art. II, §2.
13. Id., art. I, §8, cl. 15.

An important purpose of the Commander in Chief Clause is to preserve civilian supremacy. Attorney General Edward Bates explained in 1861 that the President is made Commander in Chief "not because the President is supposed to be, or commonly is, in fact, a military man, a man skilled in the art of war and qualified to marshal a host in the field of battle. No, it is for quite a different reason." A soldier knows that whatever military victories might occur, "he is subject to the orders of the *civil magistrate*, and he and his army are always 'subordinate to the civil power.'"[14]

Article I empowers Congress to declare war, raise and support armies, and make rules for the land and naval forces. The debates at the Philadelphia Convention make clear that the Commander in Chief Clause did not grant the President unilateral, independent power other than the power to "repel sudden attacks."[15] Roger Sherman said the President should be able "to repel and not to commence war."[16] Taking the country from a state of peace to a state of war was a deliberative process that required congressional debate and approval. George Mason told his colleagues that he was for "clogging rather than facilitating war."[17] At the Pennsylvania ratifying convention, James Wilson expressed the prevailing sentiment that the system of checks and balances "will not hurry us into war; it is calculated to guard against it. It will not be in the power of a single man, or a single body of men, to involve us in such distress."[18]

The framers gave Congress the power to initiate war because they believed that Presidents, in the search for fame and personal glory, would have a bias that favored war.[19] John Jay warned in Federalist No. 4 that "absolute monarchs will often make war when their nations are to get nothing by it, but for purposes and objects merely personal, such as a thirst for military glory, revenge for personal affronts, ambition, or private compacts to aggrandize or support their particular families or partisans."[20] James Madison made the same point. Writing in 1793, he called war "the true nurse of executive aggrandizement.... In war, the honours and emoluments of office are to be multiplied; and it is the executive patronage under which they are to be enjoyed. It is in

---

14. 10 Op. Att'y Gen. 74, 79 (1861) (emphasis in original).
15. 2 Farrand 318–19.
16. Id. at 318.
17. Id. at 319.
18. 2 The Debates in the Several State Conventions, on the Adoption of the Federal Constitution 528 (Elliot ed. 1896).
19. William Michael Treanor, "Fame, the Founding, and the Power to Declare War," 82 Corn. L. Rev. 695 (1997).
20. The Federalist 101 (Benjamin Fletcher Wright ed. 1961).

war, finally, that laurels are to be gathered; and it is the executive brow they are to encircle."[21]

All three branches understood that the President's unilateral power in matters of war is limited to defensive actions. Implied in the power of Congress to declare war was the President's power "to repel sudden attacks."[22] For example, when the Supreme Court upheld Lincoln's blockade on the rebellious states, Justice Robert Grier emphasized that the President as Commander in Chief "has no power to initiate or declare a war against either a foreign nation or a domestic State."[23] The executive branch took exactly the same position. During oral argument, Richard Henry Dana, Jr., who was representing the President, acknowledged that Lincoln's actions had nothing to do with "the right *to initiate a war, as a voluntary act of sovereignty*. That is vested only in Congress."[24]

The historical record is replete with examples of Congress relying on the regular legislative process, including access to national security information held by the executive branch, to control presidential actions in military affairs.[25] There is no evidence from these sources that the Commander in Chief Clause was intended to deny members of Congress information needed to supervise the executive branch and learn of agency wrongdoing.

Head of the Executive Branch

The framers placed the President at the head of the executive branch to provide for unity, responsibility, and accountability. No doubt that is an important principle for assuring that the President, under Article II, Section 3, is positioned to "take Care that the Laws be faithfully executed." The delegates at the constitutional convention rejected the idea of a plural executive, preferring to anchor that responsibility in a single individual. Said John Rutledge: "A single man would feel the greatest responsibility and administer the public affairs best."[26]

But placing the President at the head of the executive branch did not remove from Congress the power to direct certain executive activities and to gain access to information needed for the performance of its legislative duties. At the Convention, Roger Sherman considered the executive "nothing more than

---

21. 6 The Writings of James Madison 174 (Hunt ed. 1906).
22. 2 Farrand 318–19.
23. The Prize Cases, 67 U.S. 635, 668 (1863).
24. Id. at 660 (emphasis in original).
25. Louis Fisher, Presidential War Power (1995).
26. 1 Farrand 65.

an institution for carrying the will of the Legislature into effect."[27] It was never the purpose to make the President personally responsible for executing all the laws. Rather, he was to take care that the laws be faithfully executed, including laws that excluded him from some operations in the executive branch.

For example, from an early date Congress vested in certain subordinate executive officials the duty to carry out specified "ministerial" functions without interference from the President. On many occasions an Attorney General has advised Presidents that they have no legal right to interfere with administrative decisions made by the auditors and comptrollers in the Treasury Department, pension officers, and other officials.[28] The President is responsible for seeing that administrative officers faithfully perform their duties, "but the statutes regulate and prescribe these duties, and he has no more power to add to, or subtract from, the duties imposed upon subordinate executive and administrative officers by the law, than those officers have to add or subtract from his duties."[29] In several decisions the Supreme Court has recognized that Congress can impose certain duties on executive officials that are beyond the control and direction of the President.[30]

Those principles were underscored by a confrontation during the Reagan administration. In 1984, Congress passed the Competition in Contracting Act (CICA) to give the Comptroller General certain authorities over agency contracting. President Reagan signed the bill but instructed Attorney General Edwin Meese to inform all executive branch agencies how to comply with the statute "in a manner consistent with the Constitution."[31] A memorandum from the Justice Department concluded that the contested provision for the Comptroller General was unconstitutional and should not be enforced by the agencies.[32] In effect, the administration had exercised an item veto by decid-

---

27. Id.
28. 1 Op. Att'y Gen. 624 (1823); 1 Op. Att'y Gen. 636 (1824); 1 Op. Att'y Gen. 678 (1824); 1 Op. Att'y Gen. 705 (1825); 1 Op. Att'y Gen. 706 (1825); 2 Op. Att'y Gen. 480 (1831); 2 Op. Att'y Gen. 507 (1832); 2 Op. Att'y Gen. 544 (1832); 4 Op. Att'y Gen. 515 (1846); 5 Op. Att'y Gen. 287 (1851); 11 Op. Att'y Gen. 14 (1864); 13 Op. Att'y Gen. 28 (1869).
29. 19 Op. Att'y Gen. 685, 686–87 (1890).
30. E.g., Kendall v. United States, 37 U.S. 522, 610 (1838); United States v. Schurz, 102 U.S. 378 (1880); Butterworth v. Hoe, 112 U.S. 50 (1884); United States v. Price, 116 U.S. 43 (1885); United States v. Louisville, 169 U.S. 249 (1898).
31. Public Papers of the Presidents, 1984, II, at 1053.
32. Office of Legal Counsel, Department of Justice, Memorandum for the Attorney General, "Implementation of the Bid Protest Provisions of the Competition in Contracting Act," October 17, 1984, at 15.

ing what parts of a statute to carry out. This was part of a larger strategy devised by enthusiasts who believed in the theory of a "unitary executive," with all parts of the executive branch directly accountable and subordinate to the President.[33]

This theory was repeatedly struck down in the courts. In upholding the provisions of CICA, a district judge stated that the position of the Reagan administration "flatly violates the express instruction of the Constitution that the President shall 'take care that the Laws be faithfully executed.'"[34] Once a bill is enacted into law, the President executes all of it, not just the parts he favors. The district court's ruling was upheld on appeal by the Third Circuit.[35] The Ninth Circuit, in upholding the Comptroller General provision, said that once Reagan put his signature to CICA it became "part of the law of the land and the President must 'take care that [it] be faithfully executed.'"[36] In his role as head of the executive branch, the President has no authority to "employ a so-called 'line item veto'and excise or sever provisions of a bill with which he disagrees."[37] A later attempt by the Justice Department to challenge the constitutionality of CICA was also turned aside in the courts.[38]

Agencies have a direct responsibility to Congress, the body that creates them. In 1854, Attorney General Caleb Cushing advised departmental heads that they had a threefold relation: to the President, to execute his will in cases in which the President possessed a constitutional or legal discretion; to the law, which directs them to perform certain acts; and to Congress, "in the conditions contemplated by the Constitution." Agencies are created by law and "most of their duties are prescribed by law; Congress may at all times call on them for information or explanation in matters of official duty; and it may, if it sees fit, interpose by legislation concerning them, when required by the interests of the Government."[39]

---

33. For an excellent analysis of the deficiencies of this theory, see Morton Rosenberg, "Congress's Prerogative Over Agencies and Agency Decisionmakers: The Rise and Demise of the Reagan Administration's Theory of the Unitary Executive," 57 G.W. L. Rev. 627 (1989).

34. Ameron, Inc. v. U.S. Army Corps of Engineers, 610 F.Supp. 750, 755 (D. N.J. 1985). See also Ameron, Inc. v. U.S. Army Corps of Engineers, 607 F.Supp. 962 (D. N.J. 1985).

35. Ameron v. United States Army Corps of Engineers, 809 F.2d 979 (3d Cir. 1986); Ameron, Inc. v. U.S. Army Corps of Engineers, 787 F.2d 875 (3d Cir. 1986)

36. Lear Siegler, Inc., Energy Products Div. v. Lehman, 842 F.2d 1102, 1124 (9th Cir. 1988).

37. Id.

38. United States v. Instruments, S.A., Inc., 807 F.Supp. 811 (D.D.C. 1992).

39. 6 Op. Att'y Gen. 326, 344 (1854).

"Sole Organ" in Foreign Affairs

During debate in the House of Representatives in 1800, John Marshall said that the President "is the sole organ of the nation in its external relations and its sole representative with foreign nations."[40] That remark was later incorporated in Justice Sutherland's opinion in *United States* v. *Curtiss-Wright Corp.* (1936), to suggest that the President is the exclusive policymaker in foreign affairs.[41] However, Justice Sutherland wrenched Marshall's statement from context to imply a position that Marshall never held. At no time, either in 1800 or later, did Marshall ever suggest that the President could act unilaterally to make foreign policy in the face of statutory limitations.

The debate in 1800 focused on the decision of President John Adams to turn over to England someone who had been charged with murder. Because the case was already pending in an American court, some members of Congress thought that Adams should be impeached for encroaching upon the judiciary and violating the doctrine of separated powers.[42] It was at that point that Marshall intervened to say that there was no basis for impeachment. Adams, by carrying out an extradition treaty entered into between England and the United States, was not attempting to make national policy single-handedly. Instead, he was carrying out a policy made jointly by the President and the Senate (for treaties).[43] Only after the policy had been formulated through the collective effort of the executive and legislative branches (by treaty or by statute) did the President emerge as the "sole organ" in *implementing* national policy. The President merely *announced* policy; he did not alone *make* it. Consistent with that principle, Marshall later decided a case as Chief Justice of the Supreme Court and ruled that in a conflict between a presidential proclamation and a congressional statute governing the seizure of foreign vessels during wartime, the statute prevails.[44]

Sutherland's use of "sole organ" in *Curtiss-Wright* prompted Justice Robert Jackson in 1952 to say that the most that can be drawn from Sutherland's decision is the intimation that the President "might act in external affairs without congressional authority, but not that he might act contrary to an Act of Congress."[45] Jackson also noted that "much of the [Sutherland] opinion is *dic-*

---

40. Annals of Cong., 6th Cong. 613 (1800).
41. 299 U.S. 304, 319–20 (1936).
42. Annals of Cong., 6th Cong. 552 (1800) (statement of Rep. Harper).
43. Id. at 597, 613–14.
44. Little v. Barreme, 6 U.S. (2 Cr.) 169, 179 (1804).
45. Youngstown Co. v. Sawyer, 343 U.S. 579, 636 n.2 (1952).

tum."⁴⁶ In 1981, the D.C. Circuit cautioned against placing undue reliance on "certain dicta" in Sutherland's opinion: "To the extent that denominating the President as the 'sole organ' of the United States in international affairs constitutes a blanket endorsement of plenary Presidential power over any matter extending beyond the borders of this country, we reject that characterization."⁴⁷

Role of the Courts

In the period immediately after World War II, federal courts typically deferred to presidential responsibilities in military and diplomatic affairs. In 1948, the Supreme Court said it would be "intolerable that courts, without the relevant information, should review and perhaps nullify actions of the Executive taken on information properly held secret. Nor can courts sit *in camera* in order to be taken into executive confidences. But even if courts could require full disclosure, the very nature of executive decisions as to foreign policy is political, not judicial."⁴⁸ The deference here was not wholly to the President. Such decisions, said the Court, "are wholly confided by our Constitution to the political departments of the government, Executive and Legislative."⁴⁹

A few years later, in the midst of the Korean War, the Court again avoided a clash with the executive branch over national security documents. A district court had ordered the government to produce documents to permit the court to determine whether they contained privileged matter. The Supreme Court reversed, ruling that the judiciary "should not jeopardize the security which the [government's] privilege is meant to protect by insisting upon an examination of the evidence, even by the judge alone, in chambers."⁵⁰

Those attitudes have long since been superseded by statutory grants of power to the courts, discussed later, that invite judges to exercise independent judgment on matters of national security. Nevertheless, some courts continue to defer to the President. In 1980, the Fourth Circuit remarked that the "executive possesses unparalleled expertise to make the decision whether to conduct foreign intelligence surveillance, whereas the judiciary is largely in-

---

46. Id. (emphasis in original).
47. American Intern. Group v. Islamic Republic of Iran, 657 F.2d 430, 438 n.6 (D.C. Cir. 1981).
48. C.& S. Air Lines v. Waterman Corp., 333 U.S. 103, 111 (1948).
49. Id.
50. United States v. Reynolds, 345 U.S. 1, 10 (1953).

experienced in making the delicate and complex decisions that lie behind foreign intelligence surveillance."[51] The Fourth Circuit freely expressed its uneasiness in this area: "the courts are unschooled in diplomacy and military affairs, a mastery of which would be essential to passing upon an executive branch request that a foreign intelligence wiretap be authorized."[52] Although the lawsuit presented a potential conflict between the President and the judiciary—and not a clash between the President and Congress—the court called the executive branch "constitutionally designated as the pre-eminent authority in foreign affairs."[53] However obsequious federal judges decide to behave, Congress—given its explicit constitutional duties—does not have to assume the same posture.

The Pentagon Papers

In the Pentagon Papers Case in 1971, the Supreme Court decided that two newspapers were constitutionally entitled to publish a Defense Department secret study that was critical of U.S. policy in the Vietnam War. Justice Stewart wrote a concurrence that spoke approvingly of independent presidential power: "If the Constitution gives the Executive a large degree of unshared power in the conduct of foreign affairs and the maintenance of our national defense, then under the Constitution the Executive must have the largely unshared duty to determine and preserve the degree of internal security necessary to exercise that power successfully."[54]

At first glance this sentence may seem logical: If one clause is valid, the other follows. But there is no necessary linkage between the two statements. The President's largely unshared power to *conduct* foreign affairs does not imply a largely unshared power to determine the *policy* for internal security, nor does it imply a largely unshared power to provide oversight of the policy. The conduct of foreign policy usually means the implementation of national security policy arrived at jointly by Congress and the President. Conduct may be executive but the policy and the oversight is executive-legislative. That is true to an even greater extent in the "maintenance of our national defense," as Justice Stewart expressed it. Congress shares that responsibility with the Pres-

---

51. United States v. Truong Dinh Hung, 629 F.2d 908, 913 (4th Cir. 1980).
52. Id. at 913–14.
53. Id. at 914.
54. New York Times Co. v. United States, 403 U.S. 713, 728–29 (1971) (Stewart, J., concurring).

ident. In the field of foreign affairs, the Constitution does not give "a large degree of unshared power" either to Congress or to the President.

Justice Stewart offered other broad views about presidential power: "it is clear to me that it is the constitutional duty of the Executive—as a matter of sovereign prerogative and not as a matter of law as the courts know law—through the promulgation and enforcement of executive regulations, to protect the confidentiality necessary to carry out its responsibilities in the fields of international relations and national defense."[55] No one doubts that the President has important duties and prerogatives in protecting confidential information. The more difficult question is the degree to which Congress can share in those duties and prerogatives by enacting restrictive legislation and conducting oversight. On that issue, Stewart's concurrence provides no answer.

Justice Stewart did acknowledge that the President lacks a monopoly: "This is not to say that Congress and the courts have no role to play."[56] And yet he appeared to assign to Congress a narrow, subordinate role: "Undoubtedly Congress has the power to enact specific and appropriate criminal laws to protect government property and preserve government secrets."[57] In any event, a concurrence by a Justice has no authoritative value in settling or defining constitutional issues.

Two other points about the Stewart concurrence deserve comment. First, his overall analysis depends almost entirely on a single case, *Curtiss-Wright*,[58] which is itself deeply flawed. Second, after stating that presidential power in national defense and international relations is "largely unchecked by the Legislative and Judicial branches,"[59] and that there is "the absence of the governmental checks and balances present in other areas of our national life,"[60] he concluded that the Pentagon documents should be published in the newspapers. Because of what he believed to be inadequate governmental checks on presidential power, Justice Stewart declared that "the only effective restraint upon executive policy and power in the areas of national defense and international affairs may lie in an enlightened citizenry—in an informed and critical public opinion which alone can here protect the values of democratic government."[61] It was for that reason that he supported "an informed and free press" to enlighten the people.[62]

---

55. Id. at 729–30.
56. Id. at 730.
57. Id.
58. Id. at 727 n.2, 728–29 n.3 (citing United States v. Curtiss-Wright).
59. Id. at 727.
60. Id. at 728.
61. Id.
62. Id.

Recent Statutory Changes

Judicial attitudes have become somewhat more emboldened in recent decades, in part because of congressional legislation. In 1973, the Supreme Court decided that it had no authority to examine *in camera* certain documents regarding a planned underground nuclear test to sift out "nonsecret components" for their release.[63] In response, Congress passed legislation to clearly authorize courts to examine executive records in judges' chambers as part of a determination of the nine categories of exemptions in the Freedom of Information Act.[64] The Foreign Intelligence Surveillance Act of 1978 requires a court order to engage in electronic surveillance within the United States for purposes of obtaining foreign intelligence information. A special court, the Foreign Intelligence Surveillance Court (FISC), is appointed by the Chief Justice to review applications submitted by government attorneys.[65] In 1980, Congress passed the Classified Information Procedures Act (CIPA) to establish procedures in court to allow a judge to screen classified information to determine whether it could be used during the trial.[66]

These statutes bring the courts a long way in terms of attitude, procedures, and capability in passing judgment on national security matters. Even if courts were to continue to defer to the President, the same attitude should not be taken by Congress. Unlike the courts, Congress has explicit duties under the Constitution to declare war, provide for the common defense, raise and support armies, and provide and maintain a navy. Legislative expertise exists in the Armed Services Committees, the defense appropriations subcommittees, the Budget Committees, the intelligence committees, and other legislative panels.

Deference by the courts need not mean deference by Congress. Two recent decisions by the Supreme Court—one in 1988 and the other in 1989—have been misinterpreted by the executive branch and some scholars to confer an unwarranted independent authority on the part of the President in foreign affairs and national security.

---

63. EPA v. Mink, 410 U.S. 73, 81 (1973).
64. 88 Stat. 1562, §4(B) (1974); see H. Rept. No. 1380, 93d Cong., 2d Sess. 8–9, 11–12 (1974).
65. 92 Stat. 1783 (1978).
66. 94 Stat. 2025 (1980).

Department of the Navy v. Egan (1988)

The OLC memo in 1996 relied in part on *Department of the Navy* v. *Egan* to maximize presidential power.[67] However, *Egan* is fundamentally and solely a case of statutory construction.[68] It has nothing to do with the President's constitutional authority. The dispute involved the Navy's denial of a security clearance to Thomas Egan, who worked on the Trident submarine. He was subsequently removed. Egan sought review by the Merit Systems Protection Board (MSPB), but the Supreme Court upheld the Navy's action by ruling that the denial of a security clearance is a sensitive discretionary judgment call *committed by law* to the executive agency with the necessary expertise for protecting classified information.[69] The conflict in this case was within the executive branch (Navy versus the MSPB), not between Congress and the executive branch.

The focus on statutory questions was evident throughout the case. As the Justice Department noted in its brief submitted to the Supreme Court: "The issue in this case is one of statutory construction and 'at bottom...turns on congressional intent.'"[70] The parties were directed to address this question: "Whether, in the course of reviewing the removal of an employee for failure to maintain a required security clearance, the Merit Systems Protection Board is *authorized by statute* to review the substance of the underlying decision to deny or revoke the security clearance."[71]

The statutory questions centered on 5 U.S.C. §§ 7512, 7513, 7532, and 7701. The Justice Department's brief analyzed the relevant statutes and their legislative history and could find no basis for determining that Congress intended the MSPB to review the merits of security clearance determinations.[72] The entire oral argument before the Court on December 2, 1987, was devoted to the meaning of statutes and what Congress intended by them. At no time did the Justice Department suggest that classified information could be withheld from Congress.

The Court's deference to the Navy did not cast a shadow over the right of Congress to sensitive information. The Court decided merely the "narrow

---

67. OLC Memo, at 6–7.
68. 484 U.S. 518 (1988).
69. Id. at 529–30.
70. U.S. Department of Justice, "Brief for the Petitioner," Department of the Navy v. Egan, October Term, 1987, at 22 (citing Clarke v. Securities Industry Ass'n, No. 85-971, January 14, 1987).
71. Id. at (I) (emphasis added).
72. U.S. Department of Justice, "Petition for a Writ of Certiorari to the United States Court of Appeals for the Federal Circuit," Department of the Navy v. Thomas E. Egan, October Term, 1986, at 4–5, 13, 15–16, 18.

question" of whether the MSPB had *statutory* authority to review the substance of a decision to deny a security clearance.[73] Although the Court referred to independent constitutional powers of the President, including those as Commander in Chief and head of the executive branch,[74] and noted the President's responsibility with regard to foreign policy,[75] the case was decided purely on statutory grounds. In stating that courts "traditionally have been reluctant to intrude upon the authority of the Executive in military and national security affairs," the Court added this key qualification: "*unless Congress specifically has provided otherwise.*"[76] The Court appears to have borrowed this thought, and language, from the Justice Department's brief: "Absent an unambiguous grant of jurisdiction by Congress, courts have traditionally been reluctant to intrude upon the authority of the executive in military and national security affairs."[77] Nothing in the legislative history of the Civil Service Reform Act of 1978 convinced the Court that the MSPB could review, on the merits, an agency's security-clearance determination.[78]

During oral argument before the Supreme Court, the Justice Department and Egan's attorney, William J. Nold, debated the statutory issues. After the department completed its presentation, Nold told the Justices "I think that we start out with the same premise. We start out with the premise that this is a case that involves statutory interpretation." Yet Nold remarked on the department's effort to shoehorn in some constitutional qualities: "What they seem to do in my view is to start building a cloud around the statute. They start building this cloud and they call it national security, and as their argument progresses...the cloud gets darker and darker and darker, so that by the time we get to the end, we can't see the statute anymore. What we see is this cloud called national security."[79]

In citing the President's role as Commander in Chief, the Court stated that the President's authority to protect classified information "flows primarily from this constitutional investment of power in the President and exists quite apart from any explicit congressional grant."[80] If Congress had never enacted legisla-

---

73. 484 U.S. at 520.
74. Id. at 527.
75. Id. at 529.
76. Id. at 530 (emphasis added).
77. U.S. Department of Justice, "Brief for the Petitioner," Department of the Navy v. Egan, October term, 1987, at 21.
78. 484 U.S. at 531 n.6.
79. Transcript of Oral Argument, December 2, 1987, at 19.
80. 484 U.S. at 527.

tion regarding classified information, certainly the President could act in the absence of congressional authority. But if Congress acts by statute, it can narrow the President's range of action and the courts then look to congressional policy.

It is helpful to place *Egan* in the context of Justice Jackson's three categories laid out in the Steel Seizure Case of 1952: (1) when the President acts pursuant to congressional authority his authority is at its maximum, because it includes everything that he possesses under the Constitution plus what Congress has delegated to him; (2) when he acts in the absence of congressional authority he operates in a "zone of twilight" in which he and Congress share concurrent authority; (3) when he acts against the expressed or implied will of Congress, his power is at "its lowest ebb."[81] *Egan* belongs in the middle category. The President's range is broad until Congress enters the zone of twilight and exerts its own authority.

The *Garfinkel* Case

The OLC memo also misinterprets the litigation that led to the Supreme Court's decision in *American Foreign Service Assn. v. Garfinkel* (1989).[82] At various points the memo cites *Garfinkel* for the proposition that Congress cannot "divest the President of his control over national security information in the Executive Branch by vesting lower-ranking personnel in that Branch with a 'right' to furnish such information to a Member of Congress without receiving official authorization to do so."[83] Yet the progression of this case from district court to the Supreme Court and back to the district court illustrates how a lower court may exaggerate the national security powers of the President at the expense of congressional prerogatives. The district court's expansive view of executive power was quickly vacated by the Supreme Court.

In 1983, President Reagan directed that all federal employees with access to classified information sign "nondisclosure agreements" or risk the loss of their security clearance.[84] Congress, concerned about the vagueness of some terms and the loss of access to information, passed legislation to prohibit the use of appropriated funds to implement the nondisclosure policy.[85] In 1988, District Court Judge Oliver Gasch held that Congress lacked constitutional authority

---

81. Youngstown Co. v. Sawyer, 343 U.S. 579, 635–37 (1952).
82. 490 U.S. 153 (1989).
83. OLC Memo, at 3.
84. National Security Decision Directive 84; see Louis Fisher, "Congressional-Executive Struggles Over Information Secrecy Pledges," 42 Adm. L. Rev. 89, 90 (1990).
85. 101 Stat. 1329-432, §630 (1987); 102 Stat. 1756, §619 (1988).

to interfere, by statute, with nondisclosure agreements drafted by the executive branch to protect the secrecy of classified information.[86] Among other authorities, Judge Gasch relied on *Egan* and *Curtiss-Wright*.[87] From *Egan* he extracts a sentence ("The authority to protect such [national security] information falls on the President as head of the Executive Branch and as Commander in Chief") without acknowledging that *Egan* was decided on statutory, not constitutional, grounds.[88] From *Curtiss-Wright* he concludes that the "sensitive and complicated role cast for the President as this nation's emissary in foreign relations requires that congressional intrusion upon the President's oversight of national security information be more severely limited than might be required in matters of purely domestic concern."[89]

In fact, the issue in *Curtiss-Wright* was whether Congress could delegate *its* powers to the President in the field of foreign relations. The previous year the Court had struck down the National Industrial Recovery Act because it had delegated an excessive amount of legislative power to the President in the field of domestic policy.[90] The question before the Court in *Curtiss-Wright* was limited: Could Congress use more general standards when delegating its authority in foreign affairs? The Court held that more general standards were permissible because of the changing circumstances that prevail in international affairs. The issue before the Court was the extent to which Congress could delegate its power (embargo authority), not the existence of independent and autonomous powers for the President.

Having mischaracterized both Supreme Court decisions, Judge Gasch concluded that Congress had passed legislation that "impermissibly restricts the President's power to fulfill obligations imposed upon him by his express constitutional powers and the role of the Executive in foreign relations."[91]

On October 31, 1988, the Supreme Court noted probable jurisdiction in the *Garfinkel* case.[92] Both the House and the Senate submitted briefs protesting Judge Gasch's analysis of the President's power over foreign affairs. During oral argument, after Edwin Kneedler of the Justice Department spoke re-

---

86. National Federation of Federal Employees v. United States, 688 F.Supp. 671 (D.D.C. 1988).
87. Id. at 676, 684–85.
88. Id. at 685.
89. Id.
90. Schechter Poultry Corp. v. United States, 295 U.S. 495 (1935); Panama Refining Co. v. Ryan, 293 U.S. 388 (1935).
91. 688 F.Supp. at 685.
92. 488 U.S. 923 (1988).

peatedly about the President's constitutional role to control classified information, one of the Justices remarked: "But, Mr. Kneedler, I just can't—I can't avoid interrupting you with this thought. The Constitution also gives Congress the power to provide for a navy and for the armed forces, and so forth, and often classified information is highly relevant to their task."[93] The attorney for the association challenging Reagan's nondisclosure policy objected that Gasch's decision, "by declaring that the Executive Branch has such sweeping power, has impeded the kind of accommodation that should take place in this kind of controversy," and hoped that the Court "wipes that decision off the books."[94]

On April 18, 1989, the Court issued a per curiam order that vacated Judge Gasch's order and remanded the case for further consideration.[95] In doing so, the Court cautioned Judge Gasch to tread with greater caution in expounding on constitutional matters: "Having thus skirted the statutory question whether the Executive Branch's implementation of [Nondisclosure] Forms 189 and 4193 violated §630, the court proceeded to address appellees' argument that the lawsuit should be dismissed because §630 was an unconstitutional interference with the President's authority to protect the national security."[96] The Court emphasized that the district court "should not pronounce upon the relative constitutional authority of Congress and the Executive Branch unless it finds it imperative to do so. Particularly where, as here, a case implicates the fundamental relationship between the Branches, courts should be extremely careful not to issue unnecessary constitutional rulings."[97] On remand, Judge Gasch held that the plaintiffs (American Foreign Service Association and Members of Congress) failed to state a cause of action for courts to decide.[98] By dismissing the plaintiff's complaint on this ground, Judge Gasch did not address any of the constitutional issues.[99]

Settling Executive-Legislative Collisions

In the 1970s and 1980s, Congress and the executive branch clashed repeatedly over access to "national security" and "foreign affairs" documents. On

---

93. Transcript of Oral Argument, March 20, 1989, at 57–58.
94. Id. at 60.
95. American Foreign Service Assn. v. Garfinkel, 490 U.S. 153 (1989).
96. Id. at 158.
97. Id. at 161.
98. American Foreign Service Ass'n Garfinkel, 732 F.Supp. 13 (D.D.C. 1990).
99. Id. at 16.

each occasion the Justice Department insisted that the documents could not be shared with a congressional committee. In the end, the administration had to drop its pretensions to having an exclusive role in determining what to release to Congress. Federal courts applied the necessary pressure in the first dispute. In two other confrontations, the power of Congress to hold an executive official in contempt was sufficient leverage to pry loose the documents.

The AT&T Cases

The first dispute began in 1976 when Congressman John Moss and his subcommittee requested from the American Telephone and Telegraph Co. (AT&T) information on "national security" wiretaps by the administration. The company was willing to release the information, but the Justice Department intervened to prevent compliance with the subcommittee subpoena, arguing that compliance might lead to public disclosure of vital information injurious to national security. President Ford wrote directly to Congressman Moss: "I have determined that compliance with the subpoena would involve unacceptable risks of disclosure of extremely sensitive foreign intelligence and counterintelligence information and would be detrimental to the national defense and foreign policy of the United States and damaging to the national security."[100]

A district judge decided that if a final determination had to be made about the need for secrecy and the risk of disclosure, "it should be made by the constituent branch of government to which the primary role in these areas is entrusted. In the areas of national security and foreign policy, that role is given to the Executive."[101] This judicial deference to presidential power was soon overturned by the D.C. Circuit. Writing for the appellate court, Judge Harold Leventhal rejected the claim of the Justice Department that the President "retains ultimate authority to decide what risks to national security are acceptable."[102] The cases cited by the administration "do not establish judicial deference to executive determinations in the area of national security when the result of that deference would be to impede Congress in exercising its legislative powers."[103]

Leventhal urged executive and legislative officials to settle their differences out of court, pointing out that a "compromise worked out between the branches is most likely to meet their essential needs and the country's consti-

---

100. Timothy S. Robinson, "Judge Halts Hill Probe of Wiretaps," Washington Post, July 23, 1976, at A12.
101. United States v. AT&T, 419 F.Supp. 454, 461 (D.D.C. 1976).
102. United States v. American Tel. & Tel. Co., 551 F.2d 384, 392 (D.C. Cir. 1976).
103. Id.

tutional balance."[104] Continued disagreement between the Justice Department and the subcommittee forced the appellate court to intervene again to give additional guidance. Leventhal dismissed the idea that the dispute was a "political question" beyond the court's jurisdiction. When a dispute consists of a clash of authority between the two branches, "judicial abstention does not lead to orderly resolution of the dispute," for neither branch had "final authority in the area of concern." In a dispute of this nature, judicial intervention helps promote the "smooth functioning of government."[105]

Advising the parties to resolve their differences by seeking middle-ground positions, Leventhal noted that the framers, in adopting a Constitution with general and overlapping provisions, anticipated that "a spirit of dynamic compromise would promote resolution of the dispute in the manner most likely to result in efficient and effective functioning of our governmental system."[106] Each branch "should take cognizance of an implicit constitutional mandate to seek optimal accommodation through a realistic evaluation of the needs of the conflicting branches in the particular fact situation."[107] The case was finally dismissed on December 21, 1978, after the Justice Department and the subcommittee settled their differences.[108]

Proceedings against Henry Kissinger

On November 6, 1975, the House Select Committee on Intelligence issued a subpoena to Henry Kissinger, Secretary of State, commanding him to provide documents relating to covert actions.[109] After he failed to comply with the subpoena, the committee voted 10 to 2 to cite Kissinger for contempt of Congress.[110] Acting on the advice of the Justice Department, President Ford invoked executive privilege to keep the material from the committee, arguing that the documents included "recommendations from previous Secretaries of State to then Presidents," jeopardizing the internal decisionmaking process.[111] A few days later, in a letter to the committee, Ford cautioned that the dispute

---

104. Id. at 394.
105. United States v. AT&T, 567 F.2d 121, 126 (D.C. Cir. 1977).
106. Id. at 127.
107. Id.
108. House Select Committee on Congressional Operations, "Court Proceedings and Actions of Vital Interest to the Congress, Current to December 31, 1978," 95th Cong., 2d Sess. 50 (1978).
109. H. Rept. No. 94-693, 94th Cong., 4–5 (1975).
110. Id. at 2.
111. Public Papers of the Presidents, 1975, II, at 1867.

"involves grave matters affecting our conduct of foreign policy and raises questions which go to the ability of our Republic to govern itself effectively."[112] Under the pressure of the contempt citation, committee members listened to an NSC aide read verbatim from the documents concerning the covert actions. Thereafter the committee chairman announced that the White House was in "substantial compliance" with the subpoena and the planned contempt action was "moot."[113] This confrontation is discussed in detail in Chapter 6.

The James Watt Episode

The third dispute concerned a decision by Interior Secretary James Watt to withhold 31 documents from a House subcommittee in 1981. The confrontation quickly escalated to a committee subpoena for the documents and a recommendation by the Committee on Energy and Commerce that Watt be cited for contempt. Attorney General Smith advised President Reagan to invoke executive privilege on the ground that all of the documents at issue "are either necessary and fundamental to the deliberative process presently ongoing in the Executive Branch or relate to sensitive foreign policy considerations."[114] *Foreign policy*? Were the Attorney General and his legal assistants in the Justice Department unaware that Congress had a clearly legitimate and constitutionally-based reason for the information? The dispute with Watt concerned the impact of Canadian investment and energy policies on American commerce, an issue clearly within the enumerated constitutional power of Congress to "regulate Commerce with foreign Nations" and its authority to oversee the particular statute that established the nation's policy on foreign investments. The eventual outcome of this dispute demonstrated that the documents were not, as Smith argued, privileged. They could have been, and eventually were, shared with the subcommittee. The details of this dispute are included in Chapter 6.

Charges about Congressional "Leaks"

Members of the executive branch often argue that sensitive, national security information should not be shared with Congress because lawmakers are

---

112. Id. at 1887. Letter of November 19, 1975, from President Ford to Representative Otis Pike, chairman of the House Select Committee on Intelligence.
113. Pat Towell, "Contempt Action Against Kissinger Dropped," CQ Weekly Report, December 13, 1975, at 2711.
114. 43 Op. Att'y Gen. 327, 328 (1981).

likely to leak the documents or intelligence to the public. During the Iran-Contra hearings in 1987, Col. Oliver North admitted that he participated in the preparation of statements to Congress that were "erroneous, misleading, evasive, and wrong," but defended his conduct because "we have had incredible leaks from discussions with closed committees of Congress." Such leaks, he said, placed "American lives at stake."[115]

During the hearings, Senator Daniel Inouye (D-Hawaii) reacted sharply to North's claim that two U.S. Senators, after being briefed by President Reagan two hours before an air attack against Libya, had leaked the information to the press. The premature disclosure, said North, resulted in intense antiaircraft fire that caused the death of two American pilots.[116] Yet officials from the Reagan administration had been the ones to tip off the media about the imminent attack. A week before the bombing, "CBS Evening News" reported: "Top U.S. officials acknowledge that detailed military contingency plans for retaliation already exists. Said one source, 'They involve five targets in Libya.'"[117] Other media outlets, including the *Wall Street Journal*, the *New York Times*, the *Washington Post*, the Associated Press, and ABC News had been given a heads-up by administration officials.[118] So public was the planned military action "that scores of American reporters had arrived in advance in the Libyan capital of Tripoli to witness the attack."[119]

North himself had been party to leaks of national security information. In his testimony before the Iran-Contra committee, he spoke about the leak of details in the capture of terrorists charged with having hijacked the cruise ship *Achille Lauro*. He claimed that "a number" of members of Congress had divulged details of the U.S. interception of an Egyptian airliner carrying the suspected terrorists. The disclosure, he said, "very seriously compromised our intelligence activities."[120] Information on the planned interception had indeed been leaked to *Newsweek*. The media is generally loath to identify sources, but the circumstances in this case convinced the magazine to provide the name:

---

115. "Iran-Contra Investigation" (100-7, Part 1), joint hearings before the Senate Select Committee on Secret Military Assistance to Iran and the Nicaraguan Opposition and the House Select Committee to Investigate Covert Arms Transactions with Iran, 100th Cong., 1st Sess. 180 (1987).
116. Id. (100-7, Part II), at 132–33.
117. Id. at 198.
118. Id. at 198–99.
119. David B. Ottaway, "Inouye Refutes North's Charge on Leaks," Washington Post, July 15, 1987, at A6.
120. "Iran-Contra Investigation" (100-7, Part II), at 132.

"the colonel did not mention that details of the interception, first published in a Newsweek cover story, were leaked by none other than North himself."[121]

There should be little doubt that congressional leaks, compared to executive leaks, are infrequent and small in number, and that a congressional leak of sensitive data will result in the removal of the legislator from the committee. The executive branch leaks more because there are more people with access to more classified documents. Presidents have long expressed frustration about the deluge of leaks from their administrations. Based on this history, John F. Kennedy spoke frankly and accurately that "the Ship of State is the only ship that leaks at the top."[122] When President Nixon was furious about leaks, leading to the creation of a "plumbers" unit and the Watergate affair, the leaks he worried about came not from Congress but from his own administration.

A recent example of the executive custom of leaking sensitive material comes from the George W. Bush administration. After 9/11, President Bush expressed anger about leaks to the news media. In response, he issued a memo stating that only eight members of Congress could receive classified or sensitive law enforcement information.[123] A member of his own party, Senator Chuck Hagel of Nebraska, remarked: "To put out a public document telling the world he doesn't trust the Congress and we leak everything, I'm not sure that helps develop unanimity and comradeship."[124] The presidential memo was so ill-advised and impractical, with regard to the access to classified information needed by lawmakers and congressional committees, that Bush retreated within a few days.[125]

Compare this contretemps to the publication in 2002 of *Bush at War* by Bob Woodward. Officially, the administration spoke harshly against leaks to the news media. And yet Woodward was permitted to interview the top executive officials, including Bush, who formulated the war against Afghanistan.

---

121. "Two Leaks, But by Whom?," Newsweek, July 27, 1987, at 16; "Newsweek Says North Was Source of Leak," Washington Post, July 20, 1987, at A4.

122. Elie Abel, Leaking: Who Does It? Who Benefits? At What Cost? 17 (1987). For the record of Congress and the executive branch in protecting classified information, see the July 29, 1988 study by Frederick M. Kaiser, Congressional Research Service, reprinted at "Congress and the Administration's Secrecy Pledges," hearing before a subcommittee of the House Committee on Government Operations, 100th Cong., 2d Sess. 50–66 (1988).

123. Presidential Memorandum, "Disclosures to the Congress," October 5, 2001.

124. Dana Milbank and Peter Slevin, "Bush Edict on Briefings Irks Hill," Washington Post, October 10, 2001, at A1.

125. Todd S. Purdum, "Bush Lifts Some Restrictions On Classified Information," New York Times, October 11, 2001, at B11; Chuck McCutcheon, "Congress Maintains its Right To Remain in the Loop," CQ Weekly Report, October 13, 2001, at 2395–96.

More seriously, the administration allowed him access to top secret, secret, and classified documents. He had neither of the two qualifications required for such access: clearance, and a "need to know." No one in the administration reviewed or censored the manuscript prior to publication. Woodward decided for himself what information to release to the public.[126]

Congressional Access to Executive Branch Employees

In 1997, the Intelligence Committees considered legislative language to expand executive employee access to Congress. A Senate report explained that current executive branch policies on classified information "could interfere with [the Senate Intelligence Committee's] ability to learn of wrongdoing within the elements over which it has oversight responsibility."[127] In creating the Intelligence Committees in the 1970s, Congress relied heavily on those panels to guard the interests of Congress as an institution. To a great degree, Congress delegated to the committees the responsibility for monitoring and controlling the intelligence community.

The 1996 OLC memo analyzed the constitutionality of two congressional enactments concerning the rights of federal employees to provide information to Congress: 5 U.S.C. §7211 (Lloyd-LaFollette Act) and Section 625 of the Treasury, Postal Service Appropriations Act for fiscal 1997 (P.L. No. 104-208).[128] Both statutory provisions gave executive employees a right to furnish information to either House of Congress or to a committee or member thereof.

The Lloyd-LaFollette Act

The OLC memo swept broadly to challenge the constitutionality of the Lloyd-LaFollette Act, originally enacted in 1912. The statute responded to presidential efforts to block the flow of information from executive employees to Congress. For example, President Theodore Roosevelt in 1902 issued a "gag order" prohibiting employees of the executive department from seeking to influence legislation "individually or through associations" except through

---

126. Bob Woodward, Bush at War xii–xiii, 75ff, 101, 117, 119, 184, 197, 228, 246, 268, 269, 282–83, 319 (2002).
127. S. Rept. No. 105–24, 105th Cong., 1st Sess. 26 (1997).
128. OLC Memo, at 2.

the heads of the departments. Failure to abide by this presidential order could result in dismissal from government service.[129] In 1909, President William Howard Taft issued another gag order, forbidding any bureau chief or any subordinate in government to apply to either House of Congress, to any committee of Congress, or to any member of Congress, for legislation, appropriations, or congressional action of any kind, "except with the consent and knowledge of the head of the department; nor shall any such person respond to any request for information from either House of Congress, or any committee of either House of Congress, or any Member of Congress, except through, or as authorized by, the head of his department."[130]

Through language added to an appropriations bill in 1912, Congress nullified the gag orders issued by Roosevelt and Taft. The debate on this provision underscores the concern of Congress that the gag orders would put congressional committees in the position of hearing "only one side of a case": the views of Cabinet officials rather than the rank-and-file members of a department. Members refused to place the welfare of citizens "in the hands and at the mercy of the whims of any single individual, whether he is a Cabinet officer or anyone else."[131] Lawmakers wanted agency employees to express complaints about the conduct of their supervisors.[132] The stated purpose of the legislation was to ensure that government employees could exercise their constitutional rights to free speech, to peaceable assembly, and to petition the government for redress of grievances.[133]

During House debate, members viewed the gag orders as an effort to prevent Congress "from learning the actual conditions that surrounded the employees of the service."[134] If agency employees could speak only through the heads of the departments, "there is no possible way of obtaining information excepting through the Cabinet officers, and if these officers desire to withhold information and suppress the truth or to conceal their official acts it is within their power to do so."[135] One legislator remarked: "The vast army of Government employees have signed no agreement upon entering the service of the Government to give up the boasted liberty of the American citizens."[136] Even more explicit was this statement during debate in the Senate:

---

129. 48 Cong. Rec. 4513 (1912).
130. Id.
131. Id. at 4657 (statement of Rep. Reilly).
132. Id.
133. Id. at 5201 (statement of Rep. Prouty).
134. Id. at 5235 (statement of Rep. Buchanan).
135. Id. at 5634 (statement of Rep. Lloyd).
136. Id. at 5637 (statement of Rep. Wilson).

Mr. President, it will not do for Congress to permit the executive branch of this Government to deny to it the sources of information which ought to be free and open to it, and such an order as this, it seems to me, belongs in some other country than the United States.[137]

The language used to nullify the gag orders was added as Section 6 to the Postal Service Appropriations Act of 1912.[138] Section 6, known as the Lloyd-LaFollette Act, provides a number of procedural safeguards to protect agency officials from arbitrary dismissals. The final sentence of Section 6 reads: "The right of persons employed in the civil service of the United States, either individually or collectively, to petition Congress, or any Member thereof, or to furnish information to either House of Congress, or to any committee or member thereof, shall not be denied or interfered with." Section 6 was later carried forward and supplemented by the Civil Service Reform Act of 1978 and codified as permanent law.[139] The conference report on this statute elaborates on the need for executive employees to disclose information to Congress:

> The provision is intended to make clear that by placing limitations on the kinds of information any employee may publicly disclose without suffering reprisal, there is no intent to limit the information an employee may provide to Congress or to authorize reprisal against an employee for providing information to Congress. For example, 18 U.S.C. 1905 prohibits public disclosure of information involving trade secrets. That statute does not apply to transmittal of such information by an agency to Congress. Section 2302(b)(8) of this act would not protect an employee against reprisal for public disclosure of such statutorily protected information, but it is not to be inferred that an employee is similarly unprotected if such disclosure is made to the appropriate unit of the Congress. Neither title I nor any other provision of the act should be construed as limiting in any way the rights of employees to communicate with or testify before Congress.[140]

As codified in 1978, any interference with the right of executive branch employees in communicating with Congress becomes an enforceable right along with other prohibited personnel practices. The U.S. Code now provides that various qualifications to the provision on prohibited personnel practices "shall

---

137. Id. at 10674 (statement of Senator Reed).
138. 37 Stat. 555, §6 (1912).
139. 5 U.S.C. §7211 (2000).
140. S. Rept. No. 95-1272, 95th Cong., 2d Sess. 132 (1978).

not be construed to authorize the withholding of information from the Congress or the taking or any personnel action against an employee who discloses information to the Congress."[141]

Whistleblower Protection Act of 1989

Congress supplemented these federal employee protections by enacting legislation in 1989, finding that federal employees who make disclosures described in 5 U.S.C. §2302(b)(8) "serve the public interest by assisting in the elimination of fraud, waste, abuse, and unnecessary Government expenditures," and that "protecting employees who disclose Government illegality, waste, and corruption is a major step toward a more effective civil service."[142] Employees may disclose information which they reasonably believe evidences a violation of any law, rule, or regulation, or constitutes gross mismanagement, a gross waste of funds, an abuse of authority, or a substantial and specific danger to public health or safety. Such disclosures are permitted unless "specifically prohibited by law and if such information is not specifically required by Executive order to be kept secret in the interest of national defense or the conduct of foreign affairs."[143] In signing the bill, President Bush said that "a true whistleblower is a public servant of the highest order...[T]hese dedicated men and women should not be fired or rebuked or suffer financially for their honesty and good judgment."[144]

Congressional Action in 1998

In order to examine the objections raised by OLC, the Senate Select Committee on Intelligence held two days of hearings in 1998. Professor Peter Raven-Hansen and I appeared the first day to rebut OLC's position that the President has ultimate and unimpeded authority over the collection, retention, and dissemination of national security information.[145] On the second day of hearings I testified alongside an attorney from OLC.[146] Based on those hearings and its own independent staff analysis, the committee reported leg-

---

141. 5 U.S.C. §2302(b) [sentence following ¶12] (2000).
142. 103 Stat. 16, §2(a) (1989).
143. Id. at 21, §1213(a)(1).
144. Public Papers of the Presidents, 1989, I, at 391.
145. "Disclosure of Classified Information to Congress," hearings before the Senate Select Committee on Intelligence, 105th Cong., 2d Sess. 5–37 (1998).
146. Id. at 39–61 (Randolph D. Moss, Office of Legal Counsel).

islation despite claims by the Justice Department that the bill was an unconstitutional invasion of presidential prerogatives. The committee acted unanimously, voting 19 to zero to report the measure.[147] The bipartisan support for legislative prerogatives was solid. The Senate report said that the administration's "intransigence on this issue compelled the Committee to act."[148] The bill passed the Senate by a vote of 93 to one.[149]

The House Permanent Select Committee on Intelligence, taking a different approach in drafting the legislation, also rejected the administration's claim that the President exercised exclusive control over national security information. I testified before the House committee as well.[150] Like the Senate, the House committee dismissed the assertion that the President, as Commander in Chief, "has ultimate and unimpeded constitutional authority over national security, or classified, information. Rather, national security is a constitutional responsibility shared by the executive and legislative branches that proceeds according to the principles and practices of comity."[151] The two committees reported and enacted legislation with this language: "national security is a shared responsibility, requiring joint efforts and mutual respect by Congress and the President." The statute further provides that Congress, "as a co-equal branch of Government, is empowered by the Constitution to serve as a check on the executive branch; in that capacity, it has a 'need to know' of allegations of wrongdoing within the executive branch, including allegations of wrongdoing in the Intelligence Community."[152]

The text and intent of the Constitution, combined with legislative and judicial precedents over the past two centuries, provide compelling support for congressional access to national security information within the executive branch. Without that information, Congress is unable to fulfill its legislative duties under Article I of the Constitution, and the political system necessarily moves away from the republican model fashioned by the framers toward

---

147. S. Rept. No. 105-165, 105th Cong., 2d Sess. 2 (1998).
148. Id. at 5.
149. 144 Cong. Rec. S1561–65 (daily ed. March 9, 1998).
150. "Record of Proceedings on H.R. 3829, The Intelligence Community Whistleblower Protection Act," hearings before the House Permanent Select Committee on Intelligence, 106th Cong., 1st Sess. 32–53 (1998).
151. H. Rept. No. 105-747, Part 1, 105th Cong., 2d Sess. 15 (1998).
152. 112 Stat. 2413, §701(b) (1998). See H. Rept. No. 105-780, 105th Cong., 2d Sess. 19 (1998), and Thomas Newcomb, "In From the Cold: The Intelligence Community Whistleblower Protection Act," 53 Adm. L. Rev. 1235 (2001).

an executive-centered regime they feared. Part of legislative access depends on agency employees—the rank-and-file—who are willing to share information about operations within their agencies. The legislative branch has a legitimate interest in obtaining information about agency corruption and mismanagement that an administration may want to conceal.

Members of Congress are aware that the executive branch often uses the label "national security" to avoid embarrassing revelations. Although Solicitor General Erwin N. Griswold prepared a brief in 1971 that told the Supreme Court that publication of the "Pentagon Papers" would pose a "grave and immediate danger to the security of the United States,"[153] and advised the Court during oral argument that the broaching of one of the documents "would be of extraordinary seriousness to the security of the United States,"[154] he later admitted in 1989 that he had never seen "any trace of a threat to the national security from the publication" of the Pentagon Papers.[155] The principal concern of executive officials who classify documents, he said, "is not with national security, but rather with governmental embarrassment of one sort or another."[156]

---

153. 71 Landmark Briefs 127 (1975) (New York Times Co. v. United States).
154. Id. at 221.
155. Erwin N. Griswold, "Secrets Not Worth Keeping," Washington Post, February 15, 1989, at A25.
156. Id.

Conclusions

Congress needs information to perform its constitutional duties. The Supreme Court remarked in 1927: "A legislative body cannot legislate wisely or effectively in the absence of information respecting the conditions which the legislation is intended to affect or change; and where the legislative body does not itself possess the requisite information—which not infrequently is true—recourse must be had to those who do possess it."[1] To enforce these constitutional duties, Congress possesses the inherent power to issue subpoenas and to punish for contempt.

Many of the documents and expert testimony needed by lawmakers are located within executive agencies that are created, authorized, and funded by Congress. In both a legal, constitutional, and practical sense, agencies are "creatures" of Congress and must serve both the executive and legislative branches.[2] As greater portions of executive power flow to the President's office, Congress has a heightened need to obtain White House documents and compel White House aides to testify. Part of legislative access depends on executive employees—the rank-and-file—who alert Congress to problems within their agencies. On the basis of two centuries of experience, Congress knows how important it is hear from employees about agency operations that an administration would just as well keep secret.

Whether lawmakers actually receive the requested information depends on their willingness, skills, and ability to devote the energy and time it takes to overcome bureaucratic hurdles. To do that job well, lawmakers have to think of themselves as belonging to an *institution* rather than to a composite of local interests. They must regard themselves as playing an essential role in defending and maintaining a republic, bringing vigor and integrity to a system of checks and balances. This does not mean that lawmakers set aside their party obligations, particularly when the President is from their party. Those obli-

---

1. McGrain v. Daugherty, 272 U.S. 135, 175 (1927).
2. Louis Fisher, The Politics of Shared Power 106–45 (4th ed. 1998).

gations, however, often require a member of Congress to draw a line on what the administration may and may not do, for otherwise the President and the party will both suffer.

The White House and agencies have become more skilled in resisting legislative inquiries, whether they come from a Congress controlled by the President's party or the opposition party. In either case, Presidents will attempt to frustrate committee investigations that threaten to embarrass the administration or divert the White House from its chosen mission. Faced with an unwanted legislative investigation, Presidents typically promise to "cooperate fully" while at the same time perfecting efforts "to blunt, to parry, and to outlast the accusations against them."[3] Similarly, agencies dig in while flooding committees with marginal or extraneous material, announcing that they have handed over "420,000 documents" when not one is useful to the legislative inquiry.

Congress has the theoretical edge because of the abundant tools at its disposal. To convert theory to practical results requires from lawmakers an intense motivation, the staying power to cope with a long and frustrating battle, and an abiding commitment to honor their constitutional purpose. Antonin Scalia, while serving as head of the OLC, put the matter well during hearings in 1975. When congressional and presidential interests collide, the answer is likely to lie in "the hurly-burly, the give-and-take of the political process between the legislative and the executive.... [W]hen it comes to an impasse the Congress has means at its disposal to have its will prevail."[4]

Untidy as they are, political battles between Congress and the executive branch are generally effective in resolving executive privilege disputes. Courts play a minor role, which is good for the judiciary and good for the country. There is no reason to think that greater involvement by the courts would be constructive or helpful. The risk is great that the Supreme Court, in trying to settle one issue, will reach upwards and announce standards and doctrines that are too broad and awkwardly drawn. The unfortunate dicta by Chief Justice Burger in the Watergate Tapes Case, suggesting that the courts might cede ground to Presidents who claim a "need to protect military, diplomatic, or sensitive national security secrets," is one example of this trait. That issue was not before the Court, was never argued or briefed, and should not have been addressed.

---

3. Tiefer, "The Specially Investigated President," at 146.
4. "Executive Privilege—Secrecy in Government," hearings before the Subcommittee on Intergovernmental Relations of the Senate Committee on Government Operations, 94th Cong., 1st Sess. 87 (1975).

Some journalists and academics think that if the President announces that information falls within the magic categories of military, diplomatic, or national security, the other two branches (and the press) should back away respectfully. Courts sometimes retreat in the face of such presidential claims, but judicial deference comes at the cost of individual liberties and a weakened system of checks and balances. Neither Congress nor the press should follow the model of judicial acquiescence. Lawmakers, assigned specific constitutional duties over the military and national security, have no reason to defer to presidential claims or exclusive or overriding power.

Political understandings and settlements have kept executive-legislative conflicts over information to a manageable level. Legal and constitutional principles serve as guides, but no more than that. Attempts to announce precise boundaries between the two branches, indicating when Congress can and cannot have information, are not realistic or even desirable. Disputes over information invariably come with unique qualities, characteristics, and histories, both legal and political, and are not likely to be governed solely by past practices and understandings. Alexander Bickel recognized that large societies will explode if they cannot devise accommodations and middle positions to overcome conflict. His advice four decades ago remains sound today; "No good society can be unprincipled; and no viable society can be principle-ridden."[5]

---

5. Alexander M. Bickel, "Foreword: The Passive Virtues," 75 Harv. L. Rev. 40, 49 (1961).

Subject Index

Abscam, 147–48
Abzug, Bella, 150–53
Achille Lauro, 249–50
"active litigation" files, ix
Adams, John, 236
Adams, Roger, 214, 216
Addington, David, 185–90
Algerine treaty, 30–33
Alter, Jonathan, 220–21
Altman, Roger C., 204
Anderson, Jack, 72
Anderson, John, 17
Anderson, Martin, 202–03
appointments, 71–90
appropriations, 11, 27–48, 202–03, 207–08, 208–09, 224–25, 242, 252–53
Arab boycott, 112
Armey, Dick, 176, 194
arms sales, 155–56
Arthur, Chester, 19
Ashcroft, John, 106
Atkisson, John McElroy, 120
attorney-client privilege, 59, 103–04, 105, 106, 223
Azulay, Avner, 218, 223

Baird, Lourdes G., 170–71, 173
Baker, John H., 138
Baldwin, Abraham, 29

Barr, William P., 97–98
Bason, George, 100
Bates, Edward, 232
Bates, John D., 195–96
Beck, Mary, 207
Belknap, William, 49
Bell, Griffin, 121
Bennett, Donald V., 200
Bereuter, Doug, 158
Biden, Joe, 77–78
Bickel, Alexander M., 259
bill of attainder, 68
Bingham, Jonathan, 155
Bland, Theodorick, 7
Blount, Thomas, 37
Blumenthal, Sidney, 66
Boland Amendment, 45–46, 64
Bork, Robert, 77–78, 80
Boucher, Rick, 68
Boxer, Barbara, 156–57
Bradford, William, 13
Braswell, Almon Glenn, 217
Breaux, John, 67
Brennan, William, 92
Breuer, Lanny, 66
Brooks, Jack, 98–100, 100–02
Brownell, Herbert, 47
Brzezinski, Zbigniew, 202
Buchan, Philip, 116
Buchanan, Patrick, 60, 200

SUBJECT INDEX

Buck, Daniel, 14
Bundy, McGeorge, 201
Burger, Warren, 88–89, 119, 258
Burnett, John D., 21
Burton, Dan, 132–33, 185, 188, 193
Bush, George H. W., 64, 100, 212, 254
Bush, George W., 78–79, 79, 80, 106–07, 109, 187, 188, 189, 194, 198, 224, 225, 226, 250
Bush, Joel D., 4
Butterfield, Alexander, 60, 200
Buzhardt, Fred, 78, 154, 200
Byrd, Robert C., 67, 74, 224–25

Califano, Joseph A., Jr., 118–21
Calio, Nicholas, 224
Calkins, William H., 138
Cambodia, 153
campaign finance documents, 106, 107, 108, 132–33
Cannon, James M., 203
Caputo, Lisa, 204
Carroll, Mary Kate Downham, 207
Carter, Billy, 143, 202
Carter, Jimmy, 121, 123, 143, 144, 202, 215
Cartusciello, Neil S., 83
Catsimatidis, John, 220
Cavanaugh, John J., 148
censure, 51–52
census data, 167–68, 171, 174, 176, 177, 178
Central Intelligence Agency (CIA), 61, 64, 76, 147, 151, 181–82, 200–01
Charles I, 27
Chase, Jonathan, 24
Cheney, Dick, 172, 179, 183–84, 189, 190–94, 198
Churchill, Winston, 141
Cisneros, Henry, 216

Clarridge, Duane, 64
Classified Information Procedures Act (CIPA), 240
Clemency (see pardon power)
Cleveland, Grover, 19–25
Clifford, Clark, 201
Clinger, William F., Jr., 131
Clinton, Bill, 44, 52, 57, 64–69, 83, 103–04, 105, 130, 131, 133, 157–58, 203–24
Clinton, Hillary, 65, 103, 204, 206, 216–17
Clinton, Roger, 216, 217, 222
Cole, Kennedy R., 203
Collins, James M., 149
Collins, Susan, 67
Colson, Charles W., 200
commander in chief, 231–33, 242, 244, 255
commerce power, 33, 34, 40–42, 44, 125, 248
confidentiality provisions, 112–14, 115, 119, 120
contempt power, 14–17, 93, 99, 100, 102, 109, 111–34, 176, 177, 246, 247–48, 248, 257
Continental Congress, 6, 7, 8
Contras (see Iran-Contra)
Conyers, John, 167
Cox, Archibald, 60, 78
Craig, Graven W., 207
Cranston, Alan, 84
Cressman, John W., 208
Culverhouse, A.B., 206
Cushing, Caleb, 235
Cutler, Lloyd, 51, 65–66, 103–04, 121, 202, 204

Dale, Billy Ray, 206
Dana, Richard Henry, Jr., 233
Dannenhauser, Jane, 206
Daschle, Tom, 81

SUBJECT INDEX

Dean, John, 59–60, 72, 73, 74, 74–75, 199–200, 229
"decisional memoranda," 79
DeLay, Tom, 176
"deliberative" documents, ix, 78, 79, 80, 106, 108, 121–22, 124–25, 127, 134, 177, 183–84, 187, 188, 190, 191, 248
Devins, Neal, 84
Dingell, John D., 82–83, 129, 145–46, 184–85, 186, 187–88, 192–93, 194, 196
diplomatic correspondence, 13–14
Dodd, Christopher, 45
Doolin, Dennis J., 152–54
Douglas, William O., 92
Dozoretz, Beth, 218–19, 223
Duane, William, 14–16
Duncan, Charles W., Jr., 121–23
Duskin, George M., 21–24

Eagleburger, Lawrence, 82
Easley, Charles, 207
Edmunds, George F., 21, 23
Edwards, Don, 98
Edwards, James B., 123
Egan, Michael J., 119, 121
Egan, Thomas, 241–42
Eggleston, Neil, 103, 204
Ehrlichman, John, 60, 61, 62, 72, 74, 75–76, 200
Eisenhower, Dwight D., 47
Eizenstat, Stuart, 203
Ellsworth, Oliver, 8
"enforcement sensitive" documents, 102, 127, 129, 134
Engstrom, Stephen, 103
Environmental Crimes Section (DOJ), 82–84
Estrada, Miguel, 79–81, 88
Ervin, Sam, 60, 73, 75, 77
Evans, Donald L., 167–68, 171

Evans, L. J., Jr., 200

Fabiani, Mark, 106
FALN clemency, 211–16, 224
Fascell, Dante, 157
Federal Advisory Committee Act (FACA), 185, 186
Federal Bureau of Investigation (FBI), 61, 74–76, 200–01, 204, 205, 212, 216
  FBI corruption (Boston), 106–09
  FBI files, 65, 206–08
Feinstein, Dianne, 212
Fernandez, Joseph, 64
Fielding, Fred F., 125, 203
Fiers, Alan, 64
Findley, Paul, 153
Findley, William, 12
Fish, Hamilton, 101, 102
Fiske, Robert, 64–65
Fitzsimons, Thomas, 28
Flanigan, Peter M., 72–73, 199
Ford, Gerald, 43, 78, 116–17, 155–56, 209–10, 212, 246, 247–48
Foreign Intelligence Surveillance Act (FISA), 240
foreign policy considerations, 117, 124, 125, 134, 229, 230, 237, 238, 239, 240, 242, 244, 245, 245, 248, 254
Forsyth, John, 40
Foster, Vincent, 65, 205
Freedom of Information Act (FOIA), 96–97, 167, 174, 177, 178, 180, 195, 230, 240
Freeh, Louis J., 132–33
Frist, Bill, 81, 88
Fugazy, William, 220

"gag order," 252–53
Gallatin, Albert, 34

Gallegos, Gilbert G., 213–14
Gamboa, Anthony, 187–90
Garfield, James, 137
Garland, Augustus, 19, 21
Garment, Leonard, 60, 78, 200, 219
Gasch, Oliver, 243–45
Gayler, Noel, 200
Gearan, Mark D., 83, 204, 205
Gekas, George, 66
Gemmell, Nancy, 206, 207
Geneen, Harold S., 72, 73
General Accounting Office, 130, 156, 172, 173, 179–98
George, Clair, 64
Gephardt, Dick, 156, 177
Gerry, Elbridge, 6–7
Giles, William, 10, 11
Ginsburg, Martin, 221, 222
Ginsburg, Ruth Bader, 221
Gingrich, Newt, 157
Gober, Ellen J., 207
Gonzales, Alberto R., 108, 197
Goodhue, Benjamin, 28
Goodlatte, Bob, 66–67
Goodpaster, Andrew, 201
Gore, Al, 118, 119
Gorham, Deborah, 206
Gorsuch, Anne, 102, 126–30
Gorton, Slade, 67
Grant, Ulysses S., 20, 50, 58, 140–41
Grassley, Charles, 85–86, 193
Gray, C. Boyden, 85, 206
Gray, Gordon, 201
Gray, L. Patrick, Jr., 74–76
Green, Edith, 150
Green, Pincus, 217–20, 222–23
Grier, Robert, 233
Griswold, Erwin N., 72, 256

Hagel, Chuck, 150
Haig, Alexander M., Jr., 60, 78, 200, 201

Haldeman, Bob, 60, 62, 74, 200
Hall, Fawn, 202
Halperin, Morton H., 85, 201
Hamilton, Alexander, 7–9, 11–13, 33–34, 36–37
Hanson, Jean E., 204
Harris, Stanley S., 128
Hart, George L., Jr., 74
Hastert, Dennis, 176
Hatch, Orrin G., 207
Hauser, Richard, 206
Hays, Wayne, 96
Hearst, Patricia (see Patricia Hearst Shaw)
Hébert, F. Edward, 152–54
Helms, Jesse, 81–82
Helms, Richard, 200
Hernreich, Nancy, 66
Hiss, Alger, 229
Hoar, George, 24
Hochuli, Jurg E., 208
Holbrooke, Richard, 85–86
Holder, Eric, 214, 216, 218–19, 221, 223
holds, Senate, 84–88
Hoover, J. Edgar, 74, 200, 201
Horowitz, Michael, 107
House resolutions of inquiry, 135–59, 174
Huber, Carolyn, 206
Hughes, William J., 148
Huston, Tom Charles, 200–01
Hyland, William G., 201

Ickes, Harold, 204, 206
Ikuta, C. Nozomi, 214
immunity, 94–95, 218
 partial ("use") immunity, 94
 full ("transactional") immunity, 94
impeachment, 7, 24, 35, 46–69, 133, 140–41, 208, 209, 210, 236

independent counsel, 63–64, 64–65, 79, 95, 105, 108, 130, 132–33, 149, 167, 199–200, 207
Indian treaties, 29, 42
Ingalls, John J., 24
Inouye, Daniel, 249
Inslaw, Inc., 100–03
Iran-Contra affair, 44–45, 62–64, 94–95, 146–47, 149, 202, 212, 249–40
Iraq, 156–57, 158
item veto, 234–35
ITT antitrust litigation, 61, 72–74
Izard, Ralph, 8

Jackson, Andrew, 51–57, 67
Jackson, Robert H., 236–37, 243
Jay, John, 33, 232
Jay treaty, 33–39, 49
Jefferson, Thomas, 10, 16, 30–32, 39–40
Jeffords, James, 67
Johnson, Andrew, 20, 24, 57–58
Johnson, Norma Holloway, 133
Johnson, Robert H., 201
Johnston, Samuel, 8
Jones, George Fleming, 81–82
Jones, Paula, 66
Jordan, 155–56

Kalmbach, Herbert, 60, 200
Kaptur, Marcy, 157
Kehrli, Bruce A., 200
Keller, Robert F., 181
Kennedy, David, 103
Kennedy, John F., 250
Kennedy, Ted, 77, 79
Kennedy, William, 103–06
Kerrey, Bob, 67
kidnapping disputes, 97–100
Kissinger, Henry, 116–17, 201, 247–48

Klein, Joel I., 204
Kleindienst, Richard, 71–74, 199
Kneedler, Edwin, 244–45
Knox, Henry, 10–11, 13
Korean War, 237
Kucinich, Dennis, 158

LaBella, Charles G., 132–33
Laos, 142, 151–52, 153
LaRue, Fred C., 200
Laurence, John, 6
Lavelle, Rita M., 129
Lay, Kenneth L., 188
Laxalt, Paul, 77
Leach, Jim, 105–06, 167
Leahy, Patrick, 88
"leaks," 248–51
Leggett, Robert L., 154
legislative vetoes, 46–48
Leventhal, Harold, 246–47
Levi, Edward, 113–14, 115, 116, 119
Lewinsky, Monica, 65
Libby, Lewis, 219–20, 222
Libya, 143, 202, 243
Lieberman, Evelyn, 205–06
Lieberman, Joseph, 196–97
Lincoln, Abraham, 19, 233
Lincoln, Levi, 40
Lindsey, Bruce, 66, 103, 204, 206, 219, 220
"litigation sensitive" documents, 101, 102, 103, 127
Livingston, Craig, 207
Livingston, Edward, 34–35
Lloyd-LaFollette Act, 251–54
Louisiana Purchase, 39–40
Love, Margaret, 211, 212
Lundquist, Andrew, 184, 186, 188
Lyman, William, 49
Lyon, James, 103

Maclay, Samuel, 38

Maclay, William, 8–9
Madison, James, 6, 7, 12–13, 28, 29, 35, 37–38, 39, 232–33
Magruder, Jeb, 60, 200
Marceca, Anthony, 207
Marks, Marc L., 126
Marshall, John, 236
Marshall, Thurgood, 92
Marumoto, William H., 200
Mason, George, 5, 232
Mathais, Charles McC., Jr., 73
Mathews, F. David, 114–15
Mathews, Sylvia, 205
McBride, Anita, 206–07
McClory, Robert, 143
McCloskey, Paul, 122
McDougal, Susan, 216
McFarlane, Robert, 63, 202
McGregor, Clark, 200
McLaren, Richard, 72
McLarty, Thomas, 204, 206
Meese, Edwin, 62, 63, 78, 79, 101, 234
Metzenbaum, Howard, 79
Mexico, 157–58
Michel, Bob, 156
Mikva, Abner J., 157
Mills, Cheryl, 66, 215–16, 220
Mills, Roger Q., 137–38
Mitchell, George, 86–87
Mitchell, John, 72, 201
Mitchell, John H., 24
Mitchell, William, 47
Moffett, Toby, 122
Moore, Matthew, 131
Moore, Richard A., 200
Morgan, Thomas E., 155
Morris, Robert, 6–7, 136
Morton, Rogers C. B., 112–14, 119
Mosbacher, Robert, 93
Moss, John, 95–97, 113, 118, 120, 246

Motley, Langhorne, 45–46
Murphy, William, 14
Muskie, Edmund S., 164
Myers, Dee Dee, 130, 205

NAFTA, 44
national security, 170, 176, 181–82, 202, 229–56, 258, 259
Newkirk, Thomas, 121–22
Nicaraguan resistance, 146–47 (see also Iran-Contra)
Nixon, Richard, 57, 58–62, 69, 71, 74–75, 78, 199–200, 209–10, 212, 229–30, 250
Nolan, Beth, 204, 218, 219, 220, 221
Nold, William J., 242
nondisclosure agreements, 243–45
Noriega, Manuel Antonio, 99
North, Oliver, 64, 94–95, 202, 249–50
Nourse, Joseph, 8–9
Nussbaum, Bernard, 85, 103, 204, 206, 207

O'Neill, Thomas P. (Tip), Jr., 149–50
oversight, legislative, 94, 102, 113, 118, 124, 127, 134, 157, 175, 176, 177, 182, 187, 193, 194, 216, 227, 238, 239, 248, 251, 255

Page, John, 29
Panetta, Leon, 146–47, 156
pardon power, 64, 208–24
Pearce, Dutee, 54
Pelosi, Nancy, 177
Pendleton Act, 19
Pentagon Papers, 150–51, 238–39, 256
Perkins, Carl, 150
Pierce, Samuel, 93
Pinckney, Charles, 5, 15

Pinochet, Augusto, 81
Podesta, John, 204, 205, 219, 220
Poindexter, John, 63, 202
Pois, Joseph, 181
Polk, James, 49–50, 141
Pollard, Jonathan, 222
Porter, Herbert L., 200
power of the purse, 27–28, 32, 208–09
Prakash, Saikrishna, 229
predecisional documents, 107, 124–25, 177
prosecutorial documents, 106, 107, 108, 109
Puerto Rican terrorists, 208, 211–16
Pugh, James Lawrence, 23–24

Quie, Albert, 150
Quinn, John M. (Jack), 130–31, 206, 214, 218, 219, 221, 223

Ramsden, Richard J., 73
Randall, Robert, 14
Randall, Samuel J., 137–38
Randall, William J., 152–53
Randolph, Edmund, 13
Raven-Hansen, Peter, 254
Rawls, W. Lee, 100, 101, 102
Reagan, Ronald, 4, 46, 51, 62–64, 76–77, 77, 123, 124, 127, 202, 203, 234–35, 243, 245, 248, 249
Rehnquist, William H., 76–77, 166
Reid, Harry, 196
removal power, 205, 224
Reno, Janet, 64–65, 132–22
resolutions of inquiry (see House resolutions of inquiry)
Revell, Oliver B., 97
Reynolds, William Bradford, 219–20
Rhodes, John J., 146
Rich, Charles, 136
Rich, Denise, 218, 223

Rich, Marc, 208, 216, 217–24
Richards, James P., 142
Richardson, Elliot, 78
Riddleberger, Harrison H., 24
Ridge, Tom, 204, 224–26
Riegle, Donald W., Jr., 84
Rodham, Hugh, 217
Rodham, Tony, 217
Rodino, Peter, 143–44
Roelle, William, 204
Rogers, William, 50, 165
Roosevelt, Theodore, 251–52
Rosenberg, Susan L., 216
Rosenthal, Benjamin, 151, 155
Ross, Steven R., 101–02
Rostow, Walter, 201
Rounsavell, Nathaniel, 16–17
Ruckelshaus, William, 78
Ruff, Charles, 214
Rumsfeld, Don, 198
Rutledge, John, 233

Scalia, Antonin, 76–77, 163–64, 258
Schaefer, Dan, 83
Schiffer, Lois, 82–84
Schlesinger, Arthur, 201
School busing, 149–50
Schumer, Charles, 156–57
Sciaroni, Bretton G., 202
Scowcroft, Brent, 157
Secret service privilege, 65, 66
Sedgwick, Theodore, 6, 29
self-incrimination privilege, 93, 94, 141, 207, 218–19
"seven member rule," 161–78
Shaw, Patricia Hearst, 216, 219
Shays, Christopher, 193
Shenwick, Linda, 85–86
Sherburne, Jane, 105, 206
Sherman, Roger, 6, 232, 233–34
Shultz, George, 63, 64
Sirica, John, 61, 62

Sloan, Clifford, 200, 204
Sloan, Hugh W., Jr., 200
Smilie, John, 16
Smith, William, 6, 11–12, 13, 14
Smith, William French, 50, 93–94, 124, 248
Snowe, Olympia, 67
Sofaer, Abraham D., 14, 97–98
"sole organ" argument, 231, 236–37
Sorensen, Theodore, 201
Spanish Bases Treaty, 43
speech or debate clause, 92
Staats, Elmer B., 181
Stanton, Edwin, 57–58
Starr, Kenneth W., 65, 105, 207
Stephanopoulos, George, 204
Steuben, Baron von, 7–10, 136
Stevens, Ted, 67, 194–95, 224–25
Stewart, Potter, 92, 238–39
St. Clair, Arthur, 10–11, 124
Stockman, David, 123
Strachen, Gordon, 200
Strong, Caleb, 8
subpoenas, 58–59, 61–62, 73, 74, 76–77, 91–109, 113, 115, 116, 118, 120, 121, 127, 129, 131, 132, 133, 171, 173, 174, 176, 180, 196, 196–97, 215, 222–23, 246, 247–48, 248, 257
Sumter, Thomas, 29
Superfund program, 127, 129
Sutherland, George, 236–37
Synar, Mike, 126

Taft, William Howard, 252
Tauzin, W. J. "Billy," 185
Tenure of Office Act, 19, 20–25, 57–58
Thomas, Lorenzo, 58
Thomasson, Patsy, 205, 208
Thompson, Fred, 67, 193
Thornburgh, Richard, 64, 98–99, 100, 102

Tiefer, Charles, 177
Torricelli, Robert, 212–13
trade secrets, 95–97, 118–21, 253
Travelgate (see White House Travel Office)
treaties, 21, 29, 30–44, 236
Tribe, Laurence H., 44
Tripp, Linda, 206
Trott, Stephen S., 79
Truman, Harry, 47, 141
Tunney, John, 73, 74
Tutu, Desmond, 215
Tyler, John, 43–44

Velázques, Nydia, 212–13
Van Buren, Martin, 54
Van Wyck, Charles H., 24
Vance, Cyrus, 201
Vietnam War, 150–54
Vignali, Carlos, 217
Vorys, John Martin, 142

Wakefield, Thomas H., 200
Walker, David, 172, 184, 190, 191–96
Walsh, Lawrence, 63–64, 95, 149
Warner, John, 85
Washington, George, 6, 7, 10, 10–11, 13, 29, 30–32, 33–39, 49, 141
Watergate, 58–62, 74–75, 78, 199–201, 229–30, 250, 258
Watkins, David, 131, 205
Watt, James, 124–26, 248
Waxman, Henry, 167–69, 170, 174–75, 176, 184–85, 186, 187–88, 192–93, 194, 196, 214
Weinberger, Caspar, 63, 64
Wetzl, Lisa, 207
whistleblowers, 85–86, 87, 251–56
White, Harry, 138
White, Hugh Lawson, 56
White, Mary Jo, 219

White House Office of Personnel Security, 206–07
White House staff, 59–60, 63, 72–73, 75, 199–227, 257, 258
White House Travel Office, 65, 130–31, 205–06, 206–07, 224
White House-Treasury contacts, 204
Whitewater, 65, 103–06
Whitney, Charles, 14
Whittlesey, Faith Ryan, 79
Williams, Lewis, 17
Williams, Margaret A., 204, 206

Wilson, Charles, 154
Wilson, James, 5, 232
Wilson, Woodrow, 46–47
Wise, Henry A., 52–56
Wolfson, Paul, 80
Wolkinson, Herman, 3–4, 165
Woods, Rose Mary, 200
Woodward, Bob, 250–51
Woolsey, James, 85
work product doctrine, 78, 101, 103, 223
"working draft," 165–66
Wyden, Ron, 87–88

Index of Cases

American Foreign Service Assn. v. Garfinkel, 490 U.S. 153 (1989), 243–45

American Foreign Service Ass'n v. Garfinkel, 732 F.Supp. 13 (D.D.C. 1990), 243–45

American Intern. Group v. Islamic Republic of Iran, 657 F.2d 430 (D.C. Cir. 1981), 237

Ameron v. United States Army Corps of Engineers, 809 F.2d 979 (3d Cir. 1986), 235

Ameron, Inc. v. U.S. Army Corps of Engineers, 787 F.2d 875 (3d Cir. 1986), 235

Ameron, Inc. v. U.S. Army Corps of Engineers, 610 F.Supp. 750 (D.N.J. 1985), 235

Ameron, Inc. v. U.S. Army Corps of Engineers, 607 F.Supp. 962 (D.N.J. 1985), 235

Anderson v. Dunn, 6 Wheat. 204 (1821), 17, 111

Ashland Oil, Inc. v. F.T.C., 548 F.2d 977 (D.C. Cir. 1976), 97

Ashland Oil, Inc. v. FTC, 409 F.Supp. 297 (1976), 92, 95, 96

ATX, Inc. v. U.S. Department of Transportation, 41 F.3d 1522 (D.C. Cir. 1994), 92

Bowsher v. Synar, 478 U.S. 714 (1986), 48

Butterworth v. Hoe, 112 U.S. 50 (1884), 234

C.&S. Air Lines v. Waterman Corp., 333 U.S. 103 (1948), 237

Carter v. U.S. Dept. of Commerce, 307 F.3d 1084 (9th Cir. 2002), 177

Chapman, In re, 166 U.S. 661 (1897), 18

Clarke v. Securities Industry Ass'n, No. 85-971 (January 14, 1987), 141

Department of the Navy v. Egan, 484 U.S. 518 (1988), 241–43, 244

Eastland v. United States v. Servicemen's Fund, 421 U.S. 491 (1975), 19, 91, 92

EPA v. Mink, 410 U.S. 73 (1973), 240

Exxon Corp. v. FTC, 589 F.2d 582 (1978), 92

Garland, Ex parte, 71 U.S. 333 (1866), 209, 210

Gordon v. Lance, 403 U.S. 1 (1971), 89

INDEX OF CASES 271

Grand Jury Subpoenas Dated March 9, 2001, In re, 179 F.Supp.2d 270 (S.D. N.Y. 2001), 218, 223

Hart v. United States, 118 U.S. 62 (1886), 209

Independent Gasoline Marketers Council v. Duncan, 492 F.Supp. 614 (D.D.C. 1980), 123

INS v. Chadha, 462 U.S. 919 (1983), 48, 174, 175, 178

Kendall v. United States, 37 U.S. 522 (1838), 234

Kennedy v. Jones, 412 F.Supp. 353 (D.C. Cir. 1976), 78

Kennedy v. Sampson, 511 F.2d 430 (D.C. Cir. 1977), 78

Kilbourn v. Thompson, 103 U.S. 168 (1881), 17, 18

Knote v. United States, 95 U.S. 149 (1877), 209

Kona Enterprises, Inc. v. Estate of Bishop, 229 F.3d 877 (9th Cir. 2000), 173

Laura, The, 114 U.S. 411 (1885), 209

Leach v. Resolution Trust Corp., 860 F.Supp. 868 (D.D.C. 1994), 167

Lear Siegler, Inc., Energy Products Div. v. Lehman, 842 F.2d 1102 (9th Cir. 1988), 235

Little v. Barreme, 6 U.S. (2 Cr.) 169 (1804), 236

Made in The USA Foundation v. United States, 242 F.3d 1300 (11th Cir. 2001), 44

Marshall v. Gordon, 243 U.S. 521 (1917), 17

McGrain v. Daugherty, 273 U.S. 135 (1927), 3, 17, 18, 91, 176, 257

Murphy v. Ford, 390 F.Supp. 1372 (W.D. Mich. 1975), 210

National Federation of Federal Employees v. United States, 688 F.Supp. 671 (D.D.C. 1988), 244

New York Times Co. v. United States, 403 U.S. 713 (1971), 238–39, 256

Panama Refining Co. v. Ryan, 293 U.S. 388 (1935), 244

Peter Kiewit Sons' Co. v. U.S. Army Corps of Engineers, 714 F.2d 163 (D.C. Cir. 1983), 92

Pillsbury Co. v. FTC, 354 F.2d 952 (5th Cir. 1966), 92

Power Authority of the State of New York v. FERC, 743, 743 F.2d (2d Cir. 1984), 92

Prize Cases, The, 67 U.S. 635 (1863), 233

Raines v. Byrd, 521 U.S. 811 (1997), 169

Schechter Poultry Corp. v. United States, 295 U.S. 495 (1935), 244

Soucie v. David, 448 F.2d 106 (D.C. Cir. 1971), 167

State of California v. FERC, 966 F.2d 1541 (9th Cir. 1992), 92

United States v. American Tel. & Tel. Co., 551 F.2d 384 (D.C. Cir. 1976), 4

United States v. AT&T, 567 F.2d 121 (D.C. Cir. 1977), 4, 246–47

United States v. AT&T, 419 F.Supp. 454 (D.D.C. 1976), 246

United States v. Brown, 381 U.S. 437 (1965), 68
United States v. Curtiss-Wright Corp., 299 U.S. 304 (1936), 236–37, 239, 244
United States v. Instruments, S.A., Inc., 807 F.Supp. 811 (D.D.C. 1992), 235
United States v. Klein, 13 Wall. 128 (1872), 209
United States v. Louisville, 169 U.S. 249 (1898), 234
United States v. Nixon, 418 U.S. 683 (1974), 3, 61, 69, 229, 258
United States v. North, 910 F.2d 843 (D.C. Cir. 1990), 95
United States v. Poindexter, 951 F.2d 369 (D.C. Cir. 1991), 95
United States v. Price, 116 U.S. 43 (1885), 234
United States v. Reynolds, 345 U.S. 1 (1953), 237
United States v. Schurz, 102 U.S. 378 (1880), 234
United States v. Truong Dinh Hung, 629 F.2d 908 (4th Cir. 1980), 237–38
United States v. U.S. House of Representatives, 556 F.Supp. 150 (D.D.C. 1983), 128

Walker v. Cheney, 230 F.Supp.2d 51 (D.D.C. 2002), 172, 195–96
Watergate Tapes Case (see United States v. Nixon)
Watkins v. United States, 354 U.S. 178 (1957), 17, 50
Waxman v. Evans, No. 02-55825 (9th Cir. 2002), 177
Waxman v. Evans, CV 01-4530 LGB (AJWx) (D. Cal. 2002), 170, 173
Wilkinson v. United States, 365 U.S. 399 (1961), 92, 94

Youngstown Co. v. Sawyer, 343 U.S. 579 (1952), 236, 243